CW01210334

On the Edge

Merry 2024 Xmas sweetheart xx

On the Edge

MARTIN KEOWN

MICHAEL JOSEPH

PENGUIN MICHAEL JOSEPH

UK | USA | Canada | Ireland | Australia
India | New Zealand | South Africa

Penguin Michael Joseph, Penguin Random House UK,
One Embassy Gardens, 8 Viaduct Gardens, London SW11 7BW

penguin.co.uk
global.penguinrandomhouse.com

Penguin Random House UK

First published 2024

001

Copyright © Martin Keown, 2024

For picture permissions see page 331

The moral right of the author has been asserted

Penguin Random House values and supports copyright. Copyright fuels creativity, encourages diverse voices, promotes freedom of expression and supports a vibrant culture. Thank you for purchasing an authorized edition of this book and for respecting intellectual property laws by not reproducing, scanning or distributing any part of it by any means without permission. You are supporting authors and enabling Penguin Random House to continue to publish books for everyone. No part of this book may be used or reproduced in any manner for the purpose of training artificial intelligence technologies or systems. In accordance with Article 4(3) of the DSM Directive 2019/790, Penguin Random House expressly reserves this work from the text and data mining exception

Set in 13.5/16pt Garamond MT Std
Typeset by Jouve (UK), Milton Keynes
Printed and bound in Great Britain by Clays Ltd, Elcograf S.p.A.

The authorized representative in the EEA is Penguin Random House Ireland,
Morrison Chambers, 32 Nassau Street, Dublin D02 YH68

A CIP catalogue record for this book is available from the British Library

HARDBACK ISBN: 978–0–241–70782–1
TRADE PAPERBACK ISBN: 978–1–405–96850–8

www.greenpenguin.co.uk

FSC Paper | Supporting responsible forestry FSC® C018179

Penguin Random House is committed to a sustainable future for our business, our readers and our planet. This book is made from Forest Stewardship Council® certified paper.

To my mum and dad, you gave me everything and asked for nothing.

To my sister Maureen and my brothers William and John. You were my protectors when I was growing up and have always been so proud of my achievements.

To Callum and Niall, my sons, my shining lights, two gifts from God.

And of course to my darling wife Nicola, who simply means everything to me. My teenage sweetheart and best friend, who I still adore more than words can say.

Every game I played was for them.

Contents

Soaking it In	1
Daring to Dream	13
A Love Story	31
Climbing the Steps	41
Dicing with Death	59
Spreading my Wings	69
Falling from Grace	79
Playing through Pain	107
Back to the Future	127
Uncoiling the Spring	147
Boring, Boring Arsenal	169
It's Fergietime!	191
Dreams Can Come True	209
My Rival, My Partner, My Friend	221
Winning the Battle	235
Ruud Boy	241
Invincible	255
Capping it All	265

CONTENTS

The Final Frontier   299
To Play Without Fear   311
Postscript   327

Acknowledgements   329

Soaking it In

There I was, alone in the Highbury dressing room, sat in the bath, not wanting to get out.

Because when I did, my time at Arsenal, perhaps even my career, was over.

It's 17 May 2004, the night of my testimonial match. I've played almost the whole ninety minutes against an all-star England team that included Andy Cole, Ian Wright, Robbie Fowler, Paul Gascoigne and David Beckham. We've won 6–0. My final game, and another clean sheet. Yess!

I always used to be the last one out after a game – to the point where my parents used to say, 'For pity's sake, where are you?' as they waited for me, having watched everyone else head home.

But I wanted to soak it up.

As a young player coming through at Arsenal, I used to notice goalkeeper Pat Jennings soaking in a hot bath after a game, centre-back David O'Leary did the same. I looked at them and how many games they had played and thought there must be something in it. Was it the bath itself or just the relaxation? I don't know.

So I took a page out of their book after every home game and sat and soaked. I was never in a rush to leave because Highbury was my second home. A sacred, mystical place where we only got to be once or twice a week at best. 'Friggin' hell, will he ever come out?' my dad used to say.

I'd lie there and think, 'Fantastic, three points, happy days.'

People would come in and out, Vic Akers, the kit man, might be cleaning up and emptying the bigger communal baths. And I'd just relax, still hearing the crowds going past outside, taking it all in.

And here I was, one last time, my creaking body luxuriating in the water after my testimonial match, knowing that once I got out of the bath, I would no longer be an Arsenal player. No more games, no more roars of the crowd, no more team bus journeys, waiting for that magical moment when Highbury came into view. No more trophies, no more crunching tackles, no more feeling the hairs on the back of my neck stand to attention as I walked out on to the hallowed turf.

As I lay there I thought back to the hundreds of times I'd been in that dressing room over the years. The glorious victories, the humbling defeats, the anger or sheepishness after a red card, the rousing team talks, the frustration at not feeling appreciated, the pride at keeping a clean sheet.

And before then too, back to when my job as an apprentice was to clean the dressing rooms and the club's legendary coach Don Howe would be in the bath as I tidied around him, asking me questions about defending, who I rated, who I thought was the best at it in the league (Terry Butcher, and he agreed).

To the time when, as I mopped the floor, I overheard the coaches Steve Burtenshaw and Terry Burton mention my name. 'You know that Martin Keown is playing brilliantly. I reckon we ought to be thinking about him going pro. What do you think, Terry?'

'Definitely, absolutely.'

And then: 'Oh, Martin, I didn't know you were there.'

It was a moment that made me feel ten feet tall. My future, decided in the bath.

SOAKING IT IN

At that moment, all those years ago, I could only dream of everything I would go on to achieve: 449 games for my beloved Arsenal, 2 Doubles, 43 caps for England (including one captaincy), 3 FA Cups, a Cup Winners' Cup, 132 games and promotion with Aston Villa, 126 appearances for Everton, learning from brilliant minds such as Graham Taylor, Howard Kendall, George Graham, Glenn Hoddle, my idol Kevin Keegan and, of course, Arsène Wenger, the man who changed my life. 800 first class professional games!

I thought back to playing alongside brave defensive warriors like Tony Adams and Sol Campbell and marvelling at the genius of Dennis Bergkamp, Patrick Vieira, Thierry Henry, and so many more.

To the challenge of trying to stop the world's best attackers: from ingenious, speedy Brazilians Romário and Ronaldo, to Alan Shearer's strength, to Gabriel Batistuta's movement, to Ruud van Nistelrooy's mind games – more on him later.

And now it was all culminating in this perfect goodbye, a third league title, won without losing a game. A small part of a monumental moment in footballing history.

But as my fingers and toes wrinkled in the water, I knew it was time.

A few weeks earlier, I'd been in the same dressing room and was as vocal as I'd ever been. And I hadn't even been playing.

My role in the 2003/04 season was peripheral. I was still a young man, but at almost thirty-eight I was getting too old for football, my body letting me down, no longer able to consistently perform at Premier League level.

But I didn't care too much: I could tell this group was special, trying to go unbeaten, trying to win a Treble, and I felt privileged to be playing for the Arsenal and part of this special environment Arsène Wenger had created.

So even though my game time was limited, I felt I had an important role to play, to motivate, inspire and reassure.

Ahead of a big game, I'd go around telling each player how much I believed in them, 'No one is better than you, you're brilliant at this, just relax.' I always made a point of talking to Kolo Touré and giving him some personalized advice about his opponent that day. It was his first full season at centre-back, and I saw it as my job to help him succeed.

I didn't do much more because I knew my boundaries.

But there was one time when I went further, when I stood up to speak because I felt I had to.

Liverpool at home, 9 April 2004.

To understand my intervention, it's worth explaining the build-up to the game.

We had just been knocked out of the Champions League and the FA Cup in quick succession, losing 1–0 to Manchester United at Villa Park in the FA Cup semi-final and then, agonizingly, to Chelsea at Highbury in the Champions League quarter finals to a late Wayne Bridge goal.

We were still a few points clear of Chelsea in the league, but those two games had knocked the confidence and morale of the group, so I was thinking that I was going to have to work extra hard motivating my fellow players.

Yes, people look back at the Invincibles as an incredible team, and rightly so, but at that point it felt like we'd missed out. For many years a lot of that team thought about what we didn't achieve rather than what we did. And I think if you asked Arsène Wenger hand on heart, that's how he'd feel.

SOAKING IT IN

So that was the backdrop to that Liverpool match. The title or bust.

But from the whistle, it all started to go against us. Sami Hyypiä put the visitors ahead after five minutes and, never mind going the season unbeaten, at that stage, just four points clear, you could see people thinking that we could throw away the league. Confidence is very brittle and you can go a whole season unbeaten and suddenly you don't know when you're going to win your next match. The fear was there.

We equalized, but Michael Owen then put Liverpool back in front just before half-time. We looked in genuine danger of unravelling.

I was on the bench and, as was the case most of that season, couldn't directly impact what was happening on the pitch. And I tell this story not because I want to lay claim to anything that incredible team did but because it felt like an important moment in the season.

Wenger stood up and talked at half-time for a few minutes, but I didn't sense his usual energy. I felt like he wasn't rallying the troops, or they weren't responding. I looked around and saw people feeling sorry for themselves.

So I asked the boss if I could speak, and he said of course, no problem. I'd never asked permission in the past and normally, after he spoke, no one spoke. But I just felt the urge to try to help.

I took a deep breath and, forcefully but positively, said:

'Look, guys. Looking around this dressing room, there's some of the best footballers I've ever played with. But we're guilty of feeling sorry for ourselves. That's what this is. We have got to fight back. And if we get the next goal in this game, we know the lid comes off the roof here and the fans will pull us through. We need to react.'

It was not rocket science – I just said what I saw on the day – but it certainly seemed to make Thierry Henry angry in a good way.

We were level on forty-nine minutes through Robert Pires, and then Henry put us ahead a minute later. And when he scores his goal, he's pointing to where I'm sitting on the bench, as if to say, 'Fuck you, fucking don't accuse me.' Because he always saw things as motivation.

The stadium erupted, Henry completed his hat-trick not long after, the unbeaten run was back on, and then, with a few minutes to go, I got my reward.

The gaffer called me to come on and, as I was standing pitchside, he leaned across and said, 'That's for half-time. Well done.' He knew I needed games (ten, actually, in total) to get a Premier League winners' medal. And he felt I deserved one.

That game was appearance number six, so I had four matches to go to qualify for a winners' medal with seven games of the season remaining.

I'm sure some players would say they were going to respond after half-time without my intervention – and they might be right – but the boss had created an environment which encouraged people to speak up and in this key moment I felt that they needed a bit of help.

No other club I played for has ever got near to that feeling – it was intoxicating.

Sharing that success with the fans during the Wenger years was a great joy, from seeing the excitement in their faces during the warm-up, almost chuckling to one another about what they were about to witness, to us on the pitch, totally focused on our next victim. The air full of tension and belief, the fans and players in tandem; Victory Through Harmony, as it says on the club's crest (in Latin!). The football felt magical, flowing as if every move was choreographed, probing and cutting our opponents to ribbons. It was a beautiful feeling.

Then there was Wenger, the proud manager, a picture of calm, seeing everything, but saying, 'Sorry, I did not see it,' when we overstepped the mark.

It was a privilege to be part of his teams.

That Liverpool win put us seven points clear. There was no doubt we were winning the league now.

But it wasn't until the title was in the bag that the boss delivered the news I knew was coming but had been dreading.

The boss always left it late when he was telling me whether he was offering me a new deal or not, though my lack of game time that season led me to fear I might be coming to the end of my Arsenal career. I had only started one more league game since the infamous van Nistelrooy incident at Old Trafford, because Wenger kept saying, 'I'm not playing you today in case you get injured.' So what happened? I pulled a calf muscle warming up to come on as a substitute, and was out for a couple of months.

We got on the team bus to go to the last game, against Leicester, the title already secured four games earlier on enemy terrain at Tottenham, to the fans' hysterical delight.

There I was, surrounded by my teammates, my friends, my confidants, by footballing geniuses I would have done anything for. Some of the greatest players to ever play the game, riding through London, on our way to making history. The last time I was ever making that journey.

Everything was about routine on match day. You'd stay

in a hotel overnight before the game. You'd go for a ten o'clock walk, do your stretches and then have a pre-match meal. You'd go back to your room, relax and change, then you'd come down at about 1 p.m. for the team meeting. You'd wander in and the boss would be showing all our best bits from previous games on a big TV screen. It was inspirational. It turned us into fans. Everyone would be buzzing, cheering when Dennis scores, Henry scores, when I made a tackle.

Then we'd calm right down, get quieter and vow to do it all again.

Then it was time for the ride to Highbury. That day Wenger told me to sit next to him, that he wanted to talk to me. We sat, we chatted and then, as the bus wound its way through the streets of Islington, those narrow roads lined with terraced houses on either side, with the early crowds gathering, milling outside the pubs, practising their favourite Arsenal songs, he delivered the news.

'Look, I don't need you any more as a player, but I'm worried about missing you in the dressing room. But I think you can play on. So if you want to play for another club, you should. If that doesn't work out, come to speak to me.'

I was flattered. He was telling me I had a future at Arsenal beyond playing.

I said, 'I knew this was coming, boss. I knew one day that, if I hung around long enough, someone is going to say it to me: "It's over." But I've loved it.'

I felt a knot in the pit of my stomach. Even though I'd known deep down for months, the reality of saying goodbye left me feeling a mixture of hurt, emptiness and despair. I was so convinced this team was going to go on and win even more. It was like I was on a high-speed train careering through Europe and I was being made to get off. It was hard to take.

Because I loved it. Not every minute, as you'll find out reading this book, but most of it.

I saw and learned so much, which is why I wanted to write this book. There're so many stories to tell, so many people I want to pay tribute to, so many happy, sad, funny and downright bizarre moments I want to share.

Writing this book, I've had to dig deep. Some of the memories are painful, especially of the many injuries I had throughout my long career. Those memories I wanted to shut out of my life, but I surprised myself with just how much I could recall.

It sometimes required conversations with other people to make sure I got things just right.

Because, more than anything, I was determined to tell the truth. Of course, large parts of my story are just that: my story, how I saw things. Others involved might have seen them differently, but my intention is to tell you about my playing career without looking to sensationalize or wrongly point the finger at anybody, but with the whole-hearted truth in mind.

I've learned a lot doing this – about myself, about how others view me and about what I value when I look back at my life in football.

I'd like to thank Tony Adams and Arsène Wenger in particular for the time they gave me as we looked back at our relationships. The chats we had – which are chapters in the book – were truly eye-opening for me.

My sons Callum and Niall were the ones who suggested I put all these memories in a book. I've headed a lot of footballs, and with all the talk of dementia in the game, I wanted to get as much of my past on paper as possible.

Nicola and I are both incredibly proud of our two wonderful sons. When our first son Callum was born, he transformed our lives. He was like a lucky mascot. Within a month of his birth, I was making my international debut.

At school Callum showed promise, both sporting and academic. He played in midfield and had a good left foot, but he was more interested in writing and performing. He narrated the school play when he was only eight, and used to devour those Harry Potter doorstep-thick books as soon as they came out.

We weren't surprised when Callum decided to go into journalism. He started at our local paper, the *Oxford Mail*, then forged an outstanding career, specializing in business and finance journalism, although I suspect if he wanted to, he would make an equally excellent football writer. His sports knowledge is immense, he is an accomplished wordsmith and has helped me hugely in putting this book together. Thankfully, he is a fully-fledged Arsenal fan.

Callum and our lovely daughter-in-law Sophie are also the parents to our two dear grandchildren, Leo and Tilly. Leo is already two and will soon be old enough for me to tell him that his old granddad once played alongside football legends such as Patrick Vieira, Tony Adams and Thierry Henry. He probably won't believe me.

Niall always loved football and I was delighted when he started to make a career in the game. Our joy in watching him make his first team debut for Reading was indescribable. And when he turned out for the Irish Under 21 team, representing the country of my parents' birth, Nicola and I couldn't have been more proud.

But Niall had always struggled with injury, and in a final attempt to help him get back to fitness, I took him to see

Phillipe Boixel, a brilliant and intuitive osteopath, who had helped me so much at Arsenal.

Phillipe examined Niall and said he could feel an unusual degree of tension in the back of his skull. Did he have a difficult birth? I was stunned. Phillipe was spot on. When I told him the details, Phillipe said that would account for the tension, and might also have caused problems to Niall's back and knees. Again he was right. Niall had undergone several knee operations but was still struggling.

During the Covid lockdown, Niall focused all his energy on trying to regain his fitness.

He trained so hard. I've never seen anybody come close to that level of determination. Everyone in the family encouraged him, especially Victoria, his girlfriend, who fought for him every step of the way.

Finally, he chose to refocus his football ambitions, and is now an outstanding youth team coach at Oxford Utd. If he fulfils his potential, in ten years' time he'll be a notable young manager, and I'll have to interview him on the TV!

Callum and Niall are incredible young men who I would be proud to have as my friends, even if they weren't my sons.

Like everything, this book is for them, my mum and dad, my siblings and my incredible wife Nicola, who I am so blessed to have in my life.

Daring to Dream

Growing up, I knew we were different. We certainly didn't think of our family as English – the abuse we experienced saw to that. My dad, Raymond, told us that when he came to England from Northern Ireland in the 1950s, and found work in Oxford, he used to walk the streets looking for accommodation, only to find signs saying, 'No blacks, no dogs, no Irish'.

We ended up living in a little terraced house on Sunningwell Road, Oxford. There was a pub on the corner, in fact in every house we lived in there was a pub on the corner – perhaps this wasn't a coincidence.

Despite being in the heart of England, we remained very much part of an Irish community, revolving predominantly around the Catholic church. I was acutely aware that my parents' accents were at odds with the locals', and I struggled to understand what my own dad was saying half the time. It was confusing, and this confusion continued into my playing days when the great John Motson, the leading commentator of the day, had trouble with my name, so he persuaded me that it should be pronounced KEY-own, with the emphasis on the first syllable, though – as Dad often reminded me – it really was Key-OWN. Dad wasn't best pleased by this name change!

Dad was a grafter, having bravely left his home in Fermanagh, Northern Ireland, at the ripe old age of twenty-one to start a new life. On arrival, he stumbled into the field of construction, for a company called Down & Francis, where he stayed for more than four decades. He started as a welder, working more or less seven days a week, before progressing into senior management. He was eventually given a beautiful carriage clock for his services to the company; it now has pride of place on my mantelpiece.

We embraced our roots. We took extended holidays to Ireland every summer and it was fantastic. We'd pack up dad's car to the point it would be so heavy the suspension was hitting the back wheels every time we went over a bump. He'd have fluid pumped into the suspension to take the weight but then, once we were unpacked in Ireland minus the weight, the headlights would shine down on the road and you couldn't see where you were going.

We'd spend three weeks in Ireland, two of them at my granny's farm in the north of Ireland where my uncle, John Keown, was living. We'd help with the farming, baling the hay, milking cows, getting up at six in the morning. It sounds like hard work but to us kids it was great fun and a feeling of total freedom.

Then we'd go for a week in the south to see my grandfather. Ireland really does have some of the best countryside in the world, so much so that my sister Maureen got the bug and lives over there now, in Galway.

There were always Irish touches at home in Oxford. Shamrock was sent over from Galway by my grandfather Dominic Duffy by the bucketload on St Patrick's Day, and when Galway played in the All-Ireland hurling championship, we all had to endure listening to it on a rickety radio and my mum, Angela, who had been to school with one of the players, would scream, 'Yahoo!' every time he invariably scored.

But being Irish made us at times a bit of a target. My dad was an avid watcher of the TV news – we weren't allowed to say a word when it was on – and we started to become aware of the terrorist attacks by the IRA. The Birmingham bombings in 1974, in which twenty-one people were killed, created a backlash against the Irish community. I was only seven, but I was old enough to feel that members of our community were being looked at differently out of fear and anger.

My mum and dad owned a shop selling groceries and alcohol, and the idea was that Mum would be out in the shop at the front but could still care for us as we lived at the rear. It was fine for a bit, but then people boycotted the shop because we were Irish. Finances became very tight. People were writing graffiti on the windows, vandalizing the vending machines, and shouting abuse at us in the street – 'Irish bastards', and the like.

It was becoming a bit of a nightmare. And I guess that's when I realized we were being treated as scapegoats, different from everybody else.

It made me angry and determined, a pair of emotions you'll hear a lot about in this book. I just thought, 'No, this is where I grew up. This is as much my area as anybody else's and I'm not going to be intimidated by anybody.' But whenever there was something in the news, the abuse got worse.

The church community held us together, with life centred on St Dominic's hall and club, which has sadly now closed. My parents had a very strong Catholic faith, and that played a big role in my upbringing.

We moved from one side of Oxford to the other, and as I wasn't enrolled into the local Catholic school in time, I went to three schools in three years, the first being a non-Catholic school about fifty yards from our front door. On my first day, all the other kids were homesick and crying, but I was laughing, excited to get going.

Eventually I ended up in a Catholic school, and I thought I'd died and gone to heaven because everyone was massively into football, just like me. It was such a change from Church Cowley school, where you weren't even allowed to play football unless you were in the top year. So when I went to Our Lady's, it was like a release. Even better, everyone seemed to be a Liverpool fan, just like me: Kevin Keegan was my hero.

And that school made me more Irish, as everything was built around the Catholic faith. Unfortunately, when I was in class with the nuns and the teachers, all I thought about was the goals and tackles I had made and how much fun it had been. I couldn't wait to get back out into the playground and took nothing in from the lessons.

When I wasn't in school, life was centred around the local park. Bartholomew Road was on one side and Gaisford Road (where we later moved to) was on the other, filled with semi-detached houses. So if you imagine that park was Highbury, it was like I had just moved from the East Stand to the West Stand. And from five years old, I would peer out of the back-bedroom window to wait for people to turn up to play in the park, and then my dad would have to come and find me at seven or eight at night. There were some bloody good players in that park, all older than me, and some of them went on to have trials with professional clubs.

At our house on Gaisford Road, Dad had to patio the whole back garden because I was tearing up the grass playing football out there all the time.

There was a fantastic wall to pass against. The wall became my best friend, as it kept giving the ball back, whereas when I played with mates, they just ran off with it. I was also able to chip the ball up on to the roof and it would come down off the guttering at different angles. I would chest it up and hit it back on to the roof for it to roll back down again. If I got the weight of the pass wrong, the ball would go over the roof and into next-door's garden. It could be a couple of days before I could get it back, which encouraged me to work harder on my ball control.

My goal was the garage door, and I was endlessly making a racket, driving everyone mad as I aimed for the top corners, interrupted every so often by a neighbour telling me to pack it in. They can't have been surprised at my career choice.

It didn't take long until I was hooked, obsessed by the beautiful game.

In 1974, so when I was seven, on the day of the FA Cup final between Liverpool and Newcastle, I was standing in front of my parents' shop window when some Newcastle fans, who were working in the area, came in wearing black-and-white scarves and looking to buy Newcastle Brown Ale. They were buzzing, talking about the final, and when Mum told them I was crazy about football they persuaded her to let me watch the game. So she led me to the TV out the back and parked me in front of it. All the talk was about Malcolm Macdonald and Kevin Keegan and I sat transfixed for the next four hours watching the teams pull up on the bus, the fans trying to clamber into the ground without tickets, and then the game itself. I was mesmerized by the football – a goal from Steve Heighway and two from Keegan. That was me hooked.

I rushed to my mum as she was shutting up shop around five o'clock to tell her that one day I was going to be a professional footballer and play in one of those cup finals. I still remember the look she gave me of total belief in her young son. I was a very determined child and she knew I never said anything unless I truly meant it.

Dad was always emphasizing that us kids needed to make something of ourselves as very soon we would be out there working in the big, bad world, but I don't think he meant football.

He was a big fan of the TV talent show *Opportunity Knocks*. One week a young girl called Lena Zavaroni, who was only ten, a couple of years older than me at the time, started singing. Dad started tutting, looked over to us and said, 'You must be ashamed of yourselves. Look at her, such a talented young girl, doing something with her life. What are you lot doing with yours?' She won the show for a record five weeks in a row and we could hardly bear to watch as Dad tutted every time she was on. (None of us became singers.) But he planted the seed in my mind that I needed to amount to something.

Dad also taught me to whistle the theme tune of the TV show *Z Cars*, and years later, when I was at Everton, that made me feel proud as I ran out to the tune at Goodison Park.

I was a bit of a pain in the butt as a kid, to be honest – too much energy. If you gave me Coca-Cola or something, I'd be off the chart.

At home we had bunk beds and a single bed next to it, with three of us in a room – me and my brothers William and John. I was in the bottom bunk, and the bed above collapsed on me a couple of times. I'd wake up and think there had been an earthquake. Which would have been a first for Oxford.

It was a tiny room, but it never seemed to bother the three of us. We didn't know anything else. Most nights, my older brother, William, would be up talking loads. He had so much energy that he hardly slept. In fact, years later, in 1986, when I played for Arsenal, we had an away game at Oxford United, who needed to win to stay up. I stayed at home and shared my old bedroom with Will. He took advantage of this, chatting away all night. He still claims that I was knackered the next day, when Oxford won 3–0. But in fact, I was one of the few Arsenal players who put in a shift that Saturday afternoon.

John, my younger brother, had to have a light on, but I needed total darkness. So I had to wait for him to sleep every night before I could go and turn the lights off.

To say we three brothers were competitive was an understatement. Will was very athletic too, running in the 200-metre English Schools final, and Swingball in the garden was like a war zone. The ball was flying so fast you couldn't even see it. Every board game ended with one of us throwing the board over in a fit of rage. But that competitiveness helped me so much when I later played professionally, as from a very young age I had a drive to be the best.

My sister Maureen was also sporty. She was nearly six foot tall and a very accomplished netball player, while my brother John is still playing local rugby union in his fifties.

On Sundays we would go to Mass. Dad was always in our ear: stand up straight, polish your shoes, take that jumper off, change those trousers, you can't go to Mass in that. Appearance was important to him.

I remember getting in trouble for making a lot of noise in church. He picked me up when we got home and threw me on to the sofa – so that didn't happen again. But my dad wouldn't really hit you, there was just the threat of it. My mum was the one who was dishing out the wooden spoon.

As I said above, I was quite hard to handle. I just used to

go and roam the streets from the age of five. I was renting my bike out to one lad, a bit of a notorious kid, and getting 5p a day off him. One day he didn't come back. Off I went to look for him, because I had to get this bike back or the old fellow would go berserk. But I got lost and wasn't able to cross the road because the factory gates had opened at the British Leyland Cowley plant, where 20,000-plus people worked. Most employees there went to work on a bike and it was like the Tour de France for the next half an hour – little did I know that there was a pedestrian underpass I could have taken. Somebody recognized me and told my mum so she came to give me a thick ear. I thought I might get some sympathy, but no chance.

Across the road from my house was an area of waste ground which had been turned into a speedway track, and I used to ride my bike there all the time. If I wasn't there, I was playing football or hanging around the Cowley Centre shops. It was at the speedway track that I had my first stitches inserted in my head after going up a corrugated roof section, using it as a ramp like stuntman Evel Knievel and landing on my head before I reached the end of it. The first stitches of many.

When I was a bit older, we'd go to Blackbird Leys, which is an estate about half a mile away that had a notorious reputation, which was unfair, because a lot of good people lived in those homes, and still do. I'd play football there because a lot of the best players were down on that estate.

They are happy memories, but there was a lot of bullying going on. My bike was thrown into some nettles, and I didn't know what a nettle was and I went in and got stung all over.

I spoke to my brother William recently about the bullying

and we reminisced about how our dad trained us to box, how to make a fist, how to get your hands up and protect yourself.

All three of us boys joined boxing clubs, and we were doing judo, boxing, swimming, football – you name it. It was a busy time. Dad loved boxing, in particular he admired Muhammad Ali, and he used to love telling us about how Ali would predict which round he would win his fights in and then do just that. If you say something and then actually do it, it counts for double, he'd say. 'Remember that, son.'

At home, Saturday afternoons were spent watching *Grandstand*. That was me and my older brother mostly, because my dad was always working and Mum was cleaning the house from top to bottom.

There was a period in between moving houses when we stopped at my great auntie Julie's for a while, and clear as day I can remember the calmness I felt watching the wrestling on the telly and then my excitement mounting when switching from ITV to BBC1 to watch David Coleman giving the final scores while my great-uncle Andy filled in his pools coupon.

I was a Liverpool fan back then but of course I was aware of Arsenal, especially as their Double-winning team of 1971 was so revered. But they actually were struggling a bit in the years I was growing up and only won one trophy (the 1979 FA Cup) in fifteen years. Meanwhile, Liverpool won nine league titles in that time and four European Cups – no wonder I was a fan.

By this point in my life, so much had started to become about 3 p.m. on a Saturday. I still feel everything in my life is geared to that magical moment, even though nowadays games can kick off at any old time. I find myself looking at my watch and thinking, 'It's five to three.' It became another obsession, having to get fit for Saturday. Saturday 3 p.m. became the most important time in my life.

When I got to Our Lady's school they were all obsessed with football, and that gave me a platform to thrive on. Everyone was talking about what I did on the tarmac playground, how many goals I scored at lunchtime. I was building a reputation and growing my confidence.

There were two sittings for lunch and on a typical day I'd leave the team 10–0 up and come back to find them trailing, so then I had to get us back in front.

Sorry for the cliché, but football was like an addiction, a compulsion. I just had to do it. I wanted to prove I was better than the other players. It drove me and I couldn't bear losing. Still hate it.

It wasn't always easy. At about twelve or thirteen, I was very ill with chest infections and sinus problems, which were giving me major headaches. I couldn't understand why I could hardly run in games. I felt totally exhausted all the time and kept asking Dad why my mates at school had a cold for just a few days but I had this for two or three months. Eventually the doctors found I had internal bleeding, caused by anti-inflammatories which I suspect had been over-prescribed for Osgood-Schlatter disease, which is a serious inflammation of the knee that particularly affects adolescents.

My mum took my anaemia and low blood count personally and set about feeding me up with the most outrageously big dinners: two burgers, two sausages, two rashers of bacon, beans and a pan full of chips, so determined was she to get me back into peak condition.

Despite my massive calorie intake I had plateaued at this stage. Because of my illness I wasn't really standing out any more. And that's where my dad really came into play with his simplicity about how he saw the game. He wasn't someone who knew much about the ins and outs of football, but he kept accusing me of being a ball watcher. He'd say, 'All you do is effing ball watch, standing there doing eff-all. Get your friggin' foot in.' And I realized he was right. So I changed the way I played. I started to get stuck in. And I never stopped.

He was a doer, my dad, he didn't stand on ceremony. And we'd have these huge rows and discussions that would go on for hours. If I scored six goals (and I often did), it wasn't enough. But somehow I knew he believed in me and rated me. This played out in my professional career too, as I ended up responding well to managers who pushed me – as long as they gave me that same feeling of shared belief in my ability. That is where Arsène Wenger and at times Howard Kendall were fantastic, but where I struggled with George Graham and at times Graham Taylor.

My dad only really said to me how proud he was at my testimonial game and we had a quiet chat and a big hug, and then he felt his work was done in terms of me as a footballer.

My birthday present when I turned eight was to join a local football club, Garsington. We played in green, which was nice with the Irish connection. It was in the countryside, and I think my parents enjoyed going three or four miles out of town. It was an escape for them and it reminded them of home, the rambling hills. I wasn't old enough to actually play in the team and had to wait another year. But once I did play we won the league and cup Double two years on the trot. So I'd already won a couple of Doubles as a kid. One of the cup finals was at the Manor Ground, the Oxford United football ground, so locally, that was like Wembley. I excelled at Garsington, being exceptionally quick, and ran through on goal to score many times, my mum screaming, 'Yahoo!' whenever I did. In fact, I set the goal-scoring record for the Under 10s and Under 11s.

One of my dad's best friends, Tommy Gildea, took me to watch my first professional game. One afternoon he said to me that Mick Channon, the England striker, was coming to Oxford United to play for Southampton. Channon was an international player even though his team was in Division 2, and he used to do a famous 'windmill' celebration when he scored, whirling his left arm round and round. We stood at the Cuckoo Lane end and the small ground was bursting at the seams. People were climbing the floodlight pylons to watch. In those days, everyone flocked to see individuals and not necessarily the team. I was captivated by the atmosphere, and Mick Channon seemed to have so much time on the ball. He scored a hat-trick in a 4–0 victory. His arm must have been sore from all that windmilling.

Every year at Garsington, as a treat for the players, the club would organize a visit to a top-tier game.

We went to QPR v Liverpool at Loftus Road in 1975/76, the year when QPR finished second and Liverpool top. That was an incredible atmosphere. The next game we went to was Arsenal v Man United, a fixture that became so important in my life. That was the first time I ever stepped into Highbury. Our seats were in the Upper East Stand and were so far to the left of the stand we had to watch the goalmouth action through the smeary glass end wall. I couldn't even see the goal. Years later when I was playing for Arsenal, if I was feeling anxious, I'd remind myself that half the people in that stand couldn't even see me, so why should I worry if I make a mistake?

A few years later, representing the Oxford boys district

team, we headed north for a tournament, and then, straight after a game against a local Liverpool youth team, we headed to Anfield, the highlight of the trip.

But we made a big mistake. We parked up the minibus outside Anfield and these two local young kids asked, 'Can we mind your vehicle for a few bob?' The games teacher said, 'What's your game? Go on, sling your hook,' and when we came back all our bags, our boots, everything was gone, and we were supposed to be there for a week. I say *all* our stuff was gone . . . mine was the only bag that wasn't stolen, and my boots were shit from Woolworths. Everyone got a brand-new pair of boots from the insurance money, and I still had to wear the same ones. Not the last time I was robbed at Anfield!

We were watching Liverpool that day and I had never seen or heard a crowd like it. They just moved in unison, heads were swaying, and we were stood in an area so condensed that we had to be moved, and walked around the pitch to a safer spot. As I was being marched along the touchline, I was almost transported into my future life as a player as Phil Neal received the ball right next to me and I thought, 'OK, this is how the pros see it.' Neal got the ball – he was a full-back, like I was back then – and I was side by side with him. I could almost have reached out and made a tackle, if I hadn't been only twelve years old.

At that stage in my development, football completely filled my life. I was playing for my year group at school, the year above me, the county, the district and a Sunday League team. About five or six games a week, and in different positions: up front, in midfield and at the back.

I saw myself very much as a striker. And then I left Garsington and moved to the team who were second in the league the year before, Rose Hill, and that is when, by accident, I was auditioning for centre-half, which would become my future position. The manager's son was a striker. I got moved to the back. I wasn't best pleased at the time but it turns out the manager had started me on the road to my professional career.

My dad was fuming. He always saw me as a centre-forward, and refused to come to watch me until we reached the Sunday League cup final and last match of the season, a game we won, and I was given the Man of the Match award. I was running into channels, picking off the opposing attacker's runs, and it was as easy as reading a *Beano* comic, as I used to make those runs myself when playing up front. Significantly, my dad was starting to appreciate my performances again.

As I got older, my confrontational, scrapping side started to come out.

There were two Catholic middle schools: the school where my future wife, Nicola, went, called St Gregory, and St John Bosco, where I was.

When I chatted to my old team manager and PE teacher Nick Brown recently, he told me I pretty well took over the team talks at twelve years of age when we reached the school cup final. I was throwing my boots against the dressing-room wall at half-time, demanding more of my teammates, telling them we might as well all pack it in now if we didn't step up our game.

Our school team at St John Bosco was unusual too as we had a centre-forward called Kathleen Parker, playing under the alias Gary, as otherwise she wasn't allowed to play because she was a girl. It's crazy when you think about it. She was a great player and I had recommended her to Nick as we needed her in our team.

Infuriatingly, she was denied the opportunity to play in that cup final, which is pretty disgraceful, but Nick went out of his way to make sure she got a medal – typical of the man he is. Luckily, girls' and women's football is far more advanced these days.

Anyway, those two schools then merged to form one very big school, St Edmund Campion. And when we got there, if you were seen as the top dog or a hard man, there were fights.

I had a reputation for being tough on the pitch, so I was a target. There was a time when the year above tried to pick on me, but they took on more than they could chew. Another time, my sister Maureen pulled me out of a fight just in time. I was fighting all the time and having to get good at looking after myself.

Why did I get involved? Because if your mates are all pushing you to see who's the hardest, you just do.

I was talking to Arsène Wenger about this years later, and he said to me, 'I was fighting every day at school,' and I said, 'So was I.' You were fighting for something – your reputation, to defend a brother or sister. There was always somebody on the estate trying to bully you. I'd come home and the old fella used to give me the lecture about not fighting and then ask, 'By the way, did you win?'

It's funny because with my two lads, Callum and Niall, I tried to bring them up to be smart and find the right words to navigate around these things. I don't think I ever saw them in a fight.

But I'd been wired to embrace confrontation and injustice. It definitely comes from where we were brought up and what we were going through as kids with the discrimination for being Irish.

Also, my mum was always of the view that you shouldn't be afraid to get involved in other people's confrontations. She was often running into trouble breaking up fights. It's quite difficult when you're a kid to see that; I was actually looking at my mum, saying, 'No, Mum, you can't. We can't be going into that, surely.'

It was her trying to do a good thing. A lot of people just walk on by, but not our mum. And it has stuck with me.

Years later, the night before I played my first game back with Arsenal in 1993, when Nicola and I had moved back to Oxford, I was sat in my dad's front room and my sister shouted that four lads were trying to steal Nicola's car. I was downstairs with my dad, tracksuit, trainers on, in the prime of my life. I opened the front door, whooshed out, and instead of putting my hand on the five-foot wall to help me jump, I tried to leap it unaided. I clipped the wall with my left foot and went over headfirst. I did a forward roll but landed in between the four lads, who started to run. Because I was on the floor, it gave them a bit of a head start. But very quickly I was running in between them all, but I knew I could only take one out. So I just tackled one of them like a footballer (it would have been a red) and he flew into the air and landed on his chin. And then I kept running to try to get another one.

My first instinct was always just to go straight into the fire. They could have had knives. And yet if the same thing happened today, I would stupidly go and do the same thing, because I want to protect my property and I don't like people to take liberties with me. And that's a theme you'll see a lot of in this book, and one that didn't always serve me well, especially when it came to my first stint at Arsenal.

One thing I would say about my anger and seeming need for confrontation is that when I played football, it almost gave me permission to get wound up. Most people scrap when they're kids, they might scrap when they're teenagers, and then they usually go into the world and keep out of trouble except maybe getting drunk in a pub and having a punch up.

My job was quite unusual in that sense. To the point that before one game at Arsenal, I wasn't really feeling aggressive and asked Dennis Bergkamp to give me a little slap across the face to get me going. Dennis of course grinned and hit me with a massive slap that sent me halfway across the dressing room and had me chasing after him minutes before we ran out to play at Highbury.

As I said, unusual.

But then, home life had been quite unusual too.

A Love Story

My parents' relationship was complicated.

It was a massive love story between the two of them and there were so many great times. But there were difficult ones too.

Let's start with the happy memories: the smell of cooked bacon teasing us out of bed on Saturday mornings; Sunday-afternoon dinners all sat in the dining room and crowded round the telly watching sitcoms like *To the Manor Born* – my parents loved to laugh and watched every comedy show they could; great Christmases; eating toasted sandwiches on cold days; and of course those trips to Ireland that I mentioned in the last chapter.

People always used to say that Mum was stunning and looked like Jackie Kennedy. I remember watching Miss World at a young age and asking her why she hadn't entered. Looking back at pictures now, I can see the Kennedy likeness. She used to wear amazing clothes too.

My mum had such a difficult childhood, and it created huge insecurities within her. I think it stemmed from the fact that she lost her own mother at four years of age. She remembers being lifted up to see her mother one last time through a window, because she was dying with meningitis. She always felt that her world was going to disintegrate. And that created a sort of paranoia that would rear its head every so often.

I remember waking up frozen one Friday night when I was about twelve. I came downstairs and the front door was wide open. Mum was standing outside the pub at the end of the road. She'd just sprung out, having had enough of waiting for Dad to return from the pub. She thought he was up to no good and she was standing watching him through the window. She was gone for ages, and I thought, 'Mum, what are you doing?'

That's quite scary for kids. You wake up and you think, 'What's happened?'

Mum was insecure and thought that Dad was in the pub for a reason. On a Friday night my dad enjoyed the banter, he loved the craic. He had a great sense of humour. So he'd go out, he'd want to speak to the lads – he was a man's man. During the week he'd come in from work and he'd want some down time, but my mum would want to talk about her day and so there would sometimes be arguments out of nothing where he just wanted five minutes to read the paper.

When episodes like that happened or Mum and Dad started fighting, us siblings had to go into action mode, trying to pacify them. If there was a row, we'd have to get in between them.

Once my dad had had a drink, he probably reacted to her more than he should have done. And things got a bit physical. My mum was a woman who could look after herself and they'd tussle with each other. My dad never slapped her or hit her. It was almost like wrestling. She was quite a powerful woman, who had won every sports race and played camogie (a women's version of hurling) as a young girl. In fact, she was so strong that she once carried a full weights set back from the shops for me after I said I'd like some to help with my training. That can't have been easy – although it didn't look heavy in the Argos brochure! I later found out she'd charmed one man to help her onto the bus with them, and another to bring them to our front door.

There were a few instances like that where she'd pick up

a kitchen utensil and then put it down. I'd be terrified, thinking, 'What's going to happen here?' I definitely would have jumped in between them if it had escalated, but it never got to that stage.

There was difficulty between my sister, my mum and my dad, and all that is sort of intertwined. Maureen was the only daughter, getting nice presents for Christmas, and Mum was getting a frying pan. The old fella could probably have done better. It made Mum feel even more angry and insecure. I eventually took her to see someone years later to try to get some help as it became clear that there was a mental health element to her struggles.

We didn't make it easy for her because we were wild kids. I said a couple of bad things to her once, and she chased me and I tripped over and cut my eye (another trip to hospital for stitches). But you had to go full speed to get away from her. I was a bit scared of her. When you got hit with a wooden spoon, it hurt. You got the hell out of there if you could. I remember once jumping straight out of a ground-floor window to get away. I gave it five or six hours and then came back, just let her cool down. That was the best way to do it really, just get out of her way.

Other times we had to block the door to try to stop her storming out. We used to position ourselves. I'd be at the front door, my sister and brothers would post themselves strategically around the house. She had this stock answer – 'I'm off, I'm leaving' – and it was like, 'Here we go again.' We were very much trying to fight to keep our family together.

It hit me how unusual this was when I went to live with an old couple called Dot and Charlie in my early days at Arsenal. I was really shocked and amazed that there were no arguments. They looked after each other, they were gentle with each other, but without the end-of-week argument. It underlined to me how good a relationship could be.

But even though times were tough on occasion, I never thought it might be better if they split up. I couldn't contemplate that because those good times were worth fighting for.

And you have to remember that it was so hard for my mum because she didn't know she was unwell. None of it was her fault, as far as I'm concerned.

It was tough for Dad as well, as he was being painted within the family as the cause of the problem, but a lot of it was a figment of her imagination. It was a fantasy world that didn't exist and it wasn't until she got really, really bad and these stories didn't stack up that people started to say that they understood my dad better.

It all created an insecurity in us too. You'd be in class at school thinking about what a hard weekend it had been. It was a relief to get back to school, but often I was sitting there not even hearing anything, it was all just going over my head.

Not to make light of their weekend rows, but it was perfect training for becoming a professional footballer and those times after a game when it's so volatile and the manager is hammering all the players.

If Mum and Dad didn't have a row, it was always going to be a good week. Then, similarly, as a professional footballer, if you won a game at the weekend, it was a good week; if there was a row at the weekend, it was a defeat. The same continual ups and downs, the same sort of rhythm. It always built up to the weekend. But by three o'clock on a Saturday, Mum and Dad had probably come back together again. And they'd always go out on a Saturday night as a couple.

Things changed when Mum was, tragically, diagnosed with Alzheimer's. She'd been showing signs of the disease as early as her fifties. There was erratic behaviour. She packed her car full to the brim with her belongings one day and headed to Holyhead to catch the ferry to Ireland. She thought she was going to start a new life out there, but when she arrived, none of it existed and then she had to come back.

Dad would go off to work, and we never realized, but Mum was clocking up hundreds of miles in her car. She was behaving like a detective, driving around, trying to gather information on where my dad was. He was just at work.

It was all a lot, and then after we won the Double in 1997/98, they went to live in Fermanagh in Northern Ireland. They did about three years out there and we had some lovely summers with them when we took our sons, Callum and Niall, and they would meet all of their Keown cousins. My dad did up the farmhouse where he was born, did all the steels, with her helping him, just the two of them putting steels up. We'd come back every year and couldn't believe what had been done. And then he had to get her back because she needed a level of care and there wasn't enough in Fermanagh.

Their relationship became more mellow on their return to Oxford. I used to go back to visit and they'd be sat on the sofa, cuddling. My dad did an amazing job for her when she became ill: he learned to sew, to cook, to do the bedding. He said to me, 'This is the biggest fight of my life, to keep her here at home with me.' But eventually, after many years, he had to succumb and very reluctantly put her into a home.

It's so heartbreaking watching someone suffer with that disease. Mum's eighty-three now, and I'm convinced she still knows it's me when I visit. When you go in there to see her, it's always painful and emotional and a hard thing to do. But as my dad said, 'Remember, you're not going there for you, you go there for her.'

We didn't tell her when my dad died. She still doesn't know. Until he got really ill, he would go every day and he'd be there most of the day. And then, all of a sudden, he didn't come so maybe, deep down, she understands.

At the height of my success, I bought my mum a lovely watch for her birthday and she would proudly show it to everyone. It was her pride and joy. When her dementia started to really catch a hold of her, she tried to give the watch away, so we had to take it off her, which was one of the hardest things I've ever had to do.

My mum in her prime was incredible and used to work for the mobile blood donor unit. She was so full of life, always on the move, a rare force of nature.

Recently, I was at Hitchin Town to cover an FA Cup match, and this guy came up and said to me, 'How is your mum? What an amazing woman.' It was almost a story from the grave, because no one had mentioned my mum for many years in that context. What she used to do was, for every patient that came in, particularly the nervous ones, she'd start to talk about me and my football career before taking their blood. And if they were super-interested she'd give them a photograph of me, signed. And not to play favourites, she also used to slip my brother's business card with 'Executive Alarms' on it into their hand. He got loads of jobs off the back of it.

She worked so hard to feed and clothe us, so to end up in that home, resigned to her fate as one by one all of her faculties switch off, is heartbreaking.

What we pray for now is that she is released from her suffering. Because it's really painful to witness her sitting looking at the same view she's been looking at for all these years. As much as we think the home does a great job of keeping her alive, it's not a quality of life for anybody.

A LOVE STORY

No words can ever sum up the feeling of despair you have watching a loved one fade away in front of your eyes as you watch dementia rip them away.

I try to live my life and not worry about whether I will be affected by the same disease. I should really be working on a campaign for Alzheimer's to protect the current generation from any problems going forward. Or indeed dementia in general. It's a weird thing that the game I love could stop me even recognizing the people I love most of all in time to come.

The reality is, some studies show that you're five times more likely to get Alzheimer's if you played in a central defensive position. You're three times more likely if you've just played the game.

Yes, there are also a lot of footballers who don't get Alzheimer's. There are people who smoke forty cigarettes a day who don't get cancer. They're very lucky. But lots do.

The game does need to change, especially at the training ground, where traditionally you would have practised heading a lot. We just don't need to do that any more.

One good thing is that, these days, the average number of short passes has more or less doubled and it means there's fewer long balls. If I wasn't the first head on the ball when the keeper kicked it, I used to be annoyed and disgusted with myself for not winning it. But now, looking back, I'm pretty relieved that I didn't win all of them – maybe that gives me more time.

Despite all my mum's troubles, it was my dad who left us first. He died of lung cancer. He used to smoke cigars and cigarettes when I was a kid.

When I was young, around twelve, I saw a video at school encouraging people to quit smoking, and it was really quite impactful. There was a guy sitting on a stage and he'd had both legs and one arm amputated and he was smoking a cigarette. He introduced himself and said, 'Look, I've had to have all these limbs removed because of my smoking but I've kept this arm so I can continue to smoke.'

Terrified this might happen to my dad, I came home and told Dad if he carried on smoking it was going to kill him. I put my fist in his face and said, 'Pack it in, quit the smoking, fight it.' And he did.

He said to me years later that the sight of a twelve-year-old boy with his fist in his face demanding he stop was enough to make him see sense.

Before he packed up completely he kidded himself into smoking cigars, and then his pipe. One day after giving up smoking he got a massive cigar from the managing director at head office. When I got in the first team, he got the cigar out and said we should smoke it. I said, 'Not yet.' I was terrified he might start all over again, so I kept creating reasons for him not to smoke it. He then wanted to smoke it every time I achieved something: if we won something, if I played for England, if we won the Double. And all the time I kept on saying, 'No, no, Dad, we won't smoke that now, let's wait.' I kept raising the bar so he wouldn't smoke it.

I've got it in my bedroom drawer now. It reminds me of him.

As I said earlier, my dad was an incredible decision-maker. And even at the end he made his biggest decision. A consultant said he could have radiotherapy, but he was dying in front of our eyes. By the third day we were putting him in a wheelchair, and he said, 'I've decided that's it, I won't have any more treatment.' And I thought, 'Fair play to you.' Right to the end he was amazing at making decisions.

When my father was on his deathbed, he gave me a Bible,

asked me to read it and told me to go back to church, so I've been going ever since.

I had turned my back on the church because I felt like things had gone so wrong for me when I left Arsenal the first time. And I'd turn up at church and everyone wanted a chat, which at that moment was pointing out what a terrible time I was having at club level.

But going back made me feel much more part of the community. I feel like there's something else there, there's a strength that it gives me. I learn something new every time I go.

When I first went to live in London, my dad told me not to discuss religion. And so I find it difficult to even write a few sentences in this book about it. I do think we should be proud of what we believe in, but I don't want to shove it down people's throats.

I like to believe that there's a journey for everybody. It's comforting for me to think that there's a journey that I'm on. When it comes to Judgement Day, I'm probably in trouble though.

We can all do more. My brother John, a former electrician, does some voluntary work in a local church and puts the rest of us to shame. What am I doing for the community? Not a lot, really.

As is often the case, it's something that Arsène Wenger said that has stuck with me on this topic. He said that when he dies, he 'would like to be in paradise for the harmony and in hell for the company'.

Climbing the Steps

Highbury.

I can still smell and feel it now, walking from the tube station.

The anticipation rises in you as you walk towards it down the streets lined with Victorian terrace houses. The buzz as you get closer, and then, bang, there it is, like a TARDIS, a hidden gem. Behind the houses on three sides, a theatre of dreams on the working man's doorstep.

Over the years, it always felt so alive to me. In a second I can take myself back to match day, when I used to look out of the second-floor window of the old gym in the East Stand to take in the joyous sound of an expectant crowd. So many people!

That incredible place had a mystical and spiritual feel to it. The entrance to the main East Stand and the marble hall reception had a very stately appearance with a uniformed commissionaire standing either side of the double doors on match days.

And there was a sort of unwritten rule, born out of respect, that the fans never climbed the dozen or so steps to the front door. There was almost an invisible demarcation point: club members only beyond this point.

As a young and unknown player, the fans watched you walk up the stairs to the entrance, clearly wondering if you were somebody of importance. You felt very proud when the commissionaires allowed you through that grand entrance.

Once you were through the front door, there was very much an upstairs, downstairs feel and where you were in the pecking order was clearly defined.

Left was the ticket office.

Straight ahead was a door to the pitch.

To the right was a door down to the dressing rooms and a staircase up to where the board members, directors and bigwigs went.

Very rarely did you go up those stairs. Halfway up them was a picture of Arsenal winning the league championship in the 1930s and the roll of honour for Arsenal Player of the Year, a board I got on to in 1996, which is a source of immense pride for me.

It's actually something I feel is missing at the Emirates. There isn't a true front door, a place that says, 'This is Arsenal.'

I often used to get to evening training early as a young player, and it was as if I could feel the ghosts of yesteryear in the corridors and dressing rooms. It felt as though the spirit of the former players was supporting me and here with me as I walked down the tunnel on to the pitch of the dimly lit stadium and towards the Clock End, where we trained.

There was a small sign saying 'Keep off the pitch', but I would run on and score an imaginary goal and shoot back off again.

And I remember my first day there, as vivid as yesterday.

I was sitting at home watching the telly one evening and the phone rang. There were six of us spread across the seats of our three-piece suite – well, it was a five-piece suite really, because there were four armchairs – and my mum got up to answer it in the hallway.

She picked up the phone and the next thing we heard was her yahooing down the phone. And then came those life-changing words: 'Martin, it's Arsenal.' Arsenal. It still gives me shivers down the back of my neck now.

I said to my dad that it was about time too.

I had been playing in a Sunday league team (alongside midfielder Garry Parker, who went on to play for Forest, Villa, Leicester and with me for England Under 21s) and there were a lot of players in that team who were getting calls from clubs in and around London. We were about twelve or thirteen and I was desperate for my call to come and felt I deserved it.

The Arsenal club scout who found me was Terry Murphy.

He was an impressively well-dressed man, with an Arsenal tie, blazer and sheepskin coat, which was standard for scouts in those days.

I would come to learn that Terry was an immensely loyal, honourable and kind man, who carried himself with great class and represented Arsenal with dignity for many years.

(In fact, it was Terry who called me in 1993 to tell me that George Graham wanted me back from Everton. I always liked it when Terry called, because it was always good news.)

Initially there were five or six of us that they liked, and then it was down to me and a guy called Adrian Dalloway.

And things almost went very wrong from the start.

Adrian's dad volunteered to take us to London because he was born there, but I soon noticed we were travelling in the wrong direction and were on our way to Birmingham. I had to quickly point this out. It was going to be a long journey – in fact, it took three hours rather than the hour and a half it should have taken – and when we arrived, it was monsoon weather.

But despite the rush to get there and the weather conditions, ten minutes before my trial came a very significant moment in my life – I was handed an Arsenal home shirt for the first time. But with the rain hammering down and my shirt almost down to my knees, I could barely run round the pitch.

Luckily, the coach called us together and said that everything they'd written down was washed away and to come back next time, when the weather, hopefully, would be better.

So we all trotted back again a few weeks later, but this time down to the AstroTurf pitches on Market Road, formerly the old cattle market for London.

I wasn't taking any chances this time and insisted that my parents take me. We turned up two hours early for the trial and parked outside the stadium.

We went inside the marble halls to introduce ourselves to Terry and then I got on to the bus to be taken to the trial, with my parents following in the car.

I wasted no time trying to take hold of proceedings. Playing at right-back, every time I received the ball I ran with it, beating players, crossing the ball and setting up chances.

On the opposite side of the pitch, I could see Terry, in his sheepskin coat, talking to my mum and dad and I knew I was catching his eye and making a very good first impression.

Growing up, I was always more comfortable on the tarmac, and this new AstroTurf surface felt similar to those playground pitches at Our Lady's school all those years ago.

The club asked me to do two days a week training, but my headmaster, John Prangley, who had worked in the Birmingham area previously and had a lot of dealings with Aston Villa, said at first I was too young, but then he agreed to one evening a week. Regardless, I was ecstatic – I'd grabbed my chance.

To get to Arsenal on time, I needed to get a taxi and then the train and the tube.

My black cab used to sit outside the school gates waiting for me, and my mates would be shouting, 'Where are you going?' as I very self-consciously jumped into the back of the cab. Years later, I'd jump in a taxi and a driver would remind me it was him who had picked me up for those trips.

My sister Maureen, who was a sixth-former at this point, had been given the job of being my chaperone to Highbury. My dad was worried about me travelling on my own, as it had been all across the news that someone of a similar age to me had been kidnapped, and I hadn't been to London on my own before, or on the tube.

It was a fifteen-minute cab ride to the station, then we'd jump on the 16.05 to Paddington after buying tickets and chocolate mints, which Maureen wouldn't travel without.

It always felt a real buzz, travelling to the big smoke, especially when we arrived at Paddington in rush hour to a swathe of London commuters. We then had to get the tube to Arsenal station, which was originally called Gillespie Road, until the legendary manager Herbert Chapman literally put Arsenal on the (tube) map by cajoling the authorities to change the station's name.

As we emerged into the night from the tube station, although Highbury was just yards away, there was very little visual evidence that we were anywhere near a 60,000-capacity stadium. The first time, we had to ask for directions at a small kiosk just next to the station.

Walking past the houses, suddenly we could see the coveted Highbury pitch through a small gap between the East Stand and North Bank. Wow. Some of the floodlights along the East Stand would be lit up, and even though the stands were empty, it still looked awesome.

When we went through the double doors and into the

marble halls, we'd be greeted by a very polite middle-aged Irish lady dressed in an apron. She'd send me down the corridor and take Maureen to the Halfway House (a room halfway down the tunnel where refreshments were served and on match days was used as a players' lounge) for a chat and a cup of tea.

I mention this because she exemplified the warmth and hospitality at the club at that time. Her name was Maureen Byrne and, remembering her warmth and service to the club, I was able to invite her to my testimonial dinner years later, along with Pat Galligan, who manned the front door of Highbury day and night and was one of life's great characters.

Once I was inside, the art deco vibe of the building and the changing rooms' heated floors always gave me a cosy feel.

Then, stood outside the dressing-room door would be the great Alf Fields, a player in the 1930s, then a respected coach and at this point the youth team kit man. He was handing out the players' expenses forms that first evening. When I filled in the £6.50 it had cost me to travel, he said, 'Nobody charges that amount. Where are you coming from?'

When I told him Oxford, he said I had better be a good player if they were paying that much. I didn't have the bottle to ask him for my sister's expenses too!

Evening training for me was on Thursday nights and took place on a cinder surface behind the Clock End. You changed in the away team dressing rooms, and that's where I really started to feel the magic.

At that stage, I didn't see too many of the stars to come – Adams, Rocastle and Thomas – but every three months you would get a call to find out if you would carry on or not, and every three months it would be a different set of players and I was still there. It was a culling exercise, but I was surviving.

Those sessions were about proving you were the best. You had to stand out, catch the eye. And no one could get past me. In those early days, none of my inefficiencies were that apparent – I was just better than everyone else.

I used to do my training, and then we had to run like crazy to the tube station to get the last train back to Oxford.

We'd arrive back at Oxford station around midnight, so the next day tended to be a bit of a blur.

The Arsenal must have thought I had real potential, because they signed me as an associate schoolboy, which was a big first step on the ladder. Mum and Dad came to my school and the *Oxford Mail* came to take a photo of me with Eric Metcalf, my very supportive PE teacher, John Prangley, the headmaster and, of course, Terry Murphy from Arsenal.

After a while I started to play South East Counties league youth games on a Saturday morning for the club, and that was a huge wake-up call. That meant staying Friday night with Terry Murphy and his lovely wife, Pat, near Finsbury Park. Them taking me in was typical of the Arsenal family, and even now that ethos exists, with former club secretary David Miles and his wife Sue helping to look after Terry these days as he struggles with poor health.

I was still quite small at this point, but they threw me in at centre-half. It was fast and frenetic, everything happening at a crazy speed. It was like being thrown into a washing machine. But that's how you learn and, happily for me, they kept picking me and I kept progressing.

The next big landmark was playing in the FA Youth Cup. I was the only schoolboy in the team. That meant playing at Highbury in a game under the lights against Southampton, and the first-team manager, Terry Neill, turned up with all the club staff to watch. (Gary Lewin, who later became Arsenal and England physio, was the goalkeeper that night.)

Up front for Southampton, and already in the first team, was the very highly rated Danny Wallace.

Somehow, the game at Highbury held no fears for me, as I had been training regularly at the ground. It already felt like a second home. I can remember the smile on the face of Terry Burton, the youth team coach, after the game as he congratulated me on my performance. I felt euphoric, even though we lost 1–0.

The coaches were shocked that I was able to keep Wallace quiet and they offered me an apprenticeship contract on the back of that performance. Only four were handed out each year, and they felt like golden tickets.

I knew I'd taken a giant step that night. Here I was, running after somebody and getting rave reviews for doing it.

The day I signed my contract at Highbury, with my parents alongside me, we bumped into my hero, Kevin Keegan, there ahead of an Arsenal v Southampton game. My mum rushed up to him, told him how much I idolized him, but his response was a little underwhelming. 'It's just the first rung on the ladder,' he said.

It wasn't quite the answer I was hoping for, but Kevin Keegan wasn't wrong, and I guess he was just trying to give me a reality check.

The club always made a fuss of new signings, and treated us to a fancy meal in the Arsenal restaurant. There was a bottle of ketchup on the table and I was giving it a vigorous shake when my father hissed at me to put it down, because Terry Murphy was coming over to join us, and he might not approve of young players drowning their food in tomato sauce. So I put the bottle down and Terry then picked it up to apply to his own food. He gave the bottle a single shake, the top flew off, and the contents exploded out all over his shirt. He was completely mystified and I managed not to spit my food out.

And then my body got in the way.

I started to get pain in my left knee as part of my problems with Osgood-Schlatter disease. It's not uncommon for someone who is jumping and landing a lot on a young knee. And so I had to drop out of playing because it had become chronic and all the games I played as a kid were catching up with me.

Arsenal advised me ahead of the new season to take six months away from football to help clear up the problem. You can imagine how devastated I was.

Suddenly I realized that I hadn't really paid very much attention at school, so I worked my arse off, revising all my coursework in geography and history in the hope of better results.

But I was particularly annoyed by my careers teacher, who didn't seem to take me seriously when I discussed football, so I decided to give his lessons a miss and spend more time in my woodwork class on the wine table I was making, which now sits pride of place in my office.

I did, though, under pressure from my classmates, claim one more sporting achievement at school, taking part in the sports day athletics and winning the 100 metres, the 800 metres and the long jump, despite not training for months.

Finally, I healed. Finally, I was able to get back to football. And despite having started to go out with Nicola just three weeks earlier, off I went, aged only fifteen, to live in London full time.

*

When an apprentice joins the Arsenal, the club usually finds him lodgings with a family. But my experience was not straightforward to start out with.

All the landladies were allocated, so I ended up with my new youth team coach, Tommy Coleman.

Tommy had had many players stop with him over the years when he was a part-time coach, but now he was the full-time youth team manager, with Terry Burton promoted to reserve-team boss. Someone should have been looking closer at the wisdom of sending players who were directly under his management to stay with Tommy.

I had really enjoyed working with Terry, who was an outstanding coach and gave me many crucial lessons on defending, particularly in one-on-one situations.

Living with Tommy Coleman meant travelling over an hour to Highbury, as we were living in South Woodford in Essex. I might as well have been living in Oxford.

There was another player with me, Tony Rees, and he decided he couldn't bear living with the manager, so he went off and lived with a family member and I was all by myself.

I wasn't happy. I couldn't live with the manager. It was suffocating. I couldn't go out, I couldn't breathe. Imagine living with your boss.

Naively, not having thought the situation through, I had a quiet word with the head of youth team recruitment, Steve Burtenshaw, and told him that, as nice a family as they were, I didn't want to stay there. I was totally unaware of the impact that chat would have on my life and subsequent career.

A few weeks went past, then one day Tommy came back from an evening training session, walked past me, totally ignored me and went to see his wife, who lost her rag, rushed into the lounge and basically told me to sling my hook.

Burtenshaw had broken the news to Tommy.

I went upstairs and was packing when Tommy came up. I told him it was too late for me to get back to Oxford and he said I could stay one more night, but that was it, that now I had made life hell for him, he was going to make life hell for me!

And that's how it proceeded.

I think his wife thought I was ungrateful.

If someone had said to me, 'If you want to smooth your journey into the Arsenal first team, then stay where you are and keep your mouth shut,' maybe I would have listened.

It wasn't anything against Tommy or his wife, and it was a lovely house in South Woodford. I just didn't want to be with my manager twenty-four hours a day and to be living that far away from training.

I didn't anticipate what would happen, even though I ended up with Dot and Charlie in Stamford Hill.

Dot and Charlie were great, but it wasn't like living at home. Dot fed me well, but I was still always hungry. They just seemed to have no idea of how much a growing lad needed to eat. If I wanted something to eat after dinner, I had to make do with cream crackers and cheese, so I started going out every night to get a bag of chips, a gherkin and a tin of Tango.

Tony Adams had it easy because he lived at his parents'. One time I went round to Tony's house, he got a pack of four chocolate eclairs out of the fridge, and we had two each. It was quite the contrast.

In researching for this book, I found my diary from back then, which, as well as being full of lots of nice things about

Nicola, had 'payday' clearly written in it, as I needed the money for extra food.

The area – the Leabank View estate – wasn't great either. I tried to use the telephone boxes to speak to home or Nicola, but they were mostly vandalized, and there were gangs of lads looking for trouble. Some of them tried to mug me one night, but I sussed them out and got away. Four of them chased me down the road but they had no chance. My football training was a true life-saver.

Life could be boring, too, and the distractions weren't much better – one time we were made to do Steve Burtenshaw's house move as part of our apprentice tasks. It's not easy lifting a piano over a wall, let me tell you.

And then, at Arsenal, I was paying for the incident with Tommy Coleman.

Tommy made my life so difficult, tried to stall my career, curb my opportunities, intimidate me. In some ways, it's hard to write that, as Tommy is no longer around to defend himself and I know he has family. But it's also important to me that I tell the truth.

My early injuries opened the door for him to do that. Having done a pre-season the year before, I felt as if I was ready to commit totally to the challenge.

But six months of inactivity did not help. If I had been out that long with an injury in the modern game, I would've had rehabilitation before I joined the group, so it really shouldn't have come as a surprise when, just two days into my full-time career, I had to drop out of training with a pulled thigh muscle.

It's hard to quantify how much of my early development was affected by this injury – what was diagnosed initially as a mild thigh strain turned into four months out and meant

I barely kicked a ball in anger until the middle of November, the day of my sister's wedding, when I played that morning then rushed off to the church.

If you add up the time out for both injuries, I ended up being unavailable for eleven months, more or less.

Those four months were torture, watching out of the medical-room window, while everyone else was playing. I was being subjected to the football banter from Raphael Meade and Paul Vaessen, two young strikers who had broken into the first team squad. Them endlessly asking me if I was still a virgin was starting to wear me down.

Though, in one way, I got some revenge on Meade. A fair bit later I was wearing a new sheepskin coat bought for me from a market by my dad. The only thing was, it wasn't real. One day I was at a match, rubbing shoulders with Meade, who was wearing a lovely cream coat. At one point, I glanced at him and saw that the 'sheepskin' on my sleeve had come off on to his mac in the rain.

I tried to slip away, but it was tricky when the game was in full swing. He eventually looked at his sleeve and went berserk, threatening to throttle me and send me the bill for his dry-cleaning.

Thanks, Dad!

Back in that physio room, I was beginning to feel like a spare part.

That's when Tommy Coleman changed gear and put the squeeze on me, suggesting to me that the club was looking to tear up my contract because I had been injured and they hadn't been able to see me play.

All of this made me rush into trying to get back earlier, and the injury kept breaking down. I ended up with a small haematoma, which is still there to this day.

Luckily, Roy Johnson, the club physio, assured me that Tommy was talking rubbish and that the club would stand by me.

But he had created a fear, and my trust in him, and in the club, was waning.

In fact, I didn't know who to trust, as they told me the injury would only take a few weeks to heal.

In my four months out, Tony Adams was already playing the odd game for the reserves and Gus Caesar was brought in to fill in and then signed a full-time contract, both also 1966 babies.

I felt under so much pressure. That old diary I found is full of me worrying if I was going to ever be offered a full professional contract.

Tommy was relentless. He tried to block me going home at weekends while I was injured and then put me on the most difficult duties, the epitome of which was balls and bibs. Now, balls and bibs is the one job you don't want to do. You've got to count them all out (thirty-six balls and about sixty bibs), and you have to be meticulous or you'd get a bollocking. Normally, you do it for six weeks, but I was put on it for six months. Tommy, in one attempt to undermine me, secretly took two balls out of the first-team bag and then dragged me out of lunch to say that I hadn't done my job properly. I went round the fields looking for them. I had to do that every day for about two months, and I couldn't find them anywhere.

And then Terry Burton took pity on me, telling me he'd seen enough and that Tommy had hidden them in the coaches' room.

So I pumped them up and put them back in the bag. I went in to have my lunch and Tommy came in, shouting, 'Keown, what are you doing, having your lunch? Go find those balls.' But I told him I was going to finish my lunch first, as I was tired of him trying to stop me eating properly to build myself up. It was time to stand up for myself.

He wasn't happy at all when I presented the full set after lunch and asked me where I found them.

It was all just typical of him.

Tommy kept telling me I wasn't good enough, so my dad and I hatched a plan to front him up and take him on. I asked him for a list of which areas I was supposedly weak in, and it came back as long as your arm. So I decided to work on all the things he listed so there was no excuse: my heading, my passing, my communication.

And even when I later went out on loan (more on that later), I felt uncomfortable that it was often him coming to watch me play, as I knew the reports going back to Arsenal were not going to be positive.

He was denying me the best possible opportunity to be successful. It was wrong.

I slowly picked up my game and fitness, playing twenty-one games in the youth team and thirteen in the reserves in the 1982/83 season.

Meanwhile, the first team were struggling. They finished tenth that season (a Graham Taylor-led Watford were second), despite making the semi-finals of the FA and League Cups. A few months later, in December 1983, Terry Neill was sacked.

In my second season, I was still part of the youth team and under Tommy's control but I played most of the season in the reserves.

The talent in that youth team, though, was becoming clear: myself, Tony Adams, Michael Thomas, David Rocastle, Martin Hayes and others.

We won the Combination League but were unexpectedly knocked out of the FA Youth Cup by Stoke City in the semi-final.

Steve Burtenshaw, Terry Burton and Tommy Coleman, not to mention Alfie Fields, took it in turns to give us a bollocking for getting knocked out with all the talent we had. They said it was a disgrace.

Neill's sacking was bad timing for me, as I was supposed to be signing my pro contract. But him leaving meant it got delayed, while Tony had his sorted already. Financially, that was a blow too, as we were on £25 a week as an apprentice and £150 when we turned pro, the equivalent of about £650 today. I had to wait another three months for new coach Don Howe to find a slot to get the signature done.

Even that relief came with drama of its own. They were offering pro contracts to virtually the whole youth team group, and rightly so. Don said I was getting £145 a week but the rest were getting £150, because Tommy told Don I wasn't as good as the rest of the players. I was livid. So I told Don I was playing tomorrow and that he should come and watch me. And that if he still didn't think I was as good as the others, then fine. So he came and watched and pulled me in on the Monday, told me I was fantastic and that I was going to get the same as the rest of them.

And then, at last, something good happened and it made me realize I was going to have a career at the top.

Tony and I were dragged out to train against Charlie Nicholas and Tony Woodcock because they needed numbers. But they must have wanted to look at us too, and it was going to be a good test for two top young players.

It was two v two and we played like our lives depended on it, determined to prove to the coaches and each other that we were good enough. After that, I knew I was going to make it. If I could stop those two, I could stop anybody. Don Howe sent them off and said, 'I just want to say, you two, that was fantastic. If you two continue like that, the sky's the limit. Those two are top players and they couldn't get a look-in today.'

I was seventeen then, and my chances to train with the first team started to improve, especially in pre-season. Don used to do training clinics after that with us, and he used to shout, 'Get down low, get down low,' when he wanted us to defend a man coming at us. I would say that it didn't suit me doing that, it was too much hard work. Kenny Sansom was doing it because he was small, but I couldn't get that low. I was wasting energy, my legs were burning from squatting, so I said I should do it the way I wanted to.

Don watched me and said, 'That's perfect. You do it the way you want to.'

He believed in me. And it was just as well.

I always felt able to challenge Don, especially if other young players needed protecting. One pre-season when he returned to the club in 1997, we had so many youth team injuries I told him he needed to calm down the training.

He snapped back at me, saying it was none of my business, but they needed protecting, so I continued, telling him that he needed to modernize and that his book of knowledge should never be full.

Dicing with Death

There was a very loud voice in my head saying, 'You're dying.'

Survival mode kicked in. I needed to do something.

And to think this all started over a stupid broken elbow, thanks to my teammate Dave Madden.

It was 1984 and I was in a training session that got out of hand on the AstroTurf pitches behind the Clock End at Highbury. Things got very physical with Graham Rix, Stewart Robson and Madden when I launched from one tackle to the other. I was on the ground, trying to kick the ball, when Madden booted my left arm, which was supporting all my body weight and was nowhere near the ball. I had never experienced pain like it. My left elbow was dislocated and broken.

It meant I had to miss the second leg of the Junior Floodlit Cup, and I was then on a short holiday to Ireland with my family when the phone rang. It was Tommy Coleman, telling me there was no way I could put my feet up when they were all on their way to France to play in a tournament and that I was coming with them.

So, with my arm in a sling and the doctors saying I was unfit to travel (I still have the medical report), I nevertheless headed back to my digs in London for a very early morning start and sat on the steps outside Highbury feeling a bit nauseous.

I had a stomach pain, and I couldn't shift it. When we arrived in France there was a banquet for all the teams, so I decided to eat and have some fizzy drinks as I thought it might help. It didn't.

We were staying in a large dormitory, twenty or so beds in one room, and I just put my head down to sleep it off.

The next day the guys were up early and headed off for their first match. I opted out because the pain was getting worse. I was in bed all day without anything to eat or drink.

That second night I became very ill, vomiting, and the lads were moaning as I was keeping everybody awake.

The next morning I felt wretched again, in a hazy state and with my right side in agony. The boys went out again, and I was there alone again.

Through the haze of pain I realized that if I didn't take some sort of action for myself, I might not get out of there alive.

I headed outside despite not being able to stand properly. I went next door to where the Italian team were and said I needed a doctor. But no one spoke a word of English, so I got a chair and sat outside in the sun. Then, almost like a mirage in the desert, a car came through into the car park, familiar-looking and with an English number plate. It was Arsenal youth team scout Steve Rowley.

If he hadn't turned up, I'm not sure I would have survived. Years later, I always used to say to him, 'Steve, you saved my life,' even though he went off to the game rather than taking me straight to hospital.

Roy Johnson, the club physio, came back eventually with a French doctor.

'How long has he been here?' the doctor asked. After a quick examination, he said in broken English, 'He's got appendicitis.'

Roy replied, saying, 'Don't be ridiculous, check again,' as

I'd been there for three days. But they moved quickly to get an ambulance.

Roy felt the first hospital we went to was not fit for me to have my operation in so I was driven to a private hospital and taken down to the operating theatre, lying curled up in a ball to try to control the pain. When they injected me in my backside, I straightened, my appendix burst. I only found out later on that I had peritonitis, a serious medical emergency that, without treatment, can cause a whole-body infection called sepsis. And sepsis is often fatal.

At this point, due to the language barrier, we didn't even know that my appendix had burst. When I came round, I was in a lot of pain and stayed in hospital for the next four days.

Writing this now, I can hardly believe what I went through. It makes me really emotional.

I had buried those feelings and just got on with it, but what happened was so wrong. I was literally fighting for my life and, until I took matters into my own hands, nobody was helping me.

I was only in France for seven days but I lost more than a stone in weight. To get home, I was wheeled through the airport and on to the tarmac.

I gingerly climbed the stairs to the plane, where I saw my teammates looking at me open-mouthed, perhaps feeling a bit guilty for telling me to stop moaning a few nights earlier.

When we reached the UK, I was again wheeled through the airport, and my mum and dad's faces said it all. They and Nicola looked at me in horror and took me straight to the hospital, where I spent another seven days.

After finally coming home and eating my first proper meal,

the right side of my stomach came up like a balloon where my appendix scar was. So we went straight back to the hospital again, and they found that I had a huge abscess.

They opened up my insides, filled me with gauze and antibiotics and I stayed in for another twenty-four hours.

However, inside a month, I was back for pre-season training and, despite cursing my bad luck, I wasn't going to give up.

I started pre-season with a hole in my side and an elbow I couldn't fully extend. In fact, I trained with a padded patch over the hole on my stomach, which was still quite deep.

And I held out my good arm to protect my side.

It wasn't sensible, but I didn't want to face a second pre-season watching from the sidelines.

I pulled my thigh muscle after just two days of my first proper pre-season with Arsenal, when I ran into Tommy Coleman, which was bad luck. I felt like the world was against me, that I had to fight to make it, and the best way I knew how to deal with problems was with confrontation. That goes back to my parents' relationship, it goes back to being bullied for being Irish, and a whole lot more. But that combative nature, which probably slowed down my progress, also made me the player and defender I became.

My dad, as a young man, had a reputation for being able to look after himself, and people used to ask him to help solve their problems. He dealt with discrimination by fighting back. And so I learned to do the same.

I used to fight Niall Quinn all the time. We used to do an exercise where two players would go into the middle of the circle of ten players to compete for headers, and the first person to head the ball ten times was the winner. Quinn was three inches taller than me and I was put with him every time. I spent the whole exercise with his elbow in my mouth, much to Tommy's delight.

Tommy was putting me with him to try to humiliate me, thinking I would lose, but I was having none of it. It was only a matter of time before it was going to go off. He was trying to light a fire, and a few times things got heated. I was driven again by my dad telling me that you have to stand up for yourself. So, one day when training finished, Quinn and I had a proper scrap. It didn't matter to me that he was the biggest guy there.

Tommy was not impressed and told me he was going to get me thrown out of the club for fighting.

Terry Neill, given the lowdown by my friend Tommy, then told me if it happened again, I was out. That he would back me for now, but I had to control my temper.

So I came home and told Dad that we had a bit of an issue. 'I can't keep throwing punches,' I said, 'or I'll be out of the club.'

It wasn't Quinn's fault. He was just part of the environment that had been created. But I don't regret it. I regret that his elbow found its way to my face by unfair means. He started it and I was trying to finish it.

Arsenal was a hard place to be back then, a brutal, tough environment, as elite sport often is.

I bumped into former Arsenal player Brian McDermott years later at Reading, and he was sitting there with a big smile on his face. I said, 'Brian, blimey, you've changed. At Arsenal everyone would walk round you because you were such an angry man.' And he said that was just the way things were back then, it was dog eat dog. There was no mercy on that team bus. The banter was relentless. The Londoners used to ask me where my combine harvester was parked every time I opened my mouth because I was from Oxford.

At times I didn't want to speak because, every time I did, someone wanted to mimic me.

I think I had a problem in a dressing room where if I felt somebody was being underhanded, I didn't really have any time for them. I'm trying to win something and if they're trying to stop me being the best I can be, I have to try to blank them out.

What I saw around me was a load of dangerous paths, reasons to fail if I wasn't careful.

That only increased once I was in the first team.

The way it worked was that when you made it into the first team, you went into the Halfway House players' lounge after games, and it was full of the stars of the day. Most of the single lads went out on the circuit, to the nightclubs. And then the drinking sessions extended for some of the players to the Sunday afternoon and evening. Tony Adams got dragged into that, and we'll talk to him later in the book about it. But they were still winning things. They were maybe addicted to the success and addicted to the booze and everything that went with it.

Goalkeeper John Lukic once said to me that he was thinking of buying a minibus so he could pick everyone up because there were so many players who had lost their driving licences because of drink-driving.

There were, though, some very good role models in the team. Paul Davis, who'd come through the youth team a few years before me, was a lovely guy with a strong moral compass. Viv Anderson was a championship and double

European Cup winner. I liked his winning mentality. Paul Mariner was a fantastic character and jumped in to intervene when a drunk Kenny Sansom asked me out for a scrap at my very first Christmas party because he wasn't happy with me giving banter to David O'Leary two weeks earlier.

Paul said to Kenny that was what they wanted from the young players – characters, banter – so to leave me alone. I appreciated that help from Paul, God rest his soul.

Kenny and Graham Rix couldn't wait to take people out drinking with them. So I have total sympathy for what happened to Tony and Paul Merson in terms of their battles with alcohol. My dad was sending me to London with a message of 'don't piss your money up against the wall'. I remember going out to the Chase Side Tavern in Southgate and Rix telling me I couldn't sit there with an orange juice, that I'd have to buy a round. It cost me a whole week's wages. It was the last time I was there. I thought, 'What a prick.'

That just wasn't me, and still isn't. I have a pint of Guinness, I'll have a glass of red wine, but the rest of it isn't me. I've never had a cocktail in my life.

Despite, or maybe because of the combative atmosphere, the talent that came out of my Arsenal youth team was incredible.

I once heard Arsène Wenger talking about Manchester United's Class of '92, and I thought, 'Boss, you've not even looked into the depths of your own club to see what we had in '83.'

Eight of our extraordinary group of young players went on to make over 4,600 senior appearances: I made 800; Tony Adams and Paul Merson made over 700 each; Niall Quinn made over 600; Rocky Rocastle and Mickey

Thomas made over 400 each. Seven of us won league titles with the Arsenal. Six of us – me, Tony, Rocastle, Thomas, Merson and Quinn – became full internationals. And two of us captained our country – Tony Adams and myself. I'm so proud, and so lucky, to have been part of that group.

When each new generation arrives at the club, that class of '83 – as well as other big home-grown successes – should be held up as an example of how it is possible to break into the first team. Arsenal have to maintain that pathway for their future success.

I recently found my old diaries from the eighties, and I kept writing the words, 'You are good enough, you are good enough.' I was writing that for myself. Because everyone was telling me I wasn't. Every day you go in, 'You can't do this, you can't do that' – no one looks at what you *can* do.

Yet that generation was special. We used to sit in the paddocks behind the bench at Highbury – me, Tony, Rocastle and others – and we were all saying to each other that we should be in the first team.

We were watching that side of Paul Davis, Rix, Sansom, Mariner, Alan Sunderland – a team of stars and thoroughbreds, but they weren't winning titles – and some of us young guys were shouting out negative things, but then we got told off because the manager could hear us. We were becoming Arsenal fans, sitting there.

One game that really stays in the memory was the 1982 UEFA Cup tie against Spartak Moscow, when the Russians played us off the park, winning 5–2. That night, Arsenal fans were thrilled by this brilliant one-touch passing and stayed behind after the game to applaud the opposition, which, at a time when football stadiums had become pretty toxic places, with hooliganism rife, was pretty remarkable. Looking back, that game was a window into the future and the style those fans would be treated to fifteen years later, the one and two touch football that became commonplace at Highbury and that Tony and I would play a big part in. We just didn't know it at the time.

There was a lot of self-belief in that paddock. We youngsters really felt we were more talented than the first team, and things came to a head one time when we played a reserves versus first-team game and we won. We went a goal in front and ran around celebrating, and they lost the plot, Alan Sunderland grabbing me around the collar and telling me to behave myself. But that's how good we were.

On a Friday back then, everyone trained together at Highbury. And when you were an accepted member of the first-team squad, you changed in the first-team dressing room. Tony got into that so young. He was seventeen, even though he was only playing the occasional game. I was still in the reserve-team dressing room with Rocastle, Thomas and the others. And we were very determined to get there, to make it into the first-team group. The actual rooms weren't that different – the first team had better kit – but it's just about what it means, what it represents.

Tony got into the first team, and Terry Neill pulled me aside and told me I was very close, that I was doing really well, to keep working hard and I would get the chance.

I fired back at Terry, saying it was a good job I didn't get picked because if I hadn't read the papers, I wouldn't have a clue who they all were. I didn't know any of the first-team squad, as I had hardly ever trained with them.

He told me I was right, and for the next two weeks I was

training with the first team. He said if I did well, it would be a permanent move.

At the end of the two weeks he told me to get my stuff and move to the first-team dressing room, that I'd been top class.

Then I went on loan. Things were about to get exciting – and then a whole lot worse.

Spreading my Wings

By Christmas 1985, I had everything I wanted at that point in my life.

I was at Arsenal, in the first team, playing well, and I was dating Nicola.

If you'd have told me then that six months later I'd be leaving the club I loved, furious with the way I'd been treated, I'd have probably laughed at you.

But as I became a key figure for the club, things started unravelling off the field with regards to my contract. And it culminated in me making a terrible mistake.

To understand that, first we need to go back a bit in time to my loan to Brighton and my Arsenal debut.

The loan to Second Division Brighton had been the making of me. You go on loan for two reasons: to come back and get into the first team or because the club doesn't think you're good enough. I wasn't sure which category I fell into, but I hit the ground running and won the Robinson's Barley Water Young Player of the Month in my first month. The former England manager Ron Greenwood was on the panel for it, so I must have been doing something right.

I finally had my chance to play and I felt free at last, excelling under a manager, Chris Cattlin, who believed in my talent. I was given the chance to play right-back with the pace and freedom to get forward, and was flying.

Brighton, much like the demographic of its town, had become a bit of an outpost for players near the end of their careers. That team had Joe Corrigan, Jimmy Case, Frank Worthington and Dennis Mortimer, but the standout player was Danny Wilson, who clearly was destined to play at a higher level. He was a true leader too.

Arsenal regularly sent coaches and scouts to keep an eye on me – and when I looked up and saw Tommy Coleman in the stand, I wondered if I'd ever get my chance – but generally the reports were that I was flying.

I was enjoying it so much that I was determined not to go back to Arsenal and play second fiddle again and was badgering Cattlin to sign me permanently. He reassured me that Arsenal was the club for me and to go and sign a new deal with them. So I went back, and suddenly there was real hope again.

Don Howe presented a two-year contract to me but confidentially advised me not to sign it because, if I got in the first team, my money would go up massively.

I saw Don as a real father figure, I trusted him, and he was insistent that he wouldn't let me sign that second year.

And for a while, that seemed like good advice. I went back to Brighton for another loan spell, played well again at right-back, and was enjoying my football, until I was told, 'We can't really play you any more, because we want to keep the regular right-back happy.'

Bizarrely, I even played up front alongside Dean Saunders a few times that season, such was the injury crisis at the club. I grabbed a couple of goals too.

Eventually, I came back from loan with real belief in my ability. My moment had finally arrived.

John Cartwright, the assistant manager, was a great advocate for us young players, and he was virtually begging Don to put me in the team.

And one week, near the end of November, he told me

there was a chance I might get the nod. The way it worked was that every Friday three teams would get put up on a notice board outside the first-team dressing room: the youth team, reserves and first team. I stood there many times disappointed when my name was either in the youth team or the reserves, and then suddenly there it was: my name, written on the first-team squad list.

I was going to finally make my Arsenal debut, away at West Bromwich Albion.

My family came up, I was playing in central defence alongside Tommy Caton and I won Man of the Match in a 0–0 draw. Having played twenty-seven games for Brighton on loan, I actually found the game very comfortable and found first-team football easier in many ways than playing in the reserves. I played knowing that I was ready. There was no fear whatsoever. And with more at stake, everything I did was magnified, and I thrived on that.

But then the next game was in the League Cup and I was cup-tied because Don had not put a clause in my Brighton contract stopping me from playing for them in the cups. I was gutted.

So O'Leary came back into the team for a few games while I was running out for the reserves, getting a bollocking for my attitude at Portsmouth from Terry Burton after we lost a game. But then the first team lost at Southampton 3–0 and it was clear changes were needed.

We played a testimonial game for Colchester manager Mike Walker and the bosses said they were going to play me and David O'Leary in the first half and Tony and Tommy Caton in the second half and whoever fared best was going to play on Saturday against Liverpool.

I thought, 'Happy days. Finally, it's a level playing field.'

The game went well, and I felt I'd more than done myself justice, but then there was silence. We had no idea who had won the trial.

So on the Saturday morning – eleven days before Christmas – I got to Highbury and they told me I was playing. I lined up with O'Leary against Liverpool, the soon-to-be Division One champions. We won 2–0 and I didn't look back that season, the next game being a 1–0 win away at league leaders Manchester United. I played every single game, until I got suspended. O'Leary then came in for me and, when my ban was over, we played in a three to finish off the season for three games.

So of course when it came to sorting my contract, I was feeling optimistic. I was a first-team player now. Surely I could take the next step up in my earnings.

Instead, Arsenal took the piss. And this is something I've been waiting to get off my chest for almost forty years, as the story that's been out there is wide of the mark.

They offered me the same money they had the year before when Don told me not to take it – £300 a week. And I couldn't go back and sort it out with Don because he'd gone by this stage, resigning after a game against Coventry.

Suddenly I was in a building where no one seemed to recognize me. Steve Burtenshaw was telling me that I was the best young central defender in the country. And then they sat down and offered me a £50 a week raise. I thought they were kidding me – I would have had every right to swerve my car off the road, like Ashley Cole famously did when he was offered £50,000 a week (only joking, Ash).

Steve went to talk to the hierarchy for me, but he told me they weren't budging. So, not one to accept what I felt was injustice, I went to see Ken Friar to try to rescue my Arsenal career.

Ken was Arsenal through and through, an extraordinary man, who was born in Highbury, started working at the club part-time aged twelve and worked his way up through the ranks until he was managing director. Everyone at the club respected Ken, and he had a real air of gravitas. It was quite intimidating sitting opposite him.

His office was up the famous marble stairs at Highbury, along the corridor, a journey players very rarely made. He passed me the offer, which I looked at and then politely told him wasn't acceptable. And then he did the strangest thing. He opened up a huge hidden safe in the panels behind the wall and said, 'Look, let me show you the debt.' He got out an enormous ledger, and everything was in red. I said, 'Don't pay me at all then, because I don't want Arsenal being in that much debt.' He wasn't expecting me to say that, and he wasn't quite sure what to do, so he put it away and told me to talk to the new manager, George Graham, when he started at the club in the coming weeks.

When I arrived in George's office, I'd been waiting a very long time – I honestly think it was a few hours – outside in the corridor with a bunch of other players. Tony Woodcock, Niall Quinn and Paul Davis were among them.

When I went in, you couldn't help but be impressed by George. He was a striking figure, immaculately dressed – but he was in a hurry. He tapped his watch and said, 'Sorry, Martin, I've promised my wife to take her on holiday, and I haven't got much time to see you.'

I wasn't standing for that, as I'd been waiting for months

to resolve my contract issues, not to mention the three hours outside his office.

We chatted about things that were wrong with the club, certain players all taking the piss. About the team bus pulling up outside Old Trafford and us having to wait for the card game to finish before we went into the ground. About all the things I thought were unprofessional.

I told him that I didn't think the team should be rerouting through the West End to drop Charlie Nicholas and Graham Rix off on the bus after a game. He seemed shocked by what was happening.

I asked him if he'd ever seen me play and he told me yes, for Brighton against Millwall, where he was previously the manager. This is where things started to go wrong.

The thing is, I wasn't playing that day – he'd mixed me up with Gary O'Reilly – which, if you've ever seen a picture of him at the time, is fair enough. We were very similar-looking, though he was somewhat slower than me. George was insistent he'd seen me lots of times when I corrected him, but I wasn't convinced that he had any knowledge of me at all.

Our talk lasted about ten to fifteen minutes. And it turned out to be the only one we had about me.

I remember there was absolutely no compromise from George and he very sternly told me that what I was being offered was their final offer.

So I shook his hand, looked him in the eye and said, 'That's it then, I'm off.' He asked me where, and I said I didn't know, but I wasn't staying with that kind of offer.

He thought I was bluffing. But I was angry and felt let down. I'd been waiting for months for the club to do right by me, and they hadn't. I told George it was ridiculous, what they were offering. Ridiculous. And that was it. I stepped out of Highbury without even looking back, I ran for a train, sprinted all the way to the station, the anger bubbling inside of me. I thought the whole thing was bullshit. They'd been telling me I was the best in the country. But they were refusing to back it up.

By this point I had seen many young players shown the door. The world of football is ruthless. You see many young dreams crushed because players are deemed not good enough, talented people shown the door, not least Nicky Beaumont, who became a close friend while sharing digs with me, and I saw how devastating that news can be.

I felt I was now producing my side of the bargain. The club needed to show some trust, faith and reward, but it just wasn't there and so it became a point of principle. I thought, 'This club has decided many players' futures, but they're not deciding mine.'

The mistake I made was to become too emotional.

The strangest thing then happened – and looking back, it was incredibly unfortunate, not wanting to be disrespectful.

The next day I had a phone call from Graham Turner, the Aston Villa manager.

I had bumped into him at an Oxford game a while before and he'd asked me about my contract. It turns out he'd watched me for Arsenal against Liverpool and Manchester United and was really impressed with how quiet I had kept Ian Rush and Mark Hughes.

When researching for this book, I found out that Graham had seen an article in the paper mentioning that my contract was up and wouldn't be sorted until George Graham came back from holiday. So he thought I was worth a call – little did he know the state of mind I was in and what had just happened.

I guess he just rang at the right time for him and Villa, calling me as I stepped through the door from that upsetting meeting at Arsenal. My brother Will handed me the phone and, in a heartbeat, my career was heading in a different direction. I agreed to meet Graham the next day.

If I had given myself another forty-eight hours, it just wouldn't have happened because I'd have calmed down. Instead, I was still angry, like a jilted lover on the rebound.

The meeting with Graham took place at Villa chairman Doug Ellis's huge Birmingham house.

Doug's opening line to me and my dad was 'Do you like the house, as this can all be yours if you are successful at Aston Villa?'

An experienced negotiator, he saw me coming from a mile off. Here he was, the perfect stranger, pretending to be my friend and offering me the sort of terms I had expected from Arsenal.

I had asked for £50 more from Arsenal. They'd offered me £300 per week, and I said I'd take £350. They also offered me the staggeringly generous signing-on fee of £1,000. Villa offered me £25,000 signing-on fee and £600 per week. The offers were worlds apart and one club made me feel valued and special – the other didn't. I agreed to the deal.

Looking back now, though, it was a mistake, and that's nothing against Villa or Graham Turner.

I should have taken a breath, gone back to training and then worked out a new deal with Arsenal over time.

I regretted it the minute I did it. Because all I'd ever wanted was to play for Arsenal. I had climbed the mountain to get into the Arsenal first team, and now I was jumping off it – and without looking where I was landing.

I was very upset. I went on holiday with Nicola for a week

and kept waking up with a start, realizing what a mistake I'd made. It was surreal. I was bumping into Arsenal fans and people were coming up to me and patting me on the back, telling me I was brilliant, what a great season I'd had. They didn't know I had secretly signed for Villa.

Another twist to all of this is that if I'd taken advice or known how it all worked, I maybe could have got out of the Villa deal. I was still under contract with Arsenal until the end of June, but Villa had told me to sign the deal early and then they put it in a vault until I was officially available in July. I could just have gone to Arsenal and said I've made a mistake and the Villa contract would have been void. But I didn't know that at the time. If I had just called somebody at Arsenal, maybe they could have helped to unravel the mess.

I almost wasn't alone in moving. David Rocastle rang me shortly after, very angry, saying, 'If you're going, I'm going too,' and Arsenal nearly lost him as well. He told me his contract offer was disappointing and he was having the same issue.

I mentioned it to Graham Turner, but he said they'd get thrown out of the league if they took another one of Arsenal's players. (I'm pretty sure he was exaggerating!) But this is where David Dein, who had joined the Arsenal board in 1983, came into his own and sorted out Rocky's contract. David had, it appeared to me, a love for a certain type of player, the spectacular player, the maverick, game-changing player. I have no problem with that at all, because I think David is a good man, but if you're a bread-and-butter player, you didn't necessarily get the same interest from him.

So Rocastle got his raise, but the club were generally taking the young players for granted. The fee I went for tells everybody the truth – the FA Independent Transfer Tribunal decided Villa had to pay £125k, rising to £200k, for me, not the £500k Arsenal wanted. The conclusion was that if Arsenal valued me at £500k, then their contract offer did not reflect that valuation.

Despite the hike in my wages and the fact that Villa was a big, historic, special club, I was pretty angry with the whole situation. Don Howe really should have addressed my contract back in December when we were beating Liverpool and Man United, first and second in the division at that point. Don was one of the best coaches that ever lived, but he wasn't suited to management.

I bumped into him at an England Under 21s meet-up shortly after the move. He jumped at me aggressively and asked what on earth I was doing leaving Arsenal. I said, 'What do you mean? It was your fault, you should have sorted my contract out back in January when I started playing regularly in the first team. What were you doing? If you were doing your job properly, I'd still be there now!'

Falling from Grace

When I arrived at Aston Villa in July 1986 I was shocked at the lack of professionalism.

After the public announcement that I had signed, I arrived during the summer at Villa Park to pick up a snazzy sponsored car as part of my deal. I thought it'd be a brand-new, shiny affair, but what was waiting for me was a used Montego with grubby upholstery and dodgy steering. It made me wonder what other surprises were in store for me at Aston Villa.

I had taken an old schoolfriend, Bronan, with me to Birmingham, and moments after driving off in my Montego, as we sat at the traffic lights, both of us looking at the grubby dashboard and interior, a car smashed into the back of us from nowhere.

If ever there was a moment when you thought out loud, 'What else could possibly go wrong?', it was then. 'Is this for real?' I thought. 'I haven't even kicked a ball yet.'

I know this was early in proceedings, but lots of things were making me doubtful about this move.

Embarrassingly, we had to drive back to the ground to tell the office they had better inform the insurance company that someone had driven into the back of us and send the car in for repairs.

On my first day at Aston Villa's training ground, Paul Elliott rushed up to me and immediately asked me why on earth I had left Arsenal to come here.

And straight away I was thinking the same thing.

Three days into pre-season training, where we hardly did anything other than jog around a pitch, we headed out to Pisa in Italy.

I quickly learned that this wasn't part of a scheduled trip where we could train and build up for the new season. We were actually there because Pisa had expressed an interest in Simon Stainrod and the game was arranged at the last minute in the hope that Doug Ellis could offload one of his strikers. This was how Ellis was running his club.

Pisa weren't interested, and in fact wanted to sign Paul Elliott, a deal which happened a year later.

Pisa is of course famous for the Leaning Tower, and it was a bit like my career, looking like it was going to fall over.

When we came back from Italy, we had to go to the hearing I mentioned earlier, where the FA tribunal would decide how much Villa should pay Arsenal for me.

Even at the tribunal, I could have just blown the whole thing out of the water and said, 'These guys approached me illegally, ambushed me, I don't even know why I'm here.' But I just thought too much damage had been done and my dad told me to stick to the commitment I'd made to Villa. I'd left Arsenal, and that was it, and at the tribunal I was confronting two very cold strangers opposite me, Ken Friar and George Graham, both stony-faced, and not speaking. It felt really odd. And by this time I was already looking at my manager, Graham Turner, and club owner, Doug Ellis, and thinking that Doug was a bit of a cheapskate.

After the hearing, Doug was being driven by Graham in his company Rover, with me sitting in the back. And he kept on looking at the manager and tutting. I was wondering what he was tutting about, because I thought they got me pretty damn cheaply.

And then he turned to Turner and said, 'Well, we spent a lot of money this summer, a lot more than I wanted to. Certainly, today, I've paid a lot more for Martin than I thought he was worth. This had better work out, because if it doesn't, you know what's going to happen.'

I tapped Mr Ellis on the shoulder and said, 'Mr Ellis, can I just say something? I've just heard you say that, and I can't believe what you've just said, because I'm telling you now that is a bargain, and I will prove to you that's the best money you've ever spent at this football club.'

I thought, 'They don't even know what they've got in the car.' I felt like Doug had sucked me in, that the whole thing was a sham, but I was there now so I had to get on with it.

Back at Arsenal, pre-season with Don Howe had been meticulous.

There were running exercises, in and out of cones, over hurdles, everything was timed. Then there were all these sequences of training and defending, so organized, so professional. You'd do this monster cross-country run. And whatever time you achieved and where you came were really significant.

I was injured during my first two pre-seasons at Arsenal. I pulled my thigh muscle the first year; the next time I had peritonitis, and could hardly put one foot in front of the other. But the following season I was fighting fit and won the cross-country. That felt even more significant than performing on the pitch, and Terry Burton, stood next to Don, shouted, 'He's back, he's finally ready to go!' That's how it was. So the pre-seasons were really significant at Arsenal.

In contrast, at Villa, it didn't seem like there was any kind of professionalism in what we were doing, nothing was really logged. There was no real way of gauging who was fit and who wasn't. We were all running around the pitch, and half of the players were cutting corners. And then came that Pisa trip. I remember we were standing under the shower at half-time listening to the team talk, trying to get cool. And then we spent the three or four days there unable to train because it was so hot.

In Italy, not one to stand on ceremony, I went to see Ron Wylie, the first-team coach, and asked what was going on. I'd only been there a few days.

I told him the training had been a joke, and if we carried on like this, we were going to get relegated and that by now at Arsenal, we'd have done x, y and z.

He said: 'What page are you on?'

I replied, 'Sorry?'

And he said, 'You're brand new and you're on page 2 of your career, and I'm on page 222. There's more than one way to skin a cat.'

I asked him to stop talking in riddles, and he told me to relax, that it would be fine.

We did of course get relegated that season. Everyone kept saying we were too good to go down, but we weren't.

What a disastrous season that was.

Steve Hodge, the England player, had come back on a pedestal after outstanding performances in the 1986 World Cup, but he had his Maradona shirt safely tucked away and made it very clear he didn't want to be there. Others, too, were restless, and senior players were coming to the end of their careers. In fact, eleven players left when we got relegated.

Now, I still look back, shocked, at the memory of two

players sitting in the bath after a game, asking each other if they had time to play nine holes of golf at the famous Belfry golf course. If they had energy for that, they can't have been putting in everything during the match. I used to go home and fall asleep, I was so exhausted.

I was Player of the Year that fateful season, but I take no pride in that whatsoever.

I started off watching the first game of the season and then I quickly got in the team because they needed me.

Turner got sacked by mid-September after a 6–0 defeat to Nottingham Forest, and I soon realized that you've got to have good, focused people around you to be successful, people willing to fight for each other, like that group at Arsenal. And when I kept looking over my shoulder at the youthful team I'd left behind, there they were, making it to two consecutive League Cup finals and winning one of them. And I threw all that away.

It was hard to show my face around town in Birmingham. We were losing so many games. I was living alone in a hotel in the city centre for the first four months and I'd come home at weekends to Oxford. I was bored at the Holiday Inn and had gone through everything on the menu, even the children's galactic burgers. At least I could go out occasionally with some of the players, to a few nightclubs here and there. I'd never really been to any nightclubs before that.

Garry Thompson was in the Holiday Inn with me and became a good friend. He told me in amongst all the despair that I was going to be a top player and would find a way out of this carnage. I really appreciated the support from Garry, who played a major part in us getting promoted the following season.

I went to stay at the club hostel for a week. It was run by club kit man Jim Paul, and his wife Sylvia. I slept on a mattress on the floor. I'd been there before, as Villa had tried to sign me as a fourteen-year-old, making me captain during my trial before my dad persuaded me to stick with Arsenal and Terry Murphy. So the hostel was familiar, though not in a great way.

Luckily, Australian defender Tony Dorigo then suggested I stop with him. I like Tony, but his dog, Rambo, a Dobermann, was absolutely frightening, especially when it jumped up and put its paws on my shoulders to greet me. So that didn't last long.

I needed to buy a house, and that's where my dad stepped in with his advice. I bought one in leafy Streetly, where there wasn't anyone else from the squad.

In fact, Graham Taylor bought a house around the corner when he took over as manager in the summer of 1987. His was one of three very nice houses being built in a small cul-de-sac near me.

I saw a For Sale sign for the remaining two houses. When I drove in one day to have a look – I'd grown sick of the endless renovations in Streetly – I caught sight of what looked like the gaffer standing at his lounge window peering out at me.

Doing an emergency three-point turn, I got out of there as fast as I could, and the next day Graham said, 'We both know that you're not going to buy a house in that cul-de-sac, don't we, Martin?'

'Yes, boss,' I said. 'You can be sure that I'm not moving in next door to you!'

Living by myself was new to me, having been part of a family of six, and I found it a bit strange. But the house needed a total renovation so I wasted no time in sending for help from home.

My brother John came up with Bronan. They were both qualified electricians, so they did all the re-wiring, and it was just great to see familiar faces. And my other brother, William, a qualified gas engineer, came up to do the central heating and plumbing. My brother-in-law, Kieron, fitted the kitchen.

Then he decided to take out the chimney breast, and I got Nigel Spink in to re-plaster the wall. Yes, Nigel Spink, the Aston Villa goalkeeper and European Cup winner. A couple of cans and a small fee, and Nigel did a great job in half an hour. Luckily he didn't charge me his division one hourly rate.

When Kieron was there, I made him work all day. He took on some of the decorating as well, and I'd go out and get him fish and chips at about nine thirty every evening, covered in paint. After five days of this, the chip shop owner said to me, 'Wow, you're working late every night.' I explained to him that my real job was as a professional footballer. He laughed, went to the till, lifted out a £5 note, pointed to the Duke of Wellington and said, 'And he's my uncle. Now get out of my chip shop and stop taking the mickey out of me.'

Near the end of the following season, when we were about to get promoted, I went back to the fish and chip shop, and when the owner saw me at the back of the queue, he shouted out, 'Martin,' and waved me to the front, saying he was sorry he hadn't believed me and congratulating me for that year's success. The fish and chips were on him for the rest of my time in the city.

I wasn't lonely for long. I had moved in just a few days before Geoff and Chris, neighbours who became good friends. A jeweller based in the famous Jewellery Quarter in the city, Geoff would see me pulling into the drive, my phone would go in the house and he'd tell me to come over for my tea. They were a wonderful couple, who really helped me settle into Birmingham.

On the pitch, I had to get on with the footballing decision I'd made. My dad used to say, 'You've made your bed, you're going to have to lie in it. But don't lie there for long, because you need to get out of the shit.'

Things hadn't worked out with Graham Turner because Doug didn't really respect him.

But the next manager in that relegation season didn't fare much better. Billy McNeill was a European Cup winner with Celtic as a player and a successful manager with them, Aberdeen and Manchester City. His nickname soon became Billy McBingo, because he used to say the word 'bingo' so often the lads could hardly contain their laughter.

Every sentence was finished with 'Bingo!', and then one day he threw in a 'Bango!' and the room nearly erupted. It reminded me of being at school and laughing at the wrong moment so you got in trouble.

Everyone was smirking, and he could sense the disrespect.

These were do-or-die matches, but we'd come out of a meeting and someone would say, 'Did anyone hear what he said?' And then everyone would say, 'No, not a word of it, but there were fifteen bingos and even a bango.'

He was ripped apart by the guys in the dressing room, although you could see that he understood the game.

He was supportive of me. One day he pulled me to one side and asked me what I was doing at Aston Villa.

I said that I'd been asking myself that since I walked through the door. In fact, he did an article in the papers saying I should be in the England squad. He understood my position. And I appreciated that.

With three games to go to rescue our top-flight status, our

opponents were Arsenal at Highbury. This was a game I'd had my eye on ever since the fixtures were released the previous summer, a huge moment for me personally.

And on the eve of the game I would get my first harsh lesson in dealing with the national media.

The press were all over me with questions about my future at Villa and whether we could stay up. I answered by saying I was determined to be a First Division player and there was no way I'd be playing in the Second Division next year. My comments were intended to be a bullish statement, signalling that Villa were not going to go down, not on my watch.

However, that's not how they were interpreted. The headlines the next morning were all 'Keown is off.'

Going back to Highbury just ten months after leaving Arsenal and embroiled in a relegation battle was always going to be a tough experience. But I was in for a shock.

I walked out on to the pitch to a chorus of boos, both from the Arsenal fans and supporters of my new club, Aston Villa. It's not very often a player gets booed by both sets of supporters. It was totally humiliating and I felt thoroughly ashamed. We lost 2–1. It was one of the lowest moments of my career.

If journalists later in my career found me difficult to deal with, then this probably explains it. I felt they'd completely stitched me up.

I was doing my absolute utmost to get that team out of trouble, but I don't think everybody else was. People weren't focused. Neale Cooper arrived from Scotland. He'd won two Scottish league medals with Aberdeen, and he was talked about as the next Graeme Souness but rarely made it to the pitch. I ended up fighting with him in Jamaica at the end of the season after I heard him talking behind my back.

When the relegation happened and Billy McNeill was sacked, I was thinking, one hundred per cent, I needed to get out of there.

But, as is the way in football, everything was suddenly about to change and Aston Villa would make their most important appointment since winning the European Cup in 1982.

Graham Taylor made the most impactful first impression of any manager I've played for.

We were all sat in the canteen at the training ground, waiting for this mystery figure, as we hadn't been told who the new manager was going to be.

The chairman came in first. And then he introduced Graham, who we all knew about because of his successful work at Watford, where he'd taken the team into the top flight, finishing second to Liverpool in 1982–83 and reaching the FA Cup final the following year, where they lost to Everton.

Immediately he said to the chairman, 'Right, Mr Chairman, there's the door, off you go. I'm with the players now. You appointed me, and now I'm going to do my job. So if you'd like to go through the door, and let me get on with it, that would be great. I know you want to stay, but off you go.'

So Ellis left and Graham walked five paces forward and said, 'Right, see that door? Anyone who wants to go through it can fuck off. Now. There it is. Don't tell me you're not being tapped up. I've just come from another club, so I know who is making themselves available. I know who's asking to leave. So now's your chance. You won't get another. Who wants to tell me they want to leave?'

Obviously, everyone had been looking at the door because

Top left: My glamorous mother, Angela, with my dad, Raymond. He was punching above his weight, like I did with Nicola.

Top right: In the middle of a packed defence outside Mum's shop.

Centre: Me, aged about 8, with my 'best friend' the wall. Whenever I passed to the wall, I always got the ball back. No idea why they called me Martin the Trophy Hunter.

Top: Playing for St John Bosco Middle School. I'm second left on the top row next to our top striker, Kathleen Parker. Note the 1971 Arsenal FA Cup Final colours.

Bottom: Will, John, Martin and Maureen – Big Sis and The Three Musketeers.

Top: With my proud mum and dad, December 1985. Best Christmas ever, and I've still got that Arsenal top.

Bottom: Signing on as a pro, 1983, on a dizzying £150 a week. Don Howe looks like he knows he's got a bargain.

Top: The Arsenal youth team, Class of '83. A vintage year, producing future first-team players me, Tony Adams, David Rocastle, Mickey Thomas, Martin Hayes and Gus Caesar, plus (not pictured) Paul Merson and Niall Quinn. The group went on to make almost 5,000 senior appearances in professional football, including 237 International Caps.

Bottom left: Proud as anything in my Arsenal centenary shirt. I'd just made it into the first team, too.

Bottom right: Playing up front on loan to Brighton, to my dad's delight; he always wanted me to be a centre-forward.

Top: Tony and I take on the Soviet Union for the England Under 17s, March 1983.

Bottom right: Tony and I recreating our youth team partnership in the first team, 1985.

Top left: Gary Lineker realizing he's about to get done for pace, April 1986. He was the league top scorer, but he drew a blank against me that day.

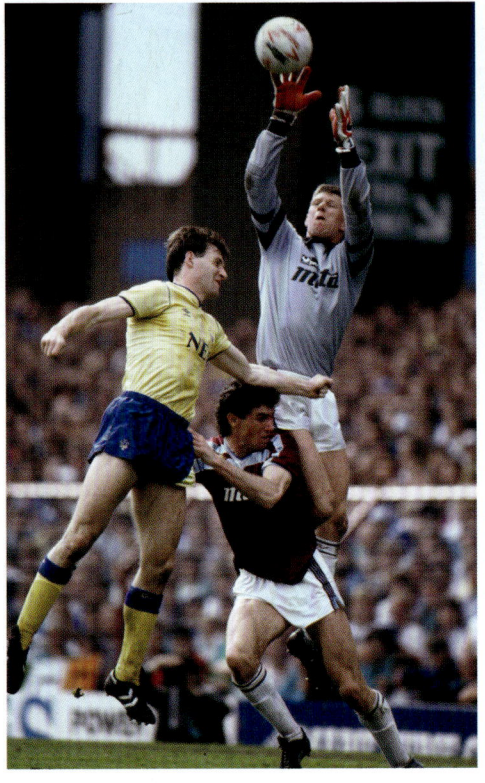

Top: Playing for Aston Villa in 1987, the season Villa were relegated. I was up against Dave Watson, my future Everton teammate.

Bottom left: Me and Nicola, just engaged, as captured by the local Birmingham newspaper, March 1988.

Left: The Zenith Data Systems Cup final, 1991. I was forced to leave the pitch after a contretemps that left me needing eighteen stitches in my lip. We were level at 1–1 when I went off but lost to Crystal Palace 4–1 after extra time.

Right: I made my England debut against France in February 1992, and managed to shackle the great Eric Cantona.

Bottom: Part of the England team against Sweden in the 1992 Euros. Competition was so tight that at half-time, when we led 1–0, we were topping our group. By full time we'd lost 2–1 and were on the plane home.

Left: In 1993, after Apartheid was abolished, Arsenal were the first overseas club to visit South Africa. I was honoured and humbled to shake hands with the great Nelson Mandela.

Bottom: Terry Murphy, the immaculately dressed Arsenal scout who discovered so many players, including David Rocastle and myself. We were both so grateful to this upright gentleman who epitomized the 'Arsenal way'.

the place was a disgrace. I certainly had been searching for an escape route. But I wasn't going to be the first to speak.

He turned to Tony Dorigo and said, 'Well, you're being tapped. One hundred per cent. I know where you're going.'

Then he said, 'The difference between me and all the previous managers is I chose Doug Ellis, he didn't choose me. I am in charge, not him. Those of you that want to stay, I'm a successful-type personality. Just take a look at my record. Look at all the promotions. We came second to Liverpool in the league. We got to the FA Cup final. And anybody who sticks with me will be successful. It's a foregone conclusion that we're going to get promoted, and this is because I'm fucking successful. I'm gonna make it happen. Who wants to be here?'

It was a wow moment.

I felt a genuine responsibility to be part of Graham's project, as I was part of the team that took Villa down and I wanted to bring them back up. He later said that if he hadn't arrived, the club could have got relegated again and again, such was the mess he found.

Graham changed the culture overnight, starting by giving us a bag with three sets of kit in it and telling us the club wasn't going to wash it for us. He wanted players who took responsibility.

He wanted a togetherness and for us to play for the community, the fans.

He wanted us to train at the ground, so we could connect more with Villa Park.

He told us that from now on everyone had to live within a ten-mile radius of the stadium and training ground. Anyone further away was told they had to move. Luckily, I was one of the closest.

I knew instantly he was the man to turn things around.

Graham was meticulous. He drilled into the players what he wanted. And the message came from the dressing room – we'd even do our warm-up in there.

Doug would come into the dressing room before the game and say, 'Good luck,' and Graham thought it was a distraction, that he was coming in at the wrong time and we needed to prepare. So one day Graham called me over and said, 'Right, sit there and watch this.' He positioned Jim Paul, the kit man, outside the door with the instruction to not let anyone in, knowing the only person Jim would let through was the chairman. Suddenly the door opened slowly and this sun-kissed hand came in. It was clearly Doug Ellis, wedding ring on. And as his hand pushed through, Graham slammed the door on his hand. We heard this 'Agh!' and then he tried to open the door again and Graham said, 'You're not coming in. I told you, that's it.' Doug never came in again – he got the message.

That next season in what is now called the Championship, I didn't have a clue who I was playing against from one week to the next. Everything was laid out for you in the top flight. You'd watch *Match of the Day*, you knew your opponent. Suddenly you have no idea and there wasn't as much information in those days.

Graham brought a team of men together, really good people. It was transformational. Twenty-two players came and went – it was like a revolving door – but a tough group emerged: Kevin Gage, Mark Lillis and Steve Sims, my defensive partner for most of the season and roommate. He got rid of Paul Elliott. Dorigo went. Andy Gray too.

I wasn't overly unhappy to see the back of Gray. I never saw the best of him. He was quick to criticize me in the heat of the moment and never took time out with a young player to try to nurture me or talk me through what he felt were my shortcomings.

Taylor gave Bernie Gallagher a chance from the reserves at left-back and he played in virtually every game. He got the best from Paul Birch and resurrected Garry Thompson and Nigel Spink, who probably had his best season since winning the European Cup. Mark Walters had been a big loss when he was snapped up by Glasgow Rangers, but Tony Daley came in to replace him and went on to play for England under Graham.

Alan McInally came down from Celtic with pace, power and directness. David Platt and Stuart Gray arrived later in the season to boost our promotion hopes.

Despite his good work, I clashed a lot with Graham. It all started in pre-season, when we'd done a load of running, some of the hardest training I've ever done in my career.

He said to us this run would be the last one of the day, so I gave it everything and we were all lying on the ground, exhausted, thinking, 'That's it for the day.'

And then he shouted really aggressively to us to get on our feet. Everyone was looking at each other, thinking he had lost the plot. Then he said he had changed his mind and that we were going to do it again.

Everyone was fuming, saying he was taking the piss.

So we did it all again and, when we finished, we were lying on the floor once more, totally exhausted.

Graham came up to me and said, 'Look, what you've learned there is that, when you thought you couldn't do another run, you're able to dig deep and find the energy to do it all again.'

And I said, 'No, I've learned that I can't trust you, that you're a liar.'

He just laughed, shook his head and walked off.

Some people might think that is a crazy thing to say to your boss. But it was the way I was feeling. His training pushed you to the absolute limit, and when you're trying to commit to somebody, you need to know you can trust them.

After a couple of weeks of endless running, the thigh injury I'd had at Arsenal came back and I had to rest – much to Graham's annoyance.

The stand-off between us was evident, and the day before the last pre-season friendly at home to Coventry, he pulled me into his office to say it was great to see me back in training but that he was massively disappointed with me as he'd hardly had a chance to see me play. He said he'd been advised to build his team around me, as I was the best player last year, but that he'd seen no evidence of that so far.

I was fuming and said it might have something to do with all that running we were doing.

I told him to take a look at me tomorrow and then tell me if he didn't think I was good enough. My opponents that day were David Speedie and Cyrille Regis, and let's just say Graham had a big smile on his face after the game and gave me the thumbs-up. I guess he'd say he got the reaction he wanted.

I suspect Graham still thought I could do with some toughening up. Years later, when Graham was England manager, Paul Ince deliberately smashed into me during England training. I jumped up, ready to have it out with him. Ince was telling everyone he was going to knock me out, and if Ian Wright hadn't got between us there would have been blood. I told Paul he could give it large out here on the pitch in front of everyone, but if he really wanted to sort it out, he could knock on my door any time he liked. (He never did. It all blew over and we ended up as good mates.)

Graham said he thought I was getting soft, and asked why I hadn't knocked Ince out there and then. But I think he only said it to get a reaction. Two days later he made Ince England captain.

We used to run so much under Graham, usually four laps around the training ground, which was almost a mile every lap. I know that because when Mark Lillis left, he got in his sponsored Montego and drove around the pitches to see how far it was.

Graham was a good runner, and if you finished behind him you had to do it all again. I used to let him go way out and then reel him in. I could see him repeatedly looking over his shoulder, desperate for me to have to do all four laps again, but I used to pip him at the line and he would go mad.

When we didn't have a midweek game, you'd turn up at the training ground and it was like an assault course, equipment and apparatus everywhere. It was all power work, which I was quite good at. And often it came with a psychological element attached.

Graham would say to us, 'What did you feel when you came to the training pitch today and you saw all the equipment out there?'

And the players would go, 'Another day of running.'

'So none of you thought, "Great, it's going to make me quicker and stronger"?'

Someone would say, 'Not really, boss.'

Then he'd spin the whole thing, tell us to get inside and that we weren't doing it now. It was done to make you think.

He was playing with us, setting challenges for the group.

As it happens, we started the promotion season badly.

In that very first meeting there was this big sales pitch, with him saying, 'I'm a successful-type personality.' But then four games in, we were third-bottom of the table. And he came in and he said, 'Guys, what do you think now? I tell you what I feel. I feel more strongly now than the day I walked in here that we're going to get promoted. I'm completely convinced.' There he was, challenging us again. He still believed it. We hadn't won a game for weeks. It was incredible to hear, and he was right.

Graham was very clear about the style of play he was looking for.

He arranged a training session at Villa Park where he set out cones between the edge of the box and the byline and he'd shout at me to hit the ball into the channel during training, with Alan McInally tasked with running after it.

The theory was that if Alan didn't beat his man, he could force a free kick, throw-in or corner. And then we meticulously worked on set plays so we'd benefit from those positions.

He even set up a throw-in competition, which Andy Gray (same name, different player, bought from Palace) won, and we launched balls into the middle of the goal on a regular basis.

Each player had their role and responsibility for attacking and defensive set pieces. I particularly liked the near-post flick-on, which I did many times, for either McInally or Garry Thompson to score.

All the fitness work began to pay off as we started to climb the table. It was high-energy, very direct football with lots of pace.

We won thirteen away games that season — it was a phenomenal effort — but we struggled at Villa Park because our opponents treated it like Wembley, saving their best performances for our amazing stadium.

We were getting good. We played Liverpool in the FA Cup fourth round that season — top of the First Division v top of the Second Division. They beat us 2–0, but we had chances and were on the way back. Villa Park was rocking. I remember thinking, 'This is why I had signed for this club.'

There were forty-four league games and I played in forty-two. I missed the last two getting injured playing for England Under 21s. And they were nerve-wracking.

Before the last match, the gaffer called me into his office, told me I had been absolutely magnificent and that Manchester United had been calling him all season about me. I had zero knowledge of this.

So he didn't want to sort out my contract yet and suggested leaving it till next season, because if we didn't go up for whatever reason, I would still definitely be playing in the top division.

It was big of him, and I appreciated that. I had absolutely no idea of United's interest, and it was never mentioned again.

I didn't have mixed feelings going into the last two games. I simply wanted success for Villa, although United would've been a huge opportunity.

I travelled on the bus for the last match of the season, Swindon away. We had been top, but then we started to buckle after we lost our assistant, Steve Harrison, in the second half of the season. He was a brilliant man who had a golden touch with the players, a unique mix of fun and laughter and a special ability to develop and nurture players.

He was great for the dressing room. We'd all sit and listen

to his stories at the back of the coach and he had us eating out of the palm of his hand. He went back to manage his beloved Watford.

Ahead of that last game against Swindon, Graham did something amazing and bizarre.

He took us out to the training pitch and brought a case of champagne with him. He brought all the staff out and all the players, and he said, 'Guys, we've blown it, really. I thought we were going to get promoted tomorrow and I bought all this champagne to celebrate because you know how certain I was that we were going to be successful, but we might as well drink it now.' So the day before the game he cracked open the champagne and the players were all drinking it. It released all the pressure.

Millwall were already up and we needed to better Middlesbrough's result at home to Leicester. And hope Bradford (at home to Ipswich) didn't better our result. So we needed to win at Swindon, but momentum was against us; our fate was no longer in our hands.

We were drawing that game and I was a nervous wreck in the stands. I couldn't watch, so I left the ground and went for a walk. It was just too unbearable. But the fans gathered outside the ground were saying our rivals were both losing, and a draw would see us promoted. I ran back five minutes before the final whistle and watched from the stands for what felt like for ever. And then, wow, we did it, and I was celebrating with everyone on the pitch.

We came back into the dressing room, but we didn't have any champagne because Graham had given it all to us the day before. So we had to go into the boardroom to borrow some champagne from Swindon. And then the celebrations started in the dressing room and then on the bus. You wished that journey could have taken a whole week to get back to Birmingham. The relegation had been the lowest point of my career, so regaining our top-flight status was massive. The lads all jumped on me and tore my shirt and pulled my tie.

It felt great to get our top-flight status back again. To walk the streets of Birmingham and, instead of hiding from everybody, instead of being blamed, to have people congratulate you. It turned out to be one of the most enjoyable seasons in my career, the feeling of promotion, that euphoria.

Doug, as a treat for the players, flew us to Majorca for a week's celebration. He had a house there he wanted us to see, and a very nice boat too. At Birmingham airport, he got out of his chauffeur-driven car, called me to the boot, and said, 'Carry that bag for me, young man.'

Well, I could hardly lift it out of the boot, it was so heavy. So I said, 'Doug, I am not your bag carrier. You take one handle and I'll take the other.'

I asked him what on earth was in the bag and he said he owned a food company and it was all the steaks for the barbecue we were having in Majorca. Typical Doug – to save a little bit of money, he was making me carry this halfway across Europe for our barbecue.

Once there, he took us out on his boat on Saturday, opening up all six Rolls-Royce engines, and we stopped in the middle of the Mediterranean, dropping anchor just before kick-off to raise a toast to those teams still in the play-off for promotion.

Despite all his broken promises and cheapskating, I have to say here that Doug's trip away was the best and only one I ever went on after winning something at the end of the season.

We were back in the big time, and delirious.

But that didn't mean things were going totally smoothly behind the scenes, or in my mind.

Over the two years with Graham I was probably pissing people off because I always kept talking about Arsenal. 'We didn't do this at Arsenal,' I'd say.

Graham was trying to get me away from this because he wanted me to be a Villa man and just think about Villa.

But what I had seen at Villa at the start was so bad and had such an impact on me that all I was thinking about deep down was seeing my contract through and getting out.

And that was wrong of me because, although I was giving everything for Villa on the pitch, I never really gave the club a chance off it. It was definitely a case of 'let's put this club back where it was and then I won't feel the guilt when I leave'.

I should have reassessed then – if only Graham would have confided in me and told me he was signing Paul McGrath.

Graham had said to me that he was going to bring in a top international player to play alongside me. He had previously bought centre-back Derek Mountfield, and it hadn't really worked. Derek had been successful at Everton but had quite a few injuries and I think he was past his best. Graham insisted that I room with him and not Steve Sims, who I'd struck up a very good relationship with. I thought he was trying to force us together unnecessarily.

The third season, back with the big boys, didn't go well. I kept getting suspended for carrying out the man marking role Graham demanded, but we managed to stay up on the final day by one point.

When I looked back recently, though, at some of the highlights, it really struck me how important David Platt, Alan McInally and Andy Gray were to keeping us up. Their flair and goal-scoring ability were crucial. At the time I probably didn't feel I was that close to Alan and David, which was completely on me.

I felt that those players were just there to use Villa as a stepping stone to other things, which proved to be the case. McInally, a huge talent, went to Bayern Munich, Platt to Italy and Andy Gray to Spurs. The irony, of course, is that I wasn't any different to them.

I have two big memories of that season football-wise. Firstly, my second return to Highbury early in the season, which, remarkably, ended in a 3–2 win for Villa. At least my own fans weren't booing me this time, though the Arsenal fans still hadn't forgiven me for leaving.

The other was the way the season finished, which completely put everything into perspective.

The horrific Hillsborough tragedy late that season, where ninety-seven fans lost their lives, meant that, understandably, a lot of games had to be postponed. So when we played our final game of the season against Coventry (a 1–1 draw), we ended up outside the relegation zone by one point, but knew that West Ham could still leapfrog us – if they beat Liverpool. That game was being played ten days later, so we were all on tenterhooks, not knowing if we'd stay up.

That day Graham told me he was too tense to listen to the game, so he went out for a run for the ninety minutes. He needn't have worried. Liverpool won 5–1 and Graham called round us all to congratulate us on staying up.

Really, I should've given it one more season at Villa. But once again, I felt upset by the way contract negotiations played out and ended up leaving.

At Christmas, when Taylor first approached me about the new contract, I was genuinely surprised he'd left it that late.

He sat me down and said he was going to offer me the biggest contract the club had ever offered a player, the same they offered to Mark Walters six months earlier when he left for Rangers.

He told me he wanted me to go away and think about it and then come back to him. But I said I didn't need to, that I could tell him now that it wasn't enough money.

'Martin, you're not listening. Go away and think about it.'

Confused, I got up and walked out of the office.

A couple of days later I went to see our club physio, Jim Walker, who was a fantastic help to me at Villa Park. I asked for his advice, and he advised me not to speak to Graham that day as we had a very important game at the weekend. Best to leave it for now.

That weekend we lost again, so I thought it best I stayed away for a bit longer still.

The next week, I played and got sent off, so I was suspended, this time for two matches.

Again, I sought advice from Jim. 'No,' he said. 'It's not a good idea to go and see him. He's even angrier with you than before.'

And so I waited. I left it until I was back in the team after my suspension.

About three or four weeks had passed by the time I finally went to see Graham again, now that things had calmed down. I walked into his office, and he just looked up and said, 'Can I help you?'

I said, 'Boss, you told me to go away and think about my new contract offer.'

'Yes, I did, but I didn't say, "Go away and take the fucking piss" – that was a month ago. Now you can fuck off out of my office and come back when I decide, not when you fucking decide!'

I couldn't believe it and, really, that was the moment I knew I was going to leave Aston Villa. Doug rang me privately and told me he'd give me what I wanted, but Graham kept telling me he was in charge of the deal and I'd better not be speaking to the chairman. It was a mess.

Then other clubs got wind of my situation and I went on an amazing tour of the country talking to potential suitors: Nottingham Forest, Derby, Manchester United and Everton.

I was using the Professional Footballers' Association as my agents at that point, and off we went to decide my future. It was a week I'll never forget, ending in my wedding to Nicola, my childhood sweetheart, who was waiting patiently to find out where she was going to live next. She'd moved to Birmingham near the end of the promotion season, but the lads joked I needed to send her away, as we started losing games.

On Monday I went to see Brian Clough.

This was at Forest's ground, and when I got there Clough was at home. So the great man gets a phone call. He's doing his rose beds, but he drives in to see me and when he arrives he's still got mud on his knees.

He walked into the meeting and said, 'Hey, young man, this had better be good. I'm doing my rose beds and got a phone call to say "Keown's in the building." So I've come in. Now don't waste my time, son.'

So I went into his office. He was with Ronnie Fenton, who was one of the coaches, and shouted to him, 'Let dog in room before thee. He talks more sense than thee. You wait outside.'

We sat and chatted for three and a half hours. He had a

three-piece suite in the office, a sofa, two chairs, a drinks cabinet in the corner and a TV, like it was a lounge.

He was sitting on the chair and I was on the sofa in the corner, and he asked if I wanted an alcoholic drink. I told him I don't really drink, and he went, 'Fuck off.' So he had a drink and I had a cup of tea.

Mr Clough was brilliant in negotiations and told me he wasn't going to be naive and push the boat out by giving me an offer so I could take it to all the other clubs. He asked me to sign a blank contract, go and talk to Alex Ferguson and the other clubs, and he'd match the best offer I got from everyone else.

And I said I couldn't do that. I'd given my word to the other managers and it wouldn't be fair not to hear what they had to say first.

The chat itself was extraordinary. It wasn't just about football but about my whole life.

He asked me about my politics. Was I Labour or Conservative? He asked me about my feelings towards women, which I felt was in some way linked to the issues he'd had and the way he'd treated Justin Fashanu, the first openly gay player in English football. Clough had at one point barred him from training.

Then it was music. I told him I was an Elton John fan and he said he was going to see him in America that summer.

He wanted to know how educated I was, what I'd achieved at school. (Not much.)

He wanted to know what I thought was my biggest attribute on the pitch. I said I was quick. And he asked, 'How quick?' I said as quick as Des Walker, and he said, 'You're going too fucking far now. Not our Des. No one is quicker than our Des.'

It has to be the most surreal meeting I've ever been in. I kept on calling him Brian and he kept saying, 'Young man, it's sir or Mr Clough.' He wasn't happy, but it was such an informal chat that I kept on talking as if he was just Brian.

He said he wanted 'one more crack at Liverpool', that he couldn't stand them and that I could help him do it. I'd seen what Forest had done, coming up from Division Two, winning two European Cups, but I just thought there was a gap appearing and I wondered whether or not Clough could still do it. I just felt it was the wrong move. I wanted to go to a bigger club.

Because Clough knew I was getting married that week, he sent flowers, chocolates and a crystal vase to Nicola. The vase is still in my cabinet now. I used to turn it around because it had a Forest emblem on it, but now I've it turned back because it's a talking point. I'm proud to have met him, and it's such a nice vase. When I eventually chose Everton, Clough rang up and said, 'Tell him I want my vase and chocolates back.'

The next day, after meeting Mr Clough, we went to Derby, and it was the complete opposite. I swear we were there for about three minutes when Derby manager Arthur Cox gave me the offer after a tiny bit of small talk and that was that. He insisted I wouldn't play at Everton as he'd tried to sign Kevin Ratcliffe from them and failed. I thought it was a negotiating tactic at the time, but it turned out to be correct.

There was some scheme where Robert Maxwell, the owner, would buy my house off me over the odds as an extra bonus. But that wasn't for me.

Then we went to see Alex Ferguson at Old Trafford,

who had been chasing me – allegedly – on and off for two seasons.

We came into the boardroom, which looks over the pitch – it was amazing. And at that point I was thinking, 'This is the club. Look at the players they've got. This could be something really big for me.'

Ferguson seemed a very mild-mannered and softly spoken man, very pleasant. I didn't see any of the anger that I came to know oh so well. We were chatting away, but I never really got the feeling he was desperate for me to sign. I just thought there was something a bit wrong.

And then Manchester United chairman Martin Edwards said, 'We're really disappointed that we can only pay you half of what you've been offered at Derby.' We asked if there was anything they could do, but they said they had financial policies and that they only paid defenders what they had offered me.

I said, 'It's not all about money. Can we go on the pitch?' And they said yes.

So Ferguson got a chain full of keys and went through them one by one, trying to open the green doors next to the turnstile. It began to sink in that this maybe wasn't going to be for me. I wasn't feeling the love. I stood back for a moment as it felt totally surreal.

There was no fanfare, they'd not rolled a red carpet out for me. Every other club was offering me way more. I was wondering if he wanted me or not. So I asked him what would he suggest I do as a father figure or a friend? What advice would he give me? And he gave me all the wrong answers. He said to me, 'You've got to think of your family.' And that's not what I wanted to hear. What I wanted to hear was: 'I want you, you sign for me. You do really well in the first two years and don't worry about the wages. I'll sort that out.' So I have no regrets about not joining the team that would turn out to be my greatest rivals.

And so to the last meeting – Everton.

I went to see manager Colin Harvey. Everton had been very successful through the eighties, they'd won a few trophies and they were playing in the cup final that summer.

And they were offering me three times what Aston Villa were. They clearly wanted me and they were a big club.

Of course Graham Taylor then put in an offer which was nearly three times what he'd offered me before. I told him I didn't know what a good deal was any more, as he'd told me that £50k a year was a fantastic amount of money at the start of all this.

It was then that he told me he was buying a top international centre-half for me to play with but he couldn't tell me who. I said, 'Graham, do you want me to stay or not? You have to tell me. We have to have this trust.' As I explained earlier, it was Paul McGrath, and I never got the opportunity to play with him. Had he told me that, it could well have changed my mind.

When I look back on it, the easy option, to take nothing away from Everton, would have been to stay at Villa. They finished second the next season. It was another one of those occasions when I thought, 'Am I able to make a decision about my career? Because wherever I go, good things happen behind me.'

But once again, I let a matter of principle get the better of me. I was off.

But the first place I was going was my honeymoon. And

as I was flying off with Nicola, Arsenal won the league at Anfield in the most dramatic fashion imaginable, with Mickey Thomas scoring the decisive goal in injury time to deny Liverpool the title. There they all were: Adams, Thomas, Quinn, Rocastle, Merson and George Graham. It could have been me. It should have been me.

Playing through Pain

I arrived at Everton in the summer of 1989, still relatively young at the age of twenty-three. I had just got married and was so excited to be joining a big club.

However, straight away I found it tough, thrust into the culture of a new football club, trying to make sense of where I was to fit in both on and off the pitch.

After a few days of training, we went away on a pre-season tour to Japan. I made the mistake of sitting in front of Neville Southall on the plane out. Throughout my career I had the privilege of playing in front of many great goalkeepers – Pat Jennings, David Seaman and Jens Lehmann. Neville was certainly in that class.

But as well as his talent, what set Neville apart was his jagged-edge tongue. His quick-witted comments kept all of us on our toes and, when the ball hit the back of the net, I quickly learned not to look at him if I didn't want to get the blame and a mouthful of abuse.

Neville had been a bin man before he made it in football, so he knew how lucky he was to be a professional footballer, and took it very seriously. His work ethic was phenomenal – he trained to a punishing schedule. But off the pitch he was witty, with a terrific sense of humour. He was quite a wordsmith; one season he persuaded me and left-back Andy Hinchcliffe that we should choose a word of the week, and try to use it as often as possible. One week the word was 'conducive' and we would say things like 'this bacon sandwich is very conducive', or 'conducive weather, isn't it?'

His humour could be cutting though. When Peter Beardsley, who had poor posture, won Everton Player of the Year, Neville, the previous winner, had to make a speech and hand over the prize, a free subscription to Sky TV, with a dish to go with it, which, Neville said, Peter could use to iron his shirts.

Still, sitting next to him on the long-haul flight to Japan was naive of me. By the time we arrived, my left shoe was missing, along with my passport, which I'd left unattended in my jacket pocket.

He'd stolen them for a laugh and creased up at the sight of me hobbling through immigration control with one shoe and no passport.

I could laugh that off, but the football side of things suddenly became much harder.

We played tour games in Japan and Thailand (Everton was quite ahead of its time in terms of spreading the club's appeal internationally), and then our last game was against a Malaysian XI.

It was before this final game that Colin Harvey dropped a bombshell. With the season opener against Coventry just eight days away, he pulled me aside and said, 'You're not going to play. Go up in the stands and watch Dave Watson and Kevin Ratcliffe play, and learn, because you're going to take over from them eventually.'

I was stunned. I told him the one discussion we had never had in our negotiations was whether he was actually going to play me, because I just assumed he would.

I recalled Arthur Cox's warning – perhaps it wasn't a bargaining tactic after all – and Clough urging me to be wary of clubs seeming too eager. It just didn't make any sense, as

Harvey had wanted me to sign so badly, even turning up to my wedding celebrations.

The deal Everton put forward was so good I thought I had better sign before it disappeared. And they were pushing me, saying, 'Are you doing this or not?'

So I sat in the stands, disgruntled, watching the team lose 2–0 at Coventry City on the first day of the 1989/90 season. In the press conference in the build-up to the game, Colin was saying, 'Martin is a great player to keep for the future. He keeps Dave Watson and Ratcliffe on their toes.'

I never signed up for that. But that's how things continued until the middle of October, when I played alongside Watson in a win over Millwall, following an injury to Ratcliffe. I finally had a run of games and was able to do my talking on the pitch.

There was a strange dynamic at Everton at that time, following the departure of Howard Kendall – the most successful manager in the club's history – two years earlier.

There was an underlying animosity between the senior players who had won trophies under Kendall and the new, younger signings. A number of experienced players had been allowed to leave, including Gary Stevens, Adrian Heath, Peter Reid, Paul Bracewell and Trevor Steven, over a two-year period of immense change at the club.

The likes of Tony Cottee, Neil McDonald, Stuart McCall and Pat Nevin were among the players brought in to replace them, along with Norman Whiteside, Peter Beagrie and myself.

Put simply, the senior players thought the new recruits weren't good enough, and they were very vocal about it.

Ratcliffe, in particular, didn't deal with my arrival in a mature way. In fact, he was quite childish about it, putting me down at every opportunity and giving me the nickname BOB (Brain of Britain) in an attempt to ridicule me.

It infuriated me. He was Everton's most successful captain and a leader at the club – he didn't need to belittle me. We were both there to do our best for Everton.

It started on the Far East tour, when one night after a few beers he said that if I took his place during that season he'd hang up his boots. He practically spat the words out. I responded, 'That's exactly what I'll make you do.'

He had seen off many young pretenders to his spot in the first team, and had the backing of his teammates to ensure he'd never be ousted.

I was determined this time it was going to be different. All this control stuff was bullshit, and I had kept far better players than Ratcliffe out of the team when I was at Arsenal. I wasn't going to back down.

His behaviour actually helped me realize later in my career just how important it was to help younger players looking to break into the team. I made sure that when Kolo Touré was brought in at Arsenal to take my place, I offered him as much guidance and support as I could – something I continued to do for him years after I retired.

(And it was really gratifying to hear how Kolo appreciated my efforts. He said, 'Martin helped me to flourish and never tried to stop me developing just because I was in competition with him. That was huge and I really respect him for that. He was a leader, always the guy who was positive in the dressing room, even when he was not starting. He taught me it's not about you, it's about the squad. Because when the team wins, you win as well. The team spirit was incredible and his role in the Invincibles was so big. He liked to laugh at himself a lot too, which is so important. You might think he's a very serious man but he's actually one of the loveliest people to be around. He knows when to make a joke and when to be serious. I can't praise him enough.')

But having the club's captain as an enemy meant I was not only out of the team but unwanted by the majority of my teammates, and it left me feeling uncomfortable.

My decision to live in Manchester in my first season at the club insulated me a bit from the full impact of the divisions within the squad.

I travelled into training each day with Dave Watson and Norman Whiteside, and being in that trio protected me from the ongoing politics. The real tensions were between two warring groups of players driving in from Southport – Kevin Sheedy, Graeme Sharp and Ian Snodin in one car, and Cottee, McCall and Beagrie in another.

I did feel a bit like Norman's gofer at times, though. When I turned up at his mansion on the way to training each morning, I'd look up to see which window he'd wave from. If he wasn't in the marital bedroom, it meant he'd been out the night before.

If he'd had a few drinks and it was his turn to drive, he would chuck down the keys to his car. So I was doing plenty of driving but not much of the thing I loved most – playing football.

My playing time began to improve in the second half of the season, though, and we finished in sixth place in the league. We did all right, but we suffered some heavy defeats. Our 6–2 loss on my return to Villa Park in November 1989 was particularly brutal for me to take. Happily, by the return game against Villa, Everton fans had actually started singing my name. I remember going into three challenges – bang, bang, bang, one after the other – and the crowd loving it. I could see some light at the end of the tunnel.

There were some really good players in that team, and I particularly enjoyed playing with Whiteside.

He signed at the same time as I did, scored thirteen goals that season and was a great talent. His career was snatched away from him, really, as he had injury issues from a young age and surgery on his knees.

When he turned up to train for the first time and we were running around the pitches, there was a constant clicking noise, as loud as someone snapping their finger. Everyone said, 'Bloody hell, Norman, what's that?'

'That's my knee,' he said.

We couldn't believe he'd passed his medical. Somebody asked him if it was painful, and he replied, 'I can't feel the knee at all, but my hammertoe is killing me.' And everyone laughed their heads off.

By the end of the first season, I was starting to really find my feet on the pitch, but off the pitch things really kicked off at the beginning of my second season, when Nicola and I decided to move to Southport. In the long term, it was a good decision and proved to be the perfect place to start a family and turn my Everton career around. But in the short term it caused me problems with the Southport mafia.

The 1990/91 season started disastrously as Everton lost their first three games. In a bid to boost morale, Colin Harvey took us all to a local Chinese restaurant for a team-bonding meal. The meal itself passed without major incident, and Colin went home, warning us not to get into any trouble.

The group then moved on to the Red Rum bar at the Carlton Hotel, and my brother Will, who was visiting from Oxford, came along too.

The mood was tense, and it worsened as more and more drinks were downed. Sheedy, one of Ratcliffe's big mates, was on his soapbox, berating all the younger players. He'd turned his attention to his next victim – Mike Milligan, who the club had signed from Oldham. He was really having a go at Milligan, saying he played like he was wearing rollerskates. It went on and on, until I felt enough was enough and jumped in to defend him.

I asked why he couldn't just make the new signings feel welcome at the club. I told him what a nightmare environment it was to come into because of the attitude of the senior players.

He then started hammering me, criticizing my ability as a footballer. I had heard it all before, and it was just football banter, so I wasn't going to rise to it, but Will was getting agitated by Sheedy's comments.

I told Will it was fine and went off to the toilet. But when I came back the rest of the group were having to separate my brother and Sheedy. While I was gone, Sheedy crossed the line with a personal attack on Will and said something I'm not going to repeat.

Will asked Sheedy outside to sort it out. Dave Watson stepped in and said to me that if Will hit Sheedy, he would then have no option but to hit Will. Instead, he suggested I take it up with Sheedy myself.

At that point we should've gone home, but we didn't. Sheedy walked out the door, tried to throw a punch at me, and I hit him back pretty hard. We were brawling in the street. Sheedy went to hospital with a cut on his eye and the story ended up in one of the papers. It was humiliating, and we were in big trouble with the club. Looking back I massively regret what happened. I would never again mix family members with my fellow players. But attacks on my family were out of bounds and I couldn't just look the other way.

The next day we came into training, the boss pulled us

both in and fined us a couple of weeks' wages. The money was donated to Alder Hey Children's Hospital.

He asked what had happened and, in fairness to Sheedy, he said, 'I take full responsibility. It was completely my fault. I had too much to drink and I had too much to say.'

I probably should have just said, 'Kev, fantastic, thank you for that,' and left it. But I said, 'No, Kev, I don't know if we can leave it here because the reason for the fight needs to come out.'

I said we weren't going to get anywhere unless we discussed the tensions in the squad. There was no unity in the dressing room. I asked for a team meeting because I didn't feel comfortable in the dressing room.

And so we got one, and it was a big mistake on my part. They just set me up.

There we all were, and Colin said, 'Martin suggested we should have a meeting. Let's get it out.' So Sheedy, who was now stone-cold sober, had nothing to say. But Ian Snodin stood up and said that the clear problem was me, saying he'd spoken to someone who was at Villa who said I was a problem there too.

What dismayed me most was that none of the group of Colin Harvey signings that I was trying to support were willing to speak up, not Cottee, McCall, Nevin, Beagrie, McDonald – none of them said a word to back me up, despite regularly hammering the senior players in private.

I was fuming, and was left wondering why I had bothered to stand up for them in the first place. Looking back, I can't blame them. They were just young lads trying to keep their heads down.

The club's new back-up goalkeeper, Gerry Peyton, stepped in to save me. Gerry, who went on to become Arsenal goalkeeping coach under Arsène Wenger and remains a close friend of mine to this day, advised me to ditch my travelling companions and car share with him. He told me I'd become very visibly part of the group the old boys didn't like – and it was something I didn't need.

Gerry's advice eventually paid dividends, and I was beginning to settle in better, but on the pitch things continued to deteriorate, until Colin Harvey was sacked at the end of October.

I felt for Colin: he was a really good guy and he loved his players. He was one of the nicest people I've ever met in the game, but he wasn't a natural manager. He was also working against the backdrop of animosity within the group which made it impossible to build a cohesive team.

He made me adapt my game, as I was used to a long ball style of play under Graham Taylor. I tried to put the ball in the channel to Graeme Sharp in training, but Colin would berate me, saying he wanted the ball played to a teammate's feet. Every training session was focused on passing, and it really improved my game. When Arsenal suddenly went passing crazy under Wenger years later, it was probably that early work I'd done under Colin that helped me.

We said our goodbyes to Colin, and it was actually quite emotional. Then, six days later, he came back through the door as the assistant to Everton's new manager, Howard Kendall, who had returned to the club from Manchester City to save the day.

It was bizarre, and it took me a while to stop calling Colin 'boss'.

I liked Howard as a manager. But I don't know if he was completely enamoured with me at first.

One day very early on, we were in a bar chatting and he

told me to get a pen. He had three bar mats and said, 'I'm going to write "Aston Villa" on the back of one.'

'Why is that?' I asked.

'Because they've come in for you,' he replied. 'I'm going to put Everton on another. And the other one I'm going to keep blank.'

What he meant was there was a third, unnamed club interested in me. Maybe it was the Arsenal?

Then he said what he was going to do was play a bit of a guessing game, because he didn't know what to do with me – keep me or let me go. He said he was worried that I'd had three big clubs already despite being only twenty-three.

So he juggled the bar mats all around, and I worked out which one Villa was. I thought maybe I was better off going back there – they were doing well under Ron Atkinson. So he stopped moving the bar mats and I picked Villa, and he went, 'No, no, not doing it. Let's do it again.' I felt like I was playing Russian roulette with my career.

Then he did it again and I picked the Villa one, and he went, 'No, that's it, you're staying. If Ron Atkinson wants you – and Ron's a bloody good judge – then I'm keeping you, that's the end of it.'

A couple of months later, I happened to be following him home in my car after one of our away games and I noticed him driving very erratically. Obviously, he had had a drink. I didn't want anything to happen to him and I didn't want to lose him as a manager.

So on the next away trip I suggested to Howard that I would take him home. I told him we'd wait until everyone had gone and he could hop in my car, I'd load up his stuff in the boot and take him home safely.

So that's what we did every away game until I left the club, and none of the rest of the squad had any idea. He would hand me his brick-sized mobile phone, state-of-the-art for the time, and tell me to call Nicola and say we were going to the Freshfield pub, which in recent years has been Jürgen Klopp's local.

We'd often chat through the tactics and how the game went. Sometimes we just played darts.

Despite our connection, it wasn't plain sailing under Howard at first. I'd finally cracked it with Colin, breaking into the first team and starting to enjoy my football.

Howard benched me for quite a long time, perhaps out of loyalty to Ratcliffe.

He was very hands on as a manager, joining in the training sessions, making things a bit brighter, a bit sharper. But results took a while to come. There was no waving of a magic wand.

He was a great talker and motivator, with a deep knowledge of the game. Considering all he achieved – with two league titles, one FA Cup and a Cup Winners' Cup he was The Toffees' greatest ever manager – I'm surprised he never managed England.

I began to win him over and became a regular starter in a back three. I finally felt I was beginning to thrive at the club.

I really loved playing at Goodison Park. There was always a fantastic atmosphere. It gave me a similar emotional connection to playing at Highbury (which was designed by the same architect, Archibald Leitch), with its steep stands close to the pitch. It was intense, but in a good way.

Until that point in my career, I'd always played for undoubtedly the biggest club in the city – Arsenal in London and Aston Villa in Birmingham. So playing second fiddle to neighbours Liverpool (sorry Everton fans), a team full of superstars, was a new experience for me.

But it taught me what a fired-up crowd can do to

world-class players, and how it can be a real leveller. In February 1991, we played Liverpool in an FA Cup fifth-round replay. The atmosphere was electric, and it was a remarkable match, ending 4–4 after we'd come from behind four times. Liverpool manager Kenny Dalglish resigned after the match, and we went on to win the replay. The game lives long in the memory of Merseyside as one of the greatest ever derbies, but it was a significant match for me personally and helped to build my career at the club.

Another big moment quickly came around the corner. Ahead of the Zenith Data Systems Cup final that year – a competition created to fill the calendar after English clubs were banned from European competition following the Heysel disaster – Howard pulled Ratcliffe and me aside.

'I want to tell you both together. Kevin, you've been a great servant for this football club, but you're not playing in this final. Martin's playing.'

All three of us started the next season, 1991/92, but Ratcliffe left shortly after, for the less competitive environment of Dundee.

Dave Watson and I then formed a really good partnership. Dave's work ethic was superb and very often when training finished he'd be in the gym, cycling to get a sweat on. I think he was hugely underrated and with a bit more pace he would surely have won more than twelve England caps.

We were probably one of the best defensive pairings in the league at that point. That's when I broke into the England squad, largely down to the Everton fans singing my name and demanding I was picked.

Everton was big on the outside but intimate on the inside, a real family club, and I felt part of that family. Like Highbury, Goodison was surrounded by streets of modest terraced houses, over which it towered like a temple. It reminded me of Arsenal.

Howard would allow local characters into the training ground canteen, including Joe, the professional burglar.

Anyone who was anyone in Liverpool was welcome, as long as they were Everton fans.

Joe would charm everyone with his stories of his successful raids and his many stays at Her Majesty's pleasure, including spending time behind bars with one of the renowned Kray twins.

Football, music and comedy were all around us. Dave Ash, who policed the training ground by day and was a well-known nightclub bouncer by night, was the heartbeat of the training ground. He treated everybody the same, he didn't give a toss about reputations and, as a kickboxer, often did more training than most of the players.

The football was interspersed with Howard's famous away trips – the boss liked to enjoy himself. He regularly wanted to go on tour, somewhere he could be with the lads and have a drink – Ireland, Barnstaple, Spain.

My initial issues settling at the club were firmly in the past. Nicola and I loved our new home, became good friends with some lovely neighbours, Dominic and Sheila Murray, who treated me like a son. They became great friends of my parents, too. Whenever Mum and Dad visited Liverpool, they'd go off to the Irish club for a dance with the Murrays, leaving Nicola and me at home with the baby, Callum, who arrived in January 1992. (Nicola's mum Maureen arrived half an hour after Callum and was a tower of strength, as usual, despite only being 4'11. She was as much a friend to me as a mother-in-law. Sadly she died in 1996 and we all miss her dreadfully.)

Callum seemed to be my lucky mascot, as his arrival

coincided with me excelling in my career. Everyone could see I was in the form of my life. They didn't know, but in fact I was suffering with a debilitating back injury that threatened my future in the game.

The problems began early in my time at Everton and, after some months of struggling with it, I went to see a specialist, someone the club physio, Les Helm, really trusted.

Neville Southall, who himself was suffering with a long-term back injury, came along too. After I spent the morning being X-rayed and scanned, the specialist told me, very matter-of-factly, that it wasn't looking good. I had early degeneration of two discs and the facet joints were very inflamed.

He told me I had three options:

1. Have an operation to remove the discs, but I'd never be the same again.
2. Pack it in.
3. Suck it up and get on with it.

I had no choice but to carry on.

Neville came with me when I went to receive my diagnosis, and I took inspiration from how he was coping with his own problems. He had a chronic back condition, and it was a miracle he was playing every Saturday. Indeed, after every away game, Neville would lie on the floor of the team coach, until they finally set up a proper bed at the back, where I later joined him, if I could find room.

By my third season at Everton, the pain was becoming too much. I would be ferried off to Arrowe Park Hospital on the Wirral to have an injection under anaesthetic into the facet joints to alleviate it. Each injection lasted for up to six weeks, then bang, the pain would return.

That season, I made it into the England squad, but I was coming home from training every day and having to lie in the recovery position just to be able to make it on to the training pitch the next day. It became a real battle. Anyone who has suffered with a bad back, which has no visible signs of pain, will know it's an injury where you are reliant on others believing the level of pain you are in. Unfortunately, I sometimes felt that the Everton club doctor simply didn't believe me.

In fact, we had to be split up by the physio, Les Helm, on one occasion when he questioned whether I was fit or not. To confuse things, I was still making it on to the pitch every Saturday, putting in performances that earned me the England call-up. And that made some people think the injury was all in my head.

Having said all that, Howard managed the situation brilliantly, though I suspected that even he didn't totally believe me. In a game away at Forest, I went out to do the warm-up as usual, but the pain was so intense I decided to walk back to the dressing room. I sat down and succumbed to the pain.

Howard asked if I could play. I told him I could, but there was no point me doing the warm-up. He told me to just sit there, then handed me a couple of strong painkillers. Everyone knew Colin Harvey was taking them for his hips so he could join in the training. In fact, with two new plastic hips, he was making it on to the training pitch more often than I was. I didn't feel any pain until half-time, and then they gave me another couple of pills.

I was somehow playing the best football of my career so far, even though I couldn't bend down to put my hand on the ball for restarts. My game developed because I realized that by doing less I was actually doing far more. Instead of charging around stupidly flying into tackles I was more assured and calm.

Because I couldn't train normally, Les, who in a previous life had been a docker and union leader and knew Liverpool and everybody in it like the back of his hand, took me to the local boxing club to train in a different way. Norman and his clicking knees were with us, too.

The boxing club was no more than a terraced house with a back room and a front room, a punch bag hanging from where the lights would normally be and ropes painted on the walls. A man in a little booth would ring the bell: three-minute rounds, five of those, two times each. Then we'd head downstairs to do a weights session using home-made dumb-bells.

Some days we would run on Crosby Beach. The soft sand was considered helpful for my back, and the howling winds made it a tough workout. Les said that if it was good enough for the famous horse Red Rum, it was good enough for me; the three-time Grand National winner had trained nearby on Southport beach.

Other days I remember us cycling on a disused railway line for hours. Without Howard's trust and Les's patience and ingenuity, I would never have made it through.

But Les was a godsend and, when I went back to Arsenal, I felt totally alone without his support around my injury.

Luckily, a miracle was ahead of me regarding my back.

When we moved back to Nicola's parents' house in Oxford, my commute to Arsenal's London Colney training ground was a good hour each way – not ideal for someone with a bad back, but I had a new car, a Saab, and the driver's seat really supported my back. In addition, the bed I was sleeping on had a solid base with very hard support.

After two weeks, Les rang me to ask how my back was, as he was fearing the worst. But somehow, changing my car and my bed had altered everything. The pain disappeared. I was waiting each day for it to break down, but it didn't. I had no problems for two or three years, until I was playing for England again, under Glenn Hoddle.

At that point, I had the same pain relief injections in my back and I never felt any severe pain again until my last two seasons.

To further complicate things during that period at Everton, my left knee became chronic, as the Osgood-Schlatters I had as a kid returned and developed into patellar tendonitis.

I was nursed through the season, but when I came back from Euro 1992 that summer, my patella tendon had partially detached from the kneecap. It required surgery and I would be out for up to three months.

As the injury occurred on international duty, I was treated like a leper. The club doctor and physio felt I shouldn't have gone to the Euros and should have rested the knee during the summer. They were probably right, but I couldn't turn down the chance to go to a major tournament.

I went off to have the operation without anyone from the club in attendance. And once it was over, they just put me into a black cab, three hours after career-saving surgery.

When I got home, I tried to get out of the black cab, but as I swung my leg round, I collapsed. I remember Trevor Murray, my neighbour and a really good friend, rushing over to help me up the stairs.

Shortly after making it back on to the pitch, my knee still in pain, I went to Cambridge to seek a second opinion. I saw a renowned knee specialist called Mr Dandy. He asked me when I was thinking of starting to play again. 'Play again?' I said. 'I've been back for over a month.'

He was flabbergasted and, once he'd picked his jaw off the floor, he told me I'd done the hard part. He'd never seen anyone recover from that sort of injury so quickly, that I'd feel some pain for about a year and then I'd be fine. He was spot on.

I returned to action just in time to play Arsenal at Highbury, and it was lucky I did. As I drove Howard back home after the game, he told me that George Graham wanted me back.

It was crunch time, because I had started tentative discussions about a new contract with Everton, but the talks weren't progressing at any speed. How did I feel? Arsenal were my childhood team, the club closest to my heart. I felt elated.

A few months passed, with no more news. The Arsenal interest seemed to have evaporated, so I went into Howard's office the day before a game to find out what was going on with my contract renewal.

I was in for a surprise. He told me that the board were not going to offer me a new deal, but instead they were going to accept an offer from Arsenal. He immediately cracked open the champagne and drank most of the bottle. I took a sip and then said my goodbyes.

He casually mentioned that the wages on offer weren't great, but I already knew that Arsenal weren't great payers. I still wanted to go back.

The club were urging me to accept the deal, as Arsenal were offering £2 million. If I had waited until the summer, my contract would've been considerably better, but Everton wouldn't have got the full £2 million.

It shows the cut-throat nature of football. Just months earlier I was recovering from major surgery, and now they wanted me gone. However, my overriding emotion was elation at being given the chance to go back to Arsenal.

I still had to pass the medical, though, and it was a very anxious time, given my injury problems. I always wondered what the report said about my back. But whatever it said, I was delighted when the move back to Arsenal went through.

Initially, I didn't pass the medical because of my knee and Arsenal sent off for a second opinion. But by that point the club had announced to the media that I had signed, so I was pretty safe. It took another nervy week behind the scenes for the OK to come through, and I was hugely relieved when it did.

More than that, I was back home.

Back to the Future

I'll always be grateful to George Graham for bringing me back to Arsenal because he gave me that chance to resolve unfinished business. It cost the club £2 million, and all for the sake of an extra £50 a week they were too stingy to pay me all those years earlier.

I invited George to my testimonial dinner in 2004. He was one of the speakers, and the first thing he said was, 'Martin could have been the most decorated football player that ever played for Arsenal Football Club. This could have been the player that played the most games for Arsenal. If only he had listened the first time around to me.' I think he wanted people to know that it was him who brought me back.

I had been desperate to get back to the club: my heart was with Arsenal.

There wasn't much fanfare when I returned. In fact, there was a cartoon in one of the newspapers of skeleton centre-halves in various states of decomposition in a closet and me going to join them, the joke being that George had signed another central defender that he didn't really need, as Tony, Bouldy, Andy Linighan and David O'Leary were already at the club.

Steve Bould, who was Tony Adams's first great centre-back partner, let me know that he wasn't over the moon that I'd returned. He was a good man, but one day after a few drinks he said to me, 'You've come to take my place.'

On top of that, there was the cloud I had left Arsenal

under, turning down what I thought was a paltry contract offer to sign for Aston Villa before George had even been in charge for a game. That was the elephant in the room, and we never discussed it.

At the time, I didn't have a desire to set the record straight with the manager, to say to him, 'This is why I left.' What was there to gain by doing that?

One player who was delighted to see me return was the wonderful Kevin Campbell, taken from us recently at a tragically early age. The first time I walked back into the dressing room he greeted me with a grin, a hug, and his habitual cry of 'Coach!' Kevin had given me that nickname when as a young nineteen-year-old pro I used to run some training sessions for the youth side. Kevin was only fifteen then, but was already a strong powerful player. One season he scored over 50 goals for the Under-18s! Now he was a first team regular and a league championship winner, and I was as pleased to see him as he was to see me.

I had to once again earn the respect of the Arsenal supporters. I certainly wasn't treated like the prodigal son on my return; in fact I think it was the complete opposite, with fans now being much more critical. I had been away for nearly seven years, become an international player and they were rightly expecting top quality from the off.

It was always going to be difficult to be the first player to replace one of those back-four members in my first season back. In my absence the Arsenal defence had become a thing of legend.

I played all across the back to give each of them valuable rest ahead of the FA Cup and League Cup finals. Every one of them was fiercely competitive and knew the strength of their unit and the reputation they had built.

During a game, Lee Dixon was constantly shouting a barrage of information at me:

'You have lost your man.'

'Your body shape is wrong.'

'Push up.'

'You should've gotten tighter there.'

All these things had me playing on the edge, but it was all healthy advice.

Where we stood on the pitch as a back four set everybody else up on the pitch. We would be on the halfway line to smother the opponent, regardless of whether there was enough pace in our back line. The message was always to push up and squeeze and only drop off when there was no pressure on the ball before it was about to be delivered by your opponent.

Opponents ran offside. We just held the line. It was expertly done.

Off the pitch, the club felt like it had been in a time capsule since I'd left, despite winning a fair few trophies. Although the ground was undergoing major redevelopment to become an all-seater, the spirit was unchanged, the backroom staff were the same – it was a really nice feeling.

One thing that surprised me, though, was how much the squad stood up to George. I remember an early game where he started to look around the room to blame people and they all started telling him to do one, and I was really amazed at that. They were all prepared to stand up for themselves and make it clear it wasn't their fault.

George's half-time team talks back then were unbelievable. He'd come in, take his jacket off, and throw it towards the coat stand and miss, like James Bond on a bad day. Gary Lewin, the physio, would run to pick it up, and George would start: 'Gary, fucking leave it. I'm up there in the directors' box and it's fucking embarrassing. That's fucking shite.'

Then he'd look around the room and pick on someone.

'Lee, what are you fucking doing?'

Lee would argue back and go off to the toilet.

'That's right, Lee, off you go and have a piss.'

Then he'd turn to Bouldie, and Bouldie would say, 'No, don't even fucking look at me. You can fucking think again.' Never did he look at Tony.

'Ian, is there any danger of you making some fucking runs?'

Ian would tell him to fuck off. And that's how it went on. I looked around the dressing room and thought, wow, does anyone respect him? It's unbelievable.

George's exit line was always, 'Make no mistake, there will be changes,' but by now the players knew his growl was worse than his bite.

The circumstances didn't make it easy for me to integrate with my new teammates.

We were all in little rooms at the training ground, which Wenger was massively against when he arrived. Instead of one dressing room, there would be about six people in one room, six in another, and so on. It wasn't great for team-bonding.

Another thing that shocked me was when we went to South Africa and there were mixed messages from George around drink. He said no alcohol was allowed on the trip and then on the plane he turned his back and Tony said, 'Get the drinks in.' Half an hour later, George joined us.

Then, when we arrived, some players went straight out on a bender and the next day the first thing we did was heading practice, because George thought everybody had a hangover. It was punishment for disobeying orders, despite the fact he'd been drinking with us.

George was like a sergeant major in lots of ways, and the day before the game he used to line us up against the wall before training for a team talk to tell us who was involved and who wasn't. He almost used to revel in it, a strong man making strong decisions.

I had a couple of run-ins with George and didn't really deal with his style of management very well. He'd just cut your legs off. He'd say to me, 'You've done well. I mean that.' And it always left me wondering why he said he meant it. It just made me feel that he never really meant it.

The biggest flashpoint was when I got taken off in a game with a few minutes to go against West Ham a few months before he left and I went absolutely berserk and battered him because Steve Bould was coming back from injury and I suspected he was trying to prepare me for getting dropped. I called him an offensive word that I'm not proud of, and his assistant, Stewart Houston, tried to calm me down. George said, 'Sit there, shut your mouth, you can have your say when I'm ready.' Which was probably the mistake he made.

I listened to him come in and give a team talk, hammering our midfield players. And then I said, 'It makes it even more unbelievable that you took me off in the game. Why did you take me off?'

He said nothing.

I told him that West Ham's centre-halves finished the game and they lost 2–0, whereas one of our centre-halves was taken off. I told him I thought that he was just a c***. And that all the players thought the same. 'It's not just me, it's everyone,' I said.

It was quite the rant.

When I got on the bus I approached him and told him I'd gone too far but that I wasn't taking that word back.

So, on the Monday, I came in and Stewart Houston was waiting for me. He grabbed me as I entered the building and took me into the weighing room.

'Martin, the boss has said we can handle this one of two ways: we can go to the press or we can do it internally. You decide.'

I told him to tell the boss not to send me some two-bob coach to talk to me about my discipline. And if he wanted to sort it out, he needed to talk to me himself. I know it was Monday and I was supposed to have calmed down, but I hadn't. I wanted to tell George I was out of there, that I'd rather be paid nothing than play for him.

The boss spoke to me the next day, and wanted me to write him a cheque as a fine, but I refused. I told him I would write one instead to Great Ormond Street Children's Hospital, which he agreed to. But I wanted to know if there would be any other comeback.

'No,' he said. 'Haven't I played you whenever you've been available? Don't worry – no problem.'

All agreed, I went back outside, he named the team and I wasn't in it. I was very close to saying, 'You can stick this club up your jacksie.'

George didn't take prisoners. His management style pushed me to the limit. When I conceded a penalty against Ipswich, soon after I returned to the Arsenal, he bollocked me at half time in front of the other players. But when I went to the toilet, he followed me and tried to apologize. I told him I didn't want special treatment. I'd make a mistake and I'd make up for it in the second half. I did and we won 2–1.

George was such a winner, but we were probably too similar, driven by that desire to succeed. He didn't realize I was already at one hundred per cent boiling point. I didn't need to explode. It took Arsène Wenger to figure me out and help unravel my angry coil.

George did make me a better defender. Once I had become part of the back four, rather than a utility player, I saw that the collective is better than any one individual. Often, at the beginning, I was dropping deeper than the others, as I thought I could deal with whoever I was playing against. But that was killing everybody else; they all had to run back with me because I was keeping my opponent onside. In those early days I didn't fully understand when to press and when to drop. But it eventually clicked.

On the pitch in my first season back (I joined in February 1993), Arsenal were in a bit of a mess. They had won just one of their last ten league games, scoring in just three of them. David Rocastle, who I admired a lot, had been sold to Leeds United. Midfielder John Jensen had arrived after a strong Euros but had little impact, and attendances were reduced as the North Bank of Highbury was being redeveloped to make it all-seater. Those of you who are old enough can surely remember the big mural behind the goal with pictures of fans. That mural caused controversy after it was pointed out that there were, remarkably, no black faces on it. To be fair to David Dein, that mistake was rectified immediately.

It was the first season of the Premier League, but it had no feel of glitz or glamour for us, as we finished tenth.

There was a huge silver lining though – the cups. Arsenal not only got to both finals, but we played – and beat – Sheffield Wednesday in dramatic circumstances twice. Not me, though, as I was cup-tied.

Two Wembley cup finals, and I couldn't play in either of them.

The League Cup – which the team almost went out of in the second round, needing penalties to beat Millwall – is famous for winning goal-scorer Steve Morrow being dropped by Tony Adams during the celebrations at Wembley. He broke his arm and didn't play again that season.

The FA Cup saw Tony score the winner in a 1–0 win in the semi-final against Tottenham, and then another unlikely final hero – Andy Linighan – netted right at the end of extra time to beat Wednesday and save the season, really.

I had come back with a completely open mind about how I was going to be at Arsenal. I was determined not to be so judgemental, not to rush in on things. So I was observing and watching everybody in that dressing room.

I just did what I was asked to do in that first year back.

That summer, which started with me being recalled to the England squad, brought more changes, with David O'Leary among those leaving. But by then I was playing regularly. And despite an opening day defeat 3–0 at home to Coventry, us drawing a ridiculous seventeen league games and going out of the domestic cups early, it was an improvement, crowned by winning our first European trophy since 1970, thanks to an Alan Smith goal against Parma in the Cup Winners' Cup final. Guess where I was? Injured, of course. I pulled my hamstring a week before the match, and George took me out for a fitness test the morning of the game, desperate for me to play. It was a very hard decision not to be a part of it. To say I was gutted was an understatement.

I could've just said I was fit but I needed to be honest and professional.

To have to sit out three finals since I'd been back felt like torture. I was, though, awarded a medal as I played in seven of the eight games to get us to the final.

But by then things were unravelling for George – on and off the pitch.

The next season was our lowest league finish since 1976 but, more worryingly, the club – and George – became embroiled in scandal.

Just to put things into context, here are some of the things we went through in that 1994/95 season:

- Finished twelfth, just six points outside the relegation zone
- Only scored in one of our opening five games
- Knocked out of the FA Cup in the third round by Millwall
- Paul Merson revealed his alcohol, drug and gambling addictions
- Somehow we reached another European final – then lost it to a freak goal from the halfway line scored by a former Spurs player
- George was sacked on the day of a game after being found guilty of taking a bung

George had taken £425,000 in cash from Norwegian agent Rune Hauge as part of the deal that saw John Jensen and Pål Lydersen move to Highbury. He convinced Arsenal to pay inflated fees for the players and then got his share.

George always insisted the money was a gift that he didn't ask for, and the club seemed to stand by him at first. Why else would they have allowed him to bring in three players – Glenn Helder, Chris Kiwomya and John Hartson – while the investigation was ongoing?

We could sense some tension though, particularly when, on the coach back from the Super Cup in Milan, David Dein sat next to George at the front of the bus and had what looked like a very tense discussion. This was just days before he was fired.

Some players were chatting about it, a bit disgruntled about the times we'd gone in for a pay rise and were told there was no money, when it turned out he had been the one taking it.

But a lot felt the club hadn't been paying people that well and that George was probably in the same boat. Also, it was well known in the game that people were on the take, and it seemed like George was simply the one who got caught.

That day he was fired. George came to the training ground, and he normally had his football kit on, but this time he was in his civies.

He got everyone outside, the whole club, and he talked then about how he was having to step aside. I don't think he used the word 'sacked' and he thanked everybody for the huge success and support they'd given him over the years.

I saw two or three senior players tear up. They'd won a lot of things together; George had put them on the map. I had a really tough exterior by that point, so I wasn't feeling sorry for him. But in a way, I look back and a lot of my toughness now has come from him, in a good way. He sometimes used to say to me, 'You're too fucking nice.' So suddenly somebody puts that on you and you use that to cope with what you're seeing in front of you. So I wasn't going to be upset. He knew what he was getting into. I just thought it was a shame that it had come to this.

BACK TO THE FUTURE

George got sacked on the morning of 21 February, leaving our assistant, Stewart Houston, to take over for that game and the rest of the season. Stewart, despite my earlier words born out of anger, was an outstanding coach, who, if he'd stayed and worked with Wenger, would have been just as successful as others. Perhaps even more so.

A look at our results in the following weeks tells you just how shaken up the club was at losing the man who had won six major trophies in nine years. We lost six out of seven league matches between 5 March and 12 April, scoring in just three games, and people were genuinely talking about us getting relegated. We were only five points off the drop at that stage, our only comfort being there were so many teams below us despite that, but as of 14 April (a day before our next game) we were only two points off the drop.

Luckily, we rallied not long after, scoring heavily again in beating Ipswich (4–1) and Aston Villa (4–0) with Ian Wright and John Hartson getting among the goals.

With Houston as caretaker manager, we very creditably got to the Cup Winners' Cup final to defend our trophy. And on that run I put in a performance I was really proud of as my man-marking skills were tested to the absolute limit.

It was the quarter-final away to French side Auxerre. Ian Wright scored the winning goal, and I kept their star man, attacking midfielder Corentin Martins, out of the game. I was playing in midfield, and the whole night I went on this ridiculous journey, following him everywhere. The only time I left him alone was to let him go to the toilet at half time. He was getting the ball off the keeper, taking it from throw-ins, we were covering every blade of grass together. I was a diligent man-marker. The role was satisfying, and my proficiency earned me the nickname The Rash.

People often ask me why I was so good at man-marking. I think it's down to a certain mentality. You have to relish the challenge of stopping the opposition's best player, and even as a kid I always had massive determination.

Most of my boyhood tussles in the park were against bigger and older boys and always seemed to be in a one v one situation and that certainly helped my development.

You have to have a mix of pace, mobility and aggression, and it's always critical to assess your opponent's strengths.

I learned how to show my opponent to the left or the right; it didn't really bother me. I realized that the key thing was how close my feet were together because being light on my feet meant I could dance in every direction, picking up the rhythm of my opponent's movement.

Invariably when you are asked to do this job at the highest level, you are playing against an elite player, who knows every trick in the book. Everything is calculated, every step, every change of pace is deliberate. But the most difficult player is the one who continually moves and protects the ball well at high speed.

You have to mirror your opponent's actions on the ball and not be fooled by body movement. If I was running with an opponent, I was always looking to swing my right leg as if I was throwing a punch. I wanted to make clean contact with the ball.

In terms of tackling, you have to go straight to the problem. Sometimes it can be like a nettle – if you grab it hard, it doesn't sting. If you're tentative, you can get badly stung.

I would work on foot patterns and concentrate on getting extra steps in so that I could push away quickly if a player was showboating, keeping my eyes fixed on the ball. Some opponents try to fool you with stepovers. You have to watch them intently. One stepover is fine, but if they do two you know they're going to take the piss and try a third. That was always my cue to tackle them, hard, smashing the ball, wiping them out, ideally without collecting a yellow!

I used to keep a mental logbook of my opponents. Some you could hit hard early, what we call a reducer. Some players never recovered from that and the game was over.

Other players would respond to that so you wouldn't do it the next time.

I would always keep prodding away, trying to unsettle my opponent. I didn't want him to be comfortable when the ball came to feet. I wanted to push him off balance. I needed him to be thinking about me, not the ball. He couldn't be the one that dictated.

I'm in charge, not him.

When my team was in possession, I made sure that I was in the right position to win the ball back if we lost it. Instinct and a desire to get to the ball first always play a major part, but if you're quick to react, your feet sort themselves out automatically so it was important not to overthink it.

And that European game against Martins was one of those occasions when it all came together. I was in midfield that day, and I ran my balls off.

After that, we scraped through the semifinals against Sampdoria on penalties. Thankfully Dave Seaman made a crucial save, because otherwise either Steve Bould or I would have had to take a pen, and we were both bricking it. Though Bouldy was on goalscoring fire, having netted two against Sampdoria in the first leg.

Now we were in another European final, against Real Zaragoza of Spain. After all the frustration of being cup-tied for both of the 1993 finals, and unavailable through injury in 1994, I actually managed to start in 1995, at Parc des Princes in Paris. However – and at this stage I was starting to think I was cursed – I got stretchered off after heading the back of Ray Parlour's head. (It was the first of two trips to the Parc des Princes, the second for England, and I was stretchered off both times.)

I was concussed, and had a depressed fracture of my nose. It was bad timing for me and the team, as I was marking Nayim, the former Spurs player, who went on to score the winning goal in extra time, lobbing our goalie David Seaman with an outrageous effort from near the halfway line. Spurs fans still celebrate that goal. Nayim claimed he meant it. David Seaman still swears it was a fluke. Either way, I like to think if I'd still been on the pitch, Nayim wouldn't have got near the ball.

It was a disappointing end to a frustrating season: finishing twelfth, the club's lowest position since 1975/76.

After George Graham's exit, Bruce Rioch arrived as manager from Bolton, who had knocked Arsenal out of the FA Cup the previous season. Bruce made a great start, at least in my estimation, when he pulled me aside and said, 'I think you can play centre midfield.'

He boosted my career because he wanted me to play, to use the ball properly. He'd stop sessions to tell you to bring the ball down rather than just help it forward. In a way he was anticipating the more sophisticated approach Arsène Wenger would bring to the club a year later.

Bruce's advice improved my passing a great deal. And in midfield, no one was as quick as I was. Nobody was as good in the air, and I found that I could use that power to good effect. I was able to drop back in and around Bouldy and Tony to cover. Eventually, Bruce reverted to a back three halfway through the season, but in both defensive and midfield roles I was able to stamp my authority on the team and when Tony was absent for a few months, Bruce handed me the captaincy, which was a hell of an honour. After my years away, I started to feel like a proper Arsenal player again.

Behind the scenes though, there were contract problems again.

Conscious of financial difficulties in the past, when I rejoined Arsenal I hired agent Tony Stephens, who had approached me offering his help.

Tony represented a small group of elite players, including David Platt. Tony persuaded Arsenal chairman Peter Hill-Wood to insert a clause in my contract saying my salary would always be on a par with the club's top earners.

But that first summer, after Arsenal won both the FA and League cups, some players signed new deals while nothing was done about adjusting my salary. For once I decided not to rock the boat, so I said nothing, preferring to assume the other players' pay had simply been raised to match mine. I was mistaken.

I waited until the end of the next season, after the Cup Winners Cup victory, when new contracts were handed out and again my pay wasn't raised to match the best paid players. I talked to Tony Stephens to do something about it. He reported back that the club had said the clause was ambiguous. These conversations apparently continued for most of the season.

Instead of resolving things for me, Tony then told me he would have to stop representing me, as Arsenal were about to sign David Platt, another of his clients, and it would be a conflict of interest for Tony to look after two teammates.

I felt let down. Tony was happy to take his commission when I re-signed for Arsenal, but now I needed his professional support, he made himself scarce. I couldn't help suspecting that he had used me to get access to the Arsenal.

I'm not obsessed with money, but I've always believed that people should be paid the right rate for the job. This mess-up rekindled the mistrust that had led me to leave the club once before. The difference was this time I couldn't bring myself to confront the people responsible.

I was particularly annoyed with chairman Peter Hill-Wood, because I felt he had broken his word. I could have employed lawyers to argue the case, but what was I going to do if I lost? Leave the club? Again? So Arsenal were let off the hook, and I had no choice but to renegotiate my deal. The parity clause was dropped.

There was another arrival at Arsenal, a far more important one. The brilliant Dutch international, Dennis Bergkamp walked through the double doors of Highbury.

What a player! Tony Adams and I had played for England against the Netherlands in April 1993, when Dennis scored a remarkable goal, chipping our goalkeeper Chris Woods first time on the volley.

So when I heard that we were signing him (for a club record £7.5 million), I knew just how good a player we were getting. It felt like a show of strength and unity from the more go-ahead board members, Danny Fiszman and David Dein, to go and get him, sending a message that the Arsenal was going in a different direction now.

When Dennis arrived, he seemed quiet at first. You could see the talent was there, but did he have the personality to make his mark in the dressing room as well as on the pitch? But he grew in confidence and started to influence games. Soon he was one of the club's key players.

He taught me so much too, taking me out on to the pitch to explain how he liked to receive the ball. 'When you're on the ball, my first movement is for the defender, not you. So if I step behind the defender, I want the ball to feet. If I want the ball in behind the defender, I will first step towards you.' This little trigger of opposite movement worked beautifully. Simple and ingenious.

I also owe him for stopping me doing something really stupid. It was years later, in 2000.

'Keown has a monkey head,' were the words ringing out around Upton Park, the angry mob of West Ham fans taunting me, goading me, trying to get a reaction and put me off my game by making monkey noises every time I touched the ball. They were even wearing T-shirts with my face on it, done up as a monkey. They had 10,000 of them printed, for God's sake.

The problem was, it was working. It was getting to me.

West Ham clearly didn't like us. We'd had some tense games against them, including a cup quarter-final penalty shootout win, and the hatred just seemed to grow and grow – probably because they almost never got the better of us.

In fact, from September 1995 – so pre-Wenger – up until February 2006, Arsenal only lost one of those derbies. One game in eleven years. And that is quite something, because going to Upton Park was difficult – the atmosphere, the nastiness, their fans made it really tough, and I always went there with an over-my-dead-body kind of attitude.

But on that day in 2000 they were trying to ridicule me and I thought it was despicable. They might have seen it as banter, but for me it wasn't. It enraged me, making fun of my looks. At that moment in time, I felt those fans were the scum of the earth.

Normally, I was quite good at not letting taunts from the crowd get to me, but that day I was close to crossing the line.

The final whistle went. Three points in the bag. Then somebody in the crowd caught my eye. He was pumped up, been in the gym, wearing one of those T-shirts, covered in tattoos, and was running along the stand to provoke me. I locked eyes. I was sick of being degraded and decided it was time to pick the biggest idiot I could find and show them all I wasn't taking the abuse any longer.

Looking back now, I was seconds away from my very own Cantona moment, from jumping into the crowd and fighting. I pointed my finger at the guy, saying, 'Come on then.' But Dennis got to me, he put his arm around me, he calmed me, he saved me.

He told me we'd done what we needed to do – win – and that was it. Don't let them get to you.

Generally, the animosity at West Ham spurred me on. Every time I played them, I almost jumped out of the ground every time I went for a header. It just propelled me to more energy. But if you look at the picture of me with Dennis that day, you can see in my face that I'm exhausted, that I'd been through an ordeal. I had been playing like a man possessed, doing whatever it took to get the three points. I had to win.

For me the abuse was awful. Nobody seemed to care though, nobody wrote about it – like it was an acceptable thing to do. No journalists showed any empathy for the amount of abuse I was getting. They seemed to think it was acceptable, a bit of fun.

By that point Dennis was established in the Premier League, a champion playing brilliant football under Arsène Wenger. But when he arrived, in time for the start of the 1995/6 season, he was still suffering the after-effects of two frustrating seasons in Milan, and he took a while to settle in. We still made a good start to that season, under Bruce, going undefeated for the first seven games. We went through a couple of rocky patches after that, but finished a respectable fifth in the table, clinching European football on the last day of the season by beating Bolton, Bruce's old club. Maybe Bruce making me captain for the last nine or ten games helped turn around our fortunes!

Despite that good finish – we'd been twelfth the year before – Bruce seemed to struggle. He had difficulty connecting with some of the star players, though I certainly could have no complaints. It didn't help that several of my teammates were going through tough times in their personal lives. Bruce had to be part-manager, part counsellor. Sometimes he would spend a whole training session off with Paul Merson, trying to advise him. Tony needed support too. Bruce was a caring man, but I think these extra pressures were getting to him, and he'd get angry and lash out at people.

It all came to a head in a pre-season game at non-league St Albans City in July 1996. Even though we went on to win 6-0, Bruce went mad at half time. He had a go at all of us, especially Ian Wright, calling him a big time Charlie who refused to make the sort of runs Bruce wanted. Then he picked up a two litre bottle of water and hurled it to the floor. It exploded like a bomb. Water and bits of plastic everywhere. We were used to George's outbursts, but most of the time he was putting on an act.

Matters worsened when we went to scorching-hot Florence for a pre-season tournament and played two forty-five minute matches in one day, losing both to Fiorentina and Benfica, who were only playing one game each. Bruce let rip at the defence, saying they were finished (I was playing in midfield at that point). He was wrong – the whole damn lot of us were less than two years away from winning the Double. But Bruce seemed to be convinced that time was up and we were past our best. He started comparing Ian's performance with players he had managed previously at Bolton. Why couldn't we be more like them? He wasn't really spreading the love.

Ian couldn't stand Bruce, to the point that he was trying to get him out of the club. One of them had to go, and it couldn't be the club's top goal-scorer. So Bruce went just days before the start of the 1996/97 season.

It can't have been easy to be the man following George Graham and all his trophies, and maybe it was to Arsène Wenger's benefit that someone else came in first, almost acting as a buffer.

Personally, Bruce gave me a much better standing within the club. He was giving someone in the middle of the bus a chance to be the captain and it gave me more confidence that what I was doing wasn't being ignored. So I feel grateful for that.

On the one hand, I was sad, as he was a decent man and I'd done well under him, being named the club's Player of the Year. But I also knew deep down that he wasn't completely right for the job.

Luckily, the next man turned out to be the perfect fit.

Uncoiling the Spring

'Boss, the guys want to go out for a drink for Nigel's birthday,' I said.

'Drink? What do you mean, drink?' replied the boss. 'It's poison. We can't go out drinking alcohol, we're at a health club.'

'Yeah, but we don't play for two weeks. Boss, I'm not asking you if we can go out for a drink. I'm just telling you these are grown men and they're going to go whether you like it or not.'

'In that case, Martin, I hold you personally responsible.'

You can guess how this story ends.

It was a couple of months into Arsène Wenger's time at the club and, with a gap between our games against Derby and Nottingham Forest, the boss had taken us to Henlow Grange for some rest, training and a change of scenery.

As I'd been captain under Bruce, I was sometimes still put forward to voice concerns for the group. So, when the team decided they wanted to go out for Nigel Winterburn's birthday, it fell to me to inform the boss. Even though I wasn't a drinker.

So off we went to a local pub.

We were a large, loud group and, although we were probably good for business, I can't imagine the locals were overly amused to have us arrive. And after a while chaos ensued.

Out of nowhere, Paul Merson went to the middle of the pub, did a forward roll, took out an imaginary gun and paraded it around the room.

The locals looked horrified. Then he blew the top of it like in a Western and put it back in his imaginary holster.

Then the drinks arrived – and it wasn't just one or two. Suddenly I thought, what have I done, taking responsibility for bringing this lot to the pub?

A few hours later, needless to say, I couldn't get them out, and there was little point trying.

Eventually, when people stumbled back to the hotel, we were not met with a warm welcome. Coach Pat Rice was tutting and the gaffer was not impressed.

You could almost see him realize just how big a cultural transformation this team needed. No more boozing, no more poison. If Arsenal were going to become great again, some drastic action was needed.

Most people think that the boss's first match in charge of Arsenal was against Blackburn on 12 October 1996. But that's not actually the case.

It was 24 September and we were heading to Cologne to play Borussia Mönchengladbach in a UEFA Cup first round, second leg, having lost the home leg 2–3. We knew Wenger was about to take over, of course – and Patrick Vieira and Remi Garde, two of his signings, had arrived already – but then there he was at the airport.

He looked like he was wearing somebody else's suit, it was so baggy, and a pair of glasses that looked like they didn't belong to him. They were huge. It was a far cry from his latter days at the club, when everything was a well-cut slimline suit. He was quite an underwhelming figure but seemed like a nice guy, smart, with a big smile. He didn't say a lot.

He was, though, involved in the preparations for the game, despite being there in theory as an observer (his official start date was October because he didn't want to breach his contract with Japanese side Nagoya Grampus Eight).

He did two things during that game that stick in my mind: he switched from a back three to a back four and he took off Tony Adams, which felt like a big deal but was the right call.

So we wondered if that was the end of the back five we'd been playing, but in fact he kept it for the rest of the season, which I thought was clever from Wenger. So many managers cannot resist making wholesale changes the second they walk in the door. The big tactical changes didn't come until 1997/98.

Then, off he flew, back to Japan for a few more weeks, with no one quite sure what to make of him.

But when he returned and started for good, it didn't take long for us to understand what he was about.

David Dein talks about what qualities a good manager needs: ability to lead the group, a good motivator, clever, a thorough understanding of opposition tactics, a great communicator and able to carry the club in front of the media.

Wenger, we soon realized, was all of those things and more, but the most immediately visible differences he made were down to how we treated our bodies and how he educated us to live a clean life and rid ourselves of that poison.

The changes to our diet came quickly. At Highbury, players had already been stopped from having alcohol in the bar after Tony discussed his problems (in Vieira's first ever team meeting!), and Merse had his troubles too.

Wenger brought in stretching after training, which nobody had seen before. Before, yes, but never after. And it wasn't long before others copied us when they saw us doing it on international duty. Now you won't find an athlete who doesn't.

Tony Colbert arrived as a sports scientist and trainer, tasked with improving our strength and conditioning. He was a great guy who I had many a positive battle with when trying to get fit, as he was a fitness fanatic who turned every exercise into a duel.

When he first joined, the boss set up a race for all the staff and we watched with delight. The fitness coach was expected to win by some distance, so you can imagine the reaction of the boss when Tony came last in the cross-country race. It was the last time, as he made sure he was super-fit in the following years.

The boss also brought in nutritionist Doctor Yann Rougier and 'Chew to Win' became a slogan. 'Guys, when you have your dinner on a Sunday, you all eat too much and eat too fast and then you fall asleep. Why do you fall asleep? Because you're using energy, the blood rushes from your head to your stomach to help you digest, but this is too much, we can't have that. We need you to chew. Chew to win so your stomach has less work to do, so it's not using as much energy and making you feel sleepy. Then we have the advantage in the game. I need you to be one hundred per cent.'

Whenever Doctor Rougier came around to us at meals, I would exaggerate the chewing when he looked at us for a laugh, and he'd join in and say, 'Very good, Martin.'

And of course *what* we were chewing changed drastically too.

We were moved to a slow-sugar diet, meaning no spikes in energy. If you eat sugar, it takes your insulin up and down, and that is bad for consistent training and performance. So we had a lot of carbohydrates, rice, pasta, vegetables and fish – food that releases energy steadily over time.

Sometimes the boss would see me eating, come over and

say, 'Oh, Martin, only one carbohydrate. Why do you have rice, pasta and mashed potato?' And I'd say, 'Because I like all three of them.' And he would reply, 'No, you have to decide which one you take because it's not good for your stomach to have all three.'

This was quite the contrast to Bruce introducing Jelly Babies and chocolate before games, and even more so to George, who would tell us on a Friday to go home and have our own food: 'We're not making your food for you here.' Instead, Wenger was saying it was the most important meal of the week and the club would gladly make it for us.

Wenger brought in parcelling our meals with yoghurt too, lining your stomach with it at the start of eating then sealing your palette with more at the end so you have a neutral taste in your mouth and don't carry on eating.

Then our chefs asked the staff at Sopwell House, where we were training, to cook the food without salt. To be fair, it still tasted nice, if a bit bland. Then they'd send instructions to hotels when we went to away games.

It was fascinating, and so well explained to us. Next was water. He told us we mustn't only drink water when we were thirsty because that is our bodies calling out for more water, and that's far too late. So everybody needed to be going to the toilet to check the colour of their wee and had to carry a water bottle with them at all times and sip it.

Oh, and it couldn't be cold water, because if it's too cold it gives you a stomach ache.

Again, a lot of this might seem like common sense now, but it was revolutionary at the time.

There was a ban on tea and coffee. The boss said, 'You're not having them because they dehydrate you.'

But the ritual of drinking tea and coffee together and the

team bonding and camaraderie that came with it were important to us. Surely suffering a bit of dehydration was worth it. I took it on myself to challenge the boss about it, but he said, 'No, it's a disaster, you're poisoning your bodies.' In the end he relented a bit and allowed tea, but not coffee.

We also negotiated ketchup back in at one stage, so he did listen sometimes.

Another obsession of the boss was that we had to keep a tracksuit top with us all the time in case we got cold as he didn't want us catching a chill. And when we met him in Zurich, which I talk about later in the book, true to form, he reached for his tracksuit top and bottle of water as we left to walk to lunch.

Back then, he didn't allow any air conditioning in the training ground either as he said it makes people sick. Another thing he was right about.

Doctor Rougier blood-tested us all and they discovered I was anaemic, which wasn't a huge surprise, as I had been as a kid. They needed to get my iron up so they gave me iron tablets, but I wasn't absorbing them so then they gave me Vitamin C on top, then some B12 and zinc. All of a sudden I had all these vitamins to take – again something that's the norm these days. Back then, other clubs looked at us suspiciously because they weren't as advanced in that area.

So next to your locker when you sat down every morning was a little pile of tablets – it became somebody's job to lay out everybody's pills. I was on board, but some of the other lads, including Dennis, used to throw them in the bin. It wasn't long before I was feeling much stronger, much quicker and had much more energy. The biggest change for me was cramp. I used to get cramps with about ten minutes to go in virtually every game, and all of that disappeared. I felt like

Top: Sergeant Major George Graham in 1995. When George spoke, everyone listened. Next to me is my great pal, Kevin Campbell, who we all sadly miss.

Bottom: Winning Arsenal Player of the Year, 1996, following in the bootsteps of legends like Frank McLintock, David Rocastle, Tony Adams and Ian Wright.

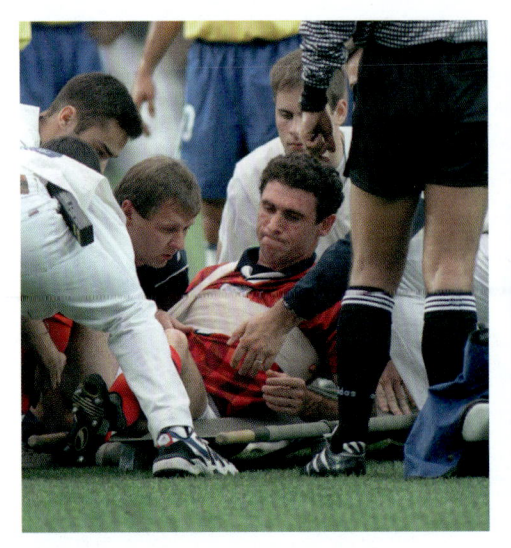

Top left: Le Tournoi was a summer tournament held a year before the 1998 World Cup finals. England won the competition, but I broke my shoulder and was sidelined until November.

Top right: Kevin Keegan's last game as England manager, and the last competitive game at the old Wembley Stadium, against Germany, in October 2000. I enjoyed playing under Kevin more than any other England manager.

Bottom: My proudest day in an England shirt, captaining my country against Finland, in 2000.

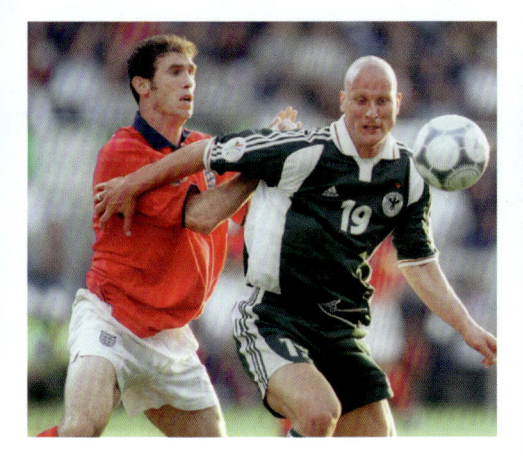

Top: Euro 2000, and our first victory over Germany in a competitive fixture since 1966, the year of my birth. I was Man of the Match for doing a marking job on the mountainous German striker, Carsten Jancker.

Right: Getting the better of World Cup winner Zinedine Zidane, February 1999. That night six Arsenal players started – four for England and two for France. In all, there were ten past, present and future Arsenal players on the pitch that night.

Bottom: About to do battle with Rivaldo, one of Brazil's brilliant number 10s, Wembley, May 2000.

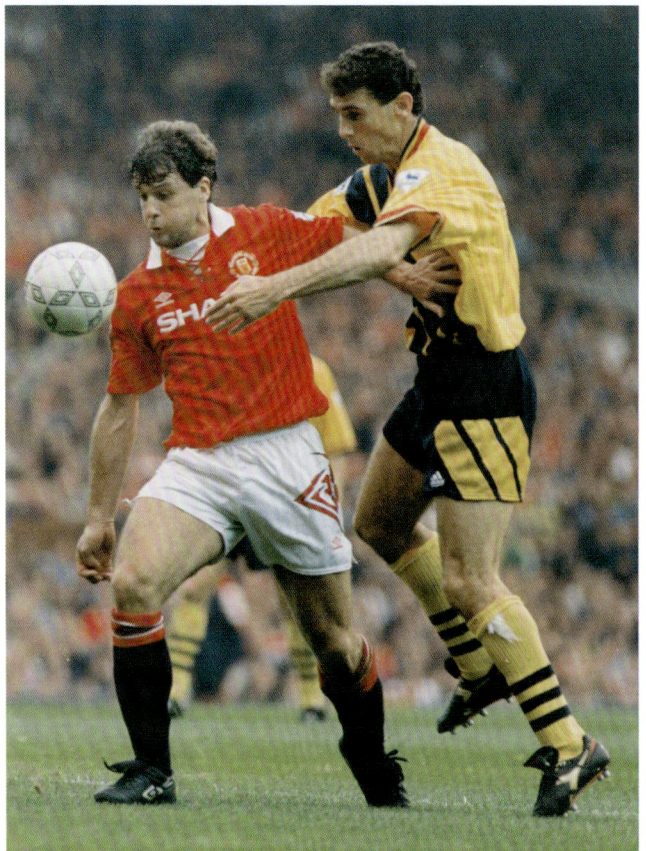

Top: Playing against Kenny Dalglish, one of the greats, in 1986.

Bottom left: Playing against an old foe, Mark Hughes. He was hard, tough and honest, and I must have faced him more often than any other player during my professional career.

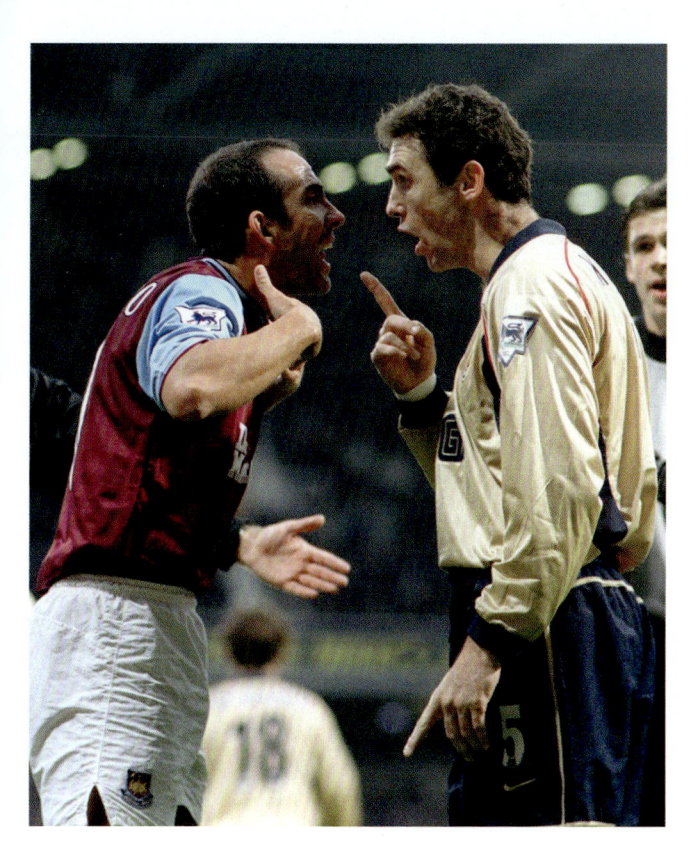

Top left: Me and Paolo Di Canio, discussing where to go for dinner after the match, December 2001.

Bottom: Arsenal beating Everton 4–0 in May 1998 to secure the Premier League title. Duncan Ferguson didn't take it well.

Top: May 1998, and Arsenal's impregnable defence celebrates winning the 1998 Premier League title, the first of the Wenger era.

Bottom: The Anglo-Dutch Comedy Club – three funny fellas and me.

Top: Completing my first league and cup double, May 1998, Wembley.

Bottom: Scoring at Leeds, April 2000. Usually Thierry scored and I chased after him. This time I was the marksman.

Top left: Dennis Bergkamp calming me down at Upton Park in October 2000, after vicious chanting by West Ham fans nearly provoked me into going over the edge.

Top right: Don't worry, it's not my blood. The FA Cup semi-final at Old Trafford, 2002.

Top: May 2002. Arsenal climb the mountain and clinch another Premier League title at Old Trafford, getting a generous round of applause from the few United fans left in the ground.

Superman. I wondered: is it the stretching? Is it the training? Is it the supplements? The food? The chewing? The sipping? I didn't know, but I knew I was going to keep doing all of it because it was making me feel magnificent.

To be clear, there was some respite from the regime, especially after games, when we had much more freedom. In the dressing room or on the bus there would be Coke, Mars bars, Snickers, KitKats, pizza – all fast-food, high-energy stuff to help us recover.

And then there was the football.

The boss took every minute of every training session. George had been pretty hands on, but Wenger was next level. He did everything, every day. Even if we won a game away from home somewhere and the left-over players had to train and the rest were indoors, he'd be out on the training pitch.

Most mornings he would be out with the equipment manager, Paul Johnson, playing little passes and then maybe taking a few shots. One memory that really sticks with me is the day the gaffer ended up in the goal as we ran past, his feet tangled in the net. The boss was always happy to see us happy, so when he saw us he just laughed with us.

Boro Primorac, one of the coaches, could play a bit, so he'd join in training, but the gaffer never did and would stand on the sidelines.

He always had a stopwatch around his neck, which he seemed obsessed with, and everything was done to the second and to the blow of the whistle.

It was a tough schedule and the boss admitted eventually that he'd made a mistake because he didn't realize how intense the games were so he then had to adjust the training. In the first pre-season, he was taking the lads (I was injured) for a run at seven o'clock in the morning, then training at 11 a.m. and again in the evening. It was too much, and we were all knackered. In time, when I went off to play for England, it felt like I could have a little break from the intensity of the training. In fact, things were so full on that the feeling from the back five was that the manager didn't want to play a five and was trying to get one of us injured so he could revert to a four.

Sessions began with a handshake. Every day the boss wanted us to shake everyone's hand while looking them in the eye to create a bond. Sometimes, I swear, he'd come round and shake mine two or three times after losing track. Then it was time to work on our technique.

The boss was a firm believer that if we came to the main core of the session and we weren't passing well enough, it was because we hadn't had a chance yet to get familiar with the ball, to get comfortable. That it was his fault if that happened, not the players'.

So quite often he'd put us into threes. One player stood between two poles with two teammates opposite, ready to serve him the ball. We did a series of little passes around these poles, all really sharp and quick-footed work.

Blow the whistle, and we worked. Blow again, and we rested. It was all a minute at a time, all done to the stopwatch. I found those little drills fantastic for footwork and control. By the time we came to the main core of the session, you were sharp and ready to go.

Core sessions were eight v eights and four v fours most of the time. Long gone were the days when we did sessions based on tackling or heading.

We also did a lot of five v twos in a small area, but that soon became a problem because the defending players would win the ball back too easily, so the boss had to make the pitch bigger so we could actually work on our passing.

That became the priority. Most of the sessions were geared to one-touch and two-touch passing. Wenger was obsessed with the idea that you mustn't take too many touches because you're killing your teammate if you don't pass quickly enough as it means he's got no time on the ball.

That meant keeping the ball on the floor, as putting the ball in the air meant it took longer to bring down and move on. At the start he wasn't quite happy with the pitches because the ball was bobbling a little, but he kept reminding us to keep the ball on the floor regardless.

It's about technique, it's about pushing through the ball. It's about not being lazy, giving more care for the person you're passing it to. It's not just dumping it on them. It's giving them a ball they can deal with.

Players in the final third would have more freedom. But our job was to get the ball to them. How many touches they needed to make in front of goal was down to them. But he always said, 'Before you pull the trigger, stop for a second, be more aware, be more collective. I want you to be greedy at the right time, but there might be a moment when you can just stop, look to your left or right and someone's in a better position.'

People were trying to say Arsenal were trying to walk the ball in at one stage, but we were simply trying to find the best chance of scoring. And when we inevitably made mistakes, he was so different from other managers. He didn't overreact, it was just a case of trying to educate and build us to what he wanted.

To help us pick the right passes, the gaffer put out mannequins and went through every player, giving us three or four options for when we had the ball. We did run-throughs and he'd tell us that, in the game, 'You know the passes that are available, you choose. That's your joy, but these are the options.'

Catering to our every need throughout that period was kit man Vic Akers, who watched the training sessions and team talks and calmness and applied them, as he won endless trophies as manager of the women's team. I don't know how he crammed it all in.

Come match day for me, it was about giving the ball on a diagonal to the best player in front of me, which was Patrick Vieira or Manu Petit – take your pick, they were both so gifted.

One other really noticeable thing was that the message for the bench was that he didn't want any coaches calling out instructions to the players.

'When you have the ball, it's your moment,' Wenger would say. It was a contrast to George but also to a lot of managers you see now. Wenger wanted to show trust in you.

That was a big change for me. As a defender growing up, the mantra I was taught was that, essentially, you're just giving it to the player in front of you who is better than you. That the midfielder has the honour of playing in midfield because he's apparently technically better than you.

George always told me to 'give it to someone who can play'; he was always closing down your thought process, even shouting instructions in your ear if you were near enough to the dugout. It was strange, as he had been a technical player, but he seemed determined to ban everything he did in his playing days.

With Wenger, it was so different and liberating. He told us to be free in our minds. 'You can play, Martin.' Of course others were technically superior to me and I tried to get them the ball, but I did it believing in myself because of him.

We didn't change our approach for anyone.

In Wenger's early teams, we had a group of physical giants complemented by some immensely talented technical players.

This team could play serious football, but if our opponent wanted to have a tear-up, they would come off second best.

Against better teams, it was harder, of course. It might sound obvious, but top players read the game better, they're more physical, they're better athletes. They're tougher, and they're more competitive.

Teams like Manchester United used to pack out the midfield, get physical and get in our faces. Vieira was often targeted. Wenger was transforming the brand of football that we were playing.

It was no longer 1–0 to the Arsenal. This was now cultured football but with the defensive steel that George instilled in us still ingrained in the team.

Off the pitch, Wenger told me he lived the same as his players: no alcohol, no late nights. He said he would not ask his players to live in a way that he was not prepared to live himself. It was impressive.

I think he had a glass of wine here and there, and I know he used to smoke during his Monaco days, but not with us.

When I went over to the staff side after I retired he'd have a glass of wine but never finish it – and it was the same again recently in Zurich. It's a typical show of control.

He was very big on principles and simplicity in his life. He used to say to me, 'One watch, one car, one wife.'

The gaffer had the most understated car in the car park, though eventually he had a deal with his sponsor. In fact, it was only me and him who didn't have posh badges on our cars — Ferraris or whatever else. I drove a Saab because of my back and the lads ripped the piss out of me for it.

The boss's advice knew no bounds. When I went shopping, he'd say, 'Martin, you must not buy a flowery shirt. If I'm buying, I buy a white shirt. Why? Because it's simple. I can wear it the first day, the second day if I cannot wash it. If you wear something that stands out, everyone is saying, "Look, he never washes." So keep things simple.'

There was advice on buying a house too. When he first arrived in north London there was no time to lose.

He decided that he needed to target and negotiate with the woman in the house, not the man, as he felt it's the woman who runs the house. When he found the house he liked, he told me he went in, looked around, said he'd take it and would give the asking price plus twenty grand on top.

But there was a catch: he wanted everything — the furniture, the cutlery, the bedding, everything. He even kept the Christmas tree! They only took their personal possessions and their clothes.

'I've got so much to do in my job I didn't have time to go and buy furniture, bedding or beds, and this house was in top condition,' he said. So the vendors accepted it there and then. When he arrived, the only thing the house didn't have was food.

When you worked with Wenger, he was giving you life lessons for free.

He gave us so much advice about our lives outside football. He loved his players more than any other manager I've played for. Any of the tension went out of my game the minute I met him, and it meant that I was more likely to win something. Before that I had ability, but I couldn't unravel the talent. But he made me successful with his belief in me. 'Martin, you'll find a way,' he'd say.

At a football club, every player is always looking out for when the boss might speak to another player, who are the lucky ones to get his attention. With Wenger it was so subtle. No one really noticed a quiet word here and a pat on the back there for a great performance the night before. At half-time there was always a compliment, he was always reassuring – but never in full view of anyone else.

He'd always find a moment, even if it was in the car park. It felt like he wasn't just the boss but also your friend.

At the start we all felt a little bit suspicious because the guy was so nice, whereas George had been the opposite. Could nice guys really win things?

But he was driven by this idea of simplicity in life, and his theory was, if you have that, you take simplicity into your game and the two are linked massively. I still try to apply that philosophy now in everything I do.

I'm pretty sure I passed that advice about plain shirts on to my sons!

Much like Wenger, I have never led a flashy life and have always tried to be sensible with money and my future. I bought properties with the money I earned from the game and was never interested in expensive holidays, cars or clothes.

I planned my career for my quality of living to go up, not down, when I finished. We lived well within our means – I was almost like a squirrel, stashing away nuts. I had seen a lot of players over the years go into financial decline, and I didn't want that to happen to us.

Then, when I finished playing, I decided to build a bigger house. I knew leaving Arsenal was going to really hurt so, to soften that blow, I wanted my home comforts to improve.

Where we lived was well tucked away in the Oxfordshire countryside, over half a mile from a main road. We had hidden our wealth from the public, but not from our children, and it had now become impossible to disguise that we were comfortably off.

It's hard to look your son in the eye when he looks around the size of the house and hears me telling him that we can't afford a new bike because I didn't want to spoil him.

But, eventually, living out of town made no sense. I felt like an estate manager, planning to get the lawn cut, maintaining the house – the upkeep was ridiculous. Then my two boys were becoming young men and because there was no or little public transport, we were ferrying them in and out at all hours of the day. So we decided to move back into Oxford so they had some independence. It was a huge change for the whole family, the boys could be independent of mum and dad's taxi service.

But as careful as I was with money, guided by my dad's voice in my head saying, 'A fool and his money are easily parted,' I, like many other footballers, got caught up in what we thought was a legitimate government-backed tax scheme run by a company called Ingenious.

The premise of the scheme was that the film industry was struggling, Chancellor Gordon Brown was appealing for people to invest in the sector. and we would receive tax relief in return.

These financial guys, they came to my house – the boys were young and playing in the kitchen with their toys – and they sat there saying how great a scheme this was and how it was a fantastic way to look after my family's future. I wasn't sure, but I got my lawyer and accountant to look at it all and they said it looked great. It wasn't, and the taxman decided that it was not legitimate, moving the goalposts.

The official letters started arriving thick and fast, demands for huge amounts. It was confusing, so I employed someone who used to work for the Inland Revenue and he went and spent a day at Ingenious Film Productions to try to work out what was going on. He came back and said I had a big problem, and that if I didn't pay the bill, it would just get bigger and bigger.

I was furious, firstly for the bad advice and secondly with myself for letting someone else make the decisions on my finances. I never have since.

Luckily, because of my property investments, I was able to find a way to pay the bill, but some others owed far more. It bankrupted people, ruined people. Some were suicidal.

Wenger's team talks were straightforward ahead of kick-off, but also really uplifting.

At the hotel before we joined the team bus, we had an in-depth meeting and Wenger would make sure the video of the previous game was running just as we walked into the room.

The reason for that was so we could relive last week's successful moments: a shot or a goal from Dennis, a superb run from Anelka, a flowing move from back to front or a crunching tackle from Tony or me – we cheered on from the sidelines as if we were watching someone else.

There we were, enjoying all the magic we were capable of. You couldn't help but be motivated.

Then he'd turn off the video and say, 'Right, gentlemen, we need to do it all again.'

In his team talk, the boss used to have two things about the opponent he would flag, and ten positive things to say about us.

If things weren't going well at half-time, you'd still see his calmness. Often he would stay outside the dressing room for those first few minutes and listen if we had a discussion amongst ourselves. Then he would come in and say, 'Quiet now. Please be calm, take a rest, use the loo, get some fluids on board.'

Then it was total quiet, with Gary Lewin milling around fixing players' strappings or Vic Akers getting fresh shirts or whatever was needed. I enjoyed the peace so I could think about my game.

I would play the game back in my head and, after ten minutes of quiet, we were ready to listen. We were thirsty for information now.

When Wenger then spoke, it was energizing. He would reaffirm his belief in us and tell us that we hadn't yet started to play. After the game and an inevitable improvement in performance, people would ask, 'What happened at half-time?' and the response would be: 'Well, the boss didn't rollick us like every other manager.'

He'd just say, 'Guys, switch on. Come on, for fuck's sake, start to play. Come on, I believe in you.'

After a few months of that bliss, I couldn't be in a dressing room for England because of all the shouting – there was no time to process anything. Arthur Cox would be telling me to sit down and listen to Kevin Keegan, and I'd be saying, 'No, I need a piss. I need to be on my own for a second.' Because that's what I'd got used to.

What of course is fascinating about all of this is that the boss was a winner, a fighter, someone who, like us, hated losing. All this calmness and simplicity didn't come easy to him. I asked him once, 'How do you stay so calm?' And he said to me, 'I am an animal, I'm a killer underneath the surface. I have to work so hard to keep this under wraps.'

He talked to me once about how he was fighting every day as a kid at school, and I know I was. So I think he liked fighters. His way round it in the early days was, famously, saying, 'I did not see it,' when we did something bad on the pitch. Of course he'd seen. And he told me years later that the less physical the team got, the more aggressive he became. Whereas at the beginning it was completely the other way around because we were a squad full of fighters.

Of course, while he valued people like me and Ray Parlour – fighters he inherited – he didn't really buy players like us in the later years. So his Arsenal went from having a perfect mix of old-style players and new-style players to, some would say, having more of an emphasis on technical ability in the years after the Invincibles.

All that makes me think that if he hadn't inherited us, he wouldn't have bought us. But there we were, and the boss not only got the best out of us and challenged us, but we got to be part of this amazing pioneering approach, bringing a different style on the pitch and way of life off it to the Premier League.

When we started becoming successful – you have to remember that Manchester United had won four of the first five Premier Leagues and came second in the other, so they were way ahead of us at the beginning – you could sense fear and reverence in our opponents.

In the seasons that followed our successes, in the tunnel I used to hear people say, 'Jeez, Vieira's even bigger than I thought he was.' People were trying to swap shirts with Dennis before the game. Sometimes it felt like we'd won before a ball had even been kicked.

At other times, things were livelier in the tunnel. Ian Wright and I had a code that I came up with if we thought things were getting tasty, as he used to get into a fair few fights. I'd say to him, 'Put the kettle on,' and that meant he needed to rush down the tunnel at half-time and prepare for a fight. And there were several, most noticeably against Coventry City one time, when things got so out of control there was a knock on the door of our changing room. It was Ken Friar, who told the boss that the police wanted to arrest three of our players. 'No, Ken, for fuck's sake, we are the home team, tell them to arrest their players,' the boss said.

Ken disappeared.

You might be reading all this thinking it sounds an amazing thing to be part of but also pretty intense.

I spoke recently to Stephen Hughes, a big part of that 1997/98 season and still a good friend, who said being on that bus with us and around that group all week was so funny and enjoyable.

And I agree – it was like reading a comic book through the week, so much fun and laughter, great banter and team spirit at its best.

Then, you'd put down the comic book for ninety minutes each Saturday or Wednesday, or whenever we had the privilege of pulling on that Arsenal shirt.

You'd go out and play this incredible, fast-flowing, aggressive, winning football.

When we returned to the dressing room, the banter and laughter would start again, and so it went on, week after week, year after year, success after success – with the odd disappointment thrown in between, of course.

When I look back at those early Wenger years, as well as the trophies and the incredible players and performances

I was honoured to be involved in, the other thing I remember is fun and happiness.

The boss wanted us to turn up at games pumped and really believing in ourselves — it's why he played those videos in the hotel beforehand. And, always someone to spot talent, he gave Paul Johnson, who was in charge of the training equipment, a far bigger job, being in charge of all travel.

On the one hand, that meant really important things like improving the hotels we stayed in and using trains instead of coaches as it reduced the travel time. That felt vital on our first trip away with him to Germany, when the coach went down a road that had a bridge we couldn't get underneath. We had to reverse the coach back and were late for the game.

We flew to most away game, even though in hindsight that was pretty controversial in terms of the environment.

The boss made sure to create the right atmosphere in the group. So, in the 1997/98 season, just as we were about to arrive at the ground, with the crowds gathering, he chose the classic Tina Turner song 'The Best' to blare out over the speakers, and I thought it fitted this group perfectly.

Five minutes out from our destination, home or away, Johnno would turn up the volume to maximum. We'd all sing it at the top of our voices and, by the time we arrived, you couldn't help but look around that bus and believe that you were simply the very best the Premier League could offer.

We were carried along with the music, and the place was buzzing. We'd literally bounce off the bus and arrive ready for the game. We were like a champagne bottle ready to be uncorked.

I can't remember what songs were played in the intervening years, but I know it was 'Dreams' by Gabrielle the next time we won the league, in 2002. And to win it at Old Trafford really was a dream — but that's for a later chapter.

We would laugh and joke in the changing room. To relax everyone before games, Ian Wright used to dance, and he claimed the boss would look at him with a disapproving stare, but I never saw that.

I was doing the Michael Jackson moonwalk myself. Dennis used to put on 'Don't Stop 'Til You Get Enough', as he knew I loved it, and I couldn't resist the urge to show people my moves. Was I any good? Absolutely not, but it certainly made people laugh. The idea was to take the tension out of the room for some of the younger players.

In that dressing room, everyone would giggle. Dennis used to mess about a lot. And it was important because, if you couldn't express yourself in there, how were you going to express yourself on the pitch in front of all those people?

The boss was very respectful of it being our place too. He used to largely steer clear of the dressing room ahead of the game. You'd find him out on the pitch, especially at away games, because he was always concerned about how the grass had been prepared for the game.

Was it cut short enough? Was it slick enough? Was there enough water on it? All attention to detail that he knew was important for our game. If someone had left the grass long to try to slow our passing game, he'd tell us, and we'd be extra determined to win.

I'd also go out pre-game to look at the grass and let the lads know if it was a day of long or medium studs. They used to take the piss out of me for doing that, but a lot of the lads would copy what I suggested. Not Thierry Henry, but I guess he could've worn slippers and still have been a class act. He didn't even tie up his shoelaces in training.

I remember one time in the 1999/2000 season, we went to Barcelona and the boss and I were taking a look at the pitch. He said to me, 'Martin, this is a disaster, the pitch is ten metres bigger than Highbury. We have ageing defenders – how can we get a result here?' It was a rare insight into what he worried about, though I don't know how it was a surprise to him – Camp Nou was hardly some stadium in a backwater of Eastern Europe!

I said, 'Boss, relax, we'll be fine.' We drew 1–1, thanks to a late Kanu goal, despite playing the latter stages with ten men after versatile defender Gilles Grimandi was sent off. Not bad, considering we were up against Rivaldo, Luís Figo, the de Boer brothers and Jari Litmanen.

By that point we were very much part of Europe's elite. And that all started with the incredible 1997/98 season.

Boring, Boring Arsenal

My phone rang and it was Bobby Armitt, Arsenal's first-team kit man. 'Martin, have you heard? There's been a fire at the training ground. They think it's Arsène.'

Now, I knew the boss was not a fan of the training complex, but burning it to the ground seemed a bit extreme.

Arsène, arson – it was a good joke at the time, but however that fire started in late 1996 (I think it was a bib that caught light in the drying room), it set the boss on a mission to get a new training ground fit for the twenty-first century.

When enquiries were made to buy our then home – the University College London playing fields, which we were sharing with the university – a price of £12 million was quoted. A bit of a liberty. Wenger, sensing an opportunity, decided to make an approach to the neighbouring local farmer, who owned all the land, 140 acres of it, to the rear of the London Colney training ground, near St Albans. His timing was perfect; a reported £6 million offer was accepted, and then the club spent another £6.5 million developing it.

Around that time they sold Nicolas Anelka to Real Madrid for £23 million, and they used about half of that money to buy the land and develop the new training complex.

The remainder was used to buy Thierry Henry, so it wasn't a bad deal all round.

Sharing with the university had not been ideal. Wenger wanted us to do extra training sessions, but the pitches were being used by students and he was tearing his hair out at the unprofessionalism of the situation. We weren't allowed to use them at all on Wednesdays, as the university had them for their sports day, and that was seen as a disaster by Wenger. He said that we needed to do our toughest session that day so our bodies recovered in time for the weekend (you usually feel most tired and stiff two days after training). Many teams trained full pelt on a Thursday after having the Wednesday off, so they would be still stiff come game day, which made no sense. Wenger wanted the hard day on the Wednesday, massage and recovery on the Thursday, then a short, sharp session on the Friday, ready to go the next day. But the university set-up made that impossible.

On top of that, there was no irrigation on the pitches, no watering of the surface, no gym — it was a mess. The boss later said he might not have stayed had the club not committed to improving the situation.

Because of the fire, we relocated our base to the hotel at Sopwell House, a short distance from our training camp, where we continued to use the pitches until October 1999.

Although, long term, we were able to move to a state-of-the-art training ground with hydro pools, seven pitches with undersoil heating, a weights room and an indoor gymnasium, short term, I am convinced Sopwell House helped to fast-track the team spirit we needed to develop with so many new players coming in from across the world.

It was a fifteen-minute coach journey from the hotel to the training ground, players only, as the boss and staff would go in their cars.

The laughter on the bus helped to gel everyone together, not least on the day Ian Wright ran out of patience with the bus driver.

Each day we would meet at the hotel and wait for the

coach to arrive. It felt like it was always late, and then the coach driver would wander into the hotel to have a drink and use the toilet, claiming that his tachograph – the device which records when a driver needs a rest – was telling him he needed to take a break.

So we'd all be sitting on the bus, waiting to leave, and it was annoying. And Ian was getting increasingly agitated each day, as he does.

Then the bus driver made a big mistake – he left the keys in the ignition.

Ian, who couldn't take it any longer, marched to the front of the bus, shouting, 'I'm going to drive this fucking bus to the training ground. I've had enough!'

Everyone was shouting back at him, 'No, Ian, you cannot be serious. Don't be stupid,' but that made him even more determined.

So he sat in the driver's seat and turned the ignition on. The engine roared, and we all looked at each other, thinking there was no way it was really going to happen.

Slowly, he put it in gear then lifted the clutch and we pulled off with the door still open. Over my shoulder, out of the back window, I could see our driver running after the bus, waving his arms for us to stop.

By this point, everybody on the bus was in hysterics as we gathered speed down a very narrow country lane which is used for school runs.

The next moment, an oncoming car came too close and suddenly there was a huge bang as our bus clipped its wing mirror.

Ian slammed on the brakes, the bus bounced to a standstill, and he legged it to the back of the bus.

With all of us sniggering and laughing, the driver of the

car, an understandably rather angry middle-aged woman, got on and said, 'I saw you, I saw you,' and even said Ian's name. She came walking down the bus to find him. 'It was you at the wheel!' she shouted at him. Ian feigned innocence, and at that moment our bus driver arrived.

Luckily, there wasn't too much damage done and the woman accepted an apology. Our driver finally got into his seat, looking thoroughly pissed off. And as he pulled off, someone shouted, 'Don't be fucking late again.'

Not all our interactions with the public were that childish and stressful, though. At the hotel, for example, the integration with guests and members was positive – most of them were fans – and seemed to make everything less stressful.

There were big changes in lots of areas behind the scenes, including the arrival of a very important guy called Sean O'Connor.

Sean is still at the club and works closely with Mikel Arteta. He became the training ground manager – he is great at his job, sees everything and is totally committed to the excellence of Arsenal. He brought along Robert Fagg, a friend who happened to be a terrific chef.

Sean was introduced to the club by Gary Lewin, showing you how everything stemmed from personal recommendations from people the club trusted. Those two were told to keep a close eye on how the food was being prepared, how much we were paying for it, and how much it would actually cost us at our new training base.

Years later I remember being particularly grateful for them when we played the Ukrainian side Shakhtar Donetsk in the Champions League in 2000.

We stayed in by some distance the worst hotel I've been to in my life – the beds had prison-like spring bases which you could feel coming through the thin mattress. Along the corridor, you could see each player go into their room and immediately come out again, saying, 'You must be joking.' In the room I was sharing with Matthew Upson, there was a patchwork of various wallpapers on one wall and bloodstains on another. Luckily, I was such good friends with Matthew that we laughed our way through it.

There was a boiler in every room so there was also a hole in the wall for ventilation, and it was like there was a gale blowing through. The electricity was governed by the local area, so at ten o'clock the lights went off and we were in total darkness. Sean and Rob came to do the food because they were worried about what we'd get served. That became the typical level of detail and professionalism introduced by Wenger.

On the pitch, in the weeks before Wenger arrived, we were nearly top of the league under Stewart and then Pat. In fact, when Arsène arrived, we'd only lost one league game.

But we faded a bit in January and February, and then the season slipped away after a ridiculous incident against Blackburn Rovers that Chris Sutton and I argue about to this day.

Stephen Hughes went down injured at Highbury, so Patrick Vieira kicked the ball out of play, as was the done thing. Then, being sportsmanlike, Blackburn gave the ball back to us from the throw-in. Nigel Winterburn had the ball at his feet, but instead of letting him run the ball out of play for a goal kick like normal, Sutton pressed him straight away. We conceded a corner, there was a bit of argy-bargy, and, you guessed it, they scored seconds later, meaning the game ended in a draw.

I went into the away dressing room to have it out with

Chris afterwards and told him he was a disgrace. I didn't hit him, but I was very close to it. There was a whole melee going on just outside the dressing room in the meantime, a mini riot. It just exploded.

Of course, we were on the wrong end of the law a couple of years later when we scored against Sheffield United after they'd kicked the ball out of play. I'm pretty sure that was Marc Overmars pretending he didn't know the rules – it was brilliant acting. Arsène offered to replay the match after the incident, and I remember the audacity of their manager Steve Bruce saying it should be at their home ground. No chance: we will replay the game, but don't take liberties.

Anyway, after that nonsense with Blackburn, we faded, drawing at Coventry and losing at home to Newcastle, who finished second to Manchester United that season.

So there was no Champions League for us, but, actually, it was a blessing in disguise. The squad would never have been big enough to cope with Champions League games and a run for the title.

It was coming up to Christmas in 1997, and life under Wenger wasn't completely smooth.

We'd lost four of our past six league games (to Derby, Liverpool, Sheffield Wednesday and Blackburn), were ten points off leaders Manchester United in fifth place and our captain, Tony Adams, had been told to take some time away by the boss after his personal struggles had led to some poor performances. The Blackburn defeat (in the season after the Sutton incident) was particularly tough on Tony, who suffered that day.

To emphasize just how bad things were, this is from a

report in the *Independent* newspaper from that game, in which we were booed off at Highbury by our own fans.

> Blackburn put paid to the notion that a challenge to Manchester United will come this season from north London. On this performance you wouldn't bet on Wenger's team with someone else's money.

I had missed the start of the season with a broken shoulder (which I got playing for England in the summer) and had not been able to do any contact work while I recovered. I was determined to return fitter than ever, so I had been doing all of the running sessions with the youth team, the under twenty-threes and the first team.

Whenever there was a running session, they'd bring me in. I was as fit as I'd ever been.

Now I was back in the team, but we were struggling and it was clear where the problem was. So the Monday after that bruising defeat to Blackburn, the boss called an emergency team meeting at Sopwell House and some home truths were heard, home truths that would set us on our way to Arsenal's first Double since 1971 – and my first major trophies at last.

I remember this meeting as clear as day. It was held in a function room in the hotel and it was a rare occasion when the boss lost his cool with Pat Rice. The boss told us we couldn't keep losing games, that if we wanted to be successful, we had to get to the bottom of the problem.

He was so wound up his usual fluent English deserted him, and what he was trying to say was not very clear. Pat intervened and said, 'Look, what I think the boss is trying to say is . . .' but it obviously wasn't quite right, as the boss jumped in and told him to shut up. 'No, Pat, that is not what I am trying to say.' We all looked at each other, pretty stunned.

What came out eventually was that we in defence felt that the midfield was not doing enough to help us out and we were being exposed. We just weren't getting enough people behind the ball.

After that, players higher up the pitch started contributing more defensively, and it made a big difference. The team's balance was better.

Tony, at this point, had been sent away to France for one month. The boss made the call to protect him.

In Tony's absence, as always, I struck up a good partnership with Steve Bould, and results started picking up.

Playing alongside Steve was always a pleasure. I felt our games complemented each other well and Steve certainly didn't get enough credit for the ability he had.

Whenever Tony didn't play, I remember the back four getting together and saying, 'Let's make sure the first headline isn't how much Arsenal missed Tony.'

That was the level of respect he was shown by the media. He was guaranteed an 8/10 in the paper in every game.

In 1993, on my return to Arsenal, Tony was quite a different person from the one I knew in our early days together. He had become an iconic figure, was club captain and had achieved many successes, won many medals and many personal accolades. He'd also opened up on his struggles with alcohol.

Before I left Arsenal in 1986, from the age of sixteen I had played with Tony in the youth team, reserves and first team on many occasions, some forty games, but I never really felt that our promising partnership from those early days had fulfilled its potential.

But once he returned from France, focused and fresh, now at last there was an opportunity for me and Tony to re-establish our former on-field relationship, and in those remaining games of that season it really took off.

With me now fully in tune with the high line and the offside call, nothing could get past us – blocks, tackles, headers. 'Over my dead body' became Tony's stock shout to the troops.

I could have gone to war with that team.

If our opponent wanted to be physical, we could match them easily. And at the same time I never saw another team outplay us with our passing game. It was a total joy.

In many ways, that group were pioneers for how Wenger's teams were going to play for the next twenty years.

We were building a new reputation for Arsenal, one far removed from the 1–0 of the Arsenal cliché from the early nineties.

Suddenly, almost overnight, we were re-branded and repackaged, playing with such freedom, expression and cutting-edge football.

By the time our good run came together that season, the team had a real international feel about it. But that was some turnaround from Wenger's first league game against Blackburn, when Patrick was the only foreign player in the starting XI (Dennis was injured). For those of you trying to remember, the team was Seaman; Dixon, Bould, Adams, Keown, Winterburn; Vieira, Platt, Merson; Wright, Hartson.

But at the height of the Double season, the team looked a lot different.

Dave Seaman was such a cool character, never ruffled. The mark of a top goalkeeper is being able to make important saves when they've had little to do for most of the game. That top-level concentration and readiness to be there when needed.

Nigel Winterburn on the left of defence was the master at winning the ball early off his opponent. He was like a Jack Russell snapping at your heels.

Lee Dixon to my right was quick, and so well schooled on defending. I never had to even look over my right shoulder because he told me everything that was happening behind me, constantly commentating to me during the game.

Both were among the greatest servants for the football club and immensely proud and determined men.

In front of us were probably two of the best midfielders to ever pull on an Arsenal shirt in Petit and Vieira. They were in a weekly contest to decide who was going to be Man of the Match.

Vieira was an extraordinary player. Arsenal had signed him, on Arsène's recommendation, while our new manager was still seeing out his contract in Japan. Pat Rice wasn't sure what to make of the newcomer, and when Arsène phoned Patrick to ask how he was settling in, Patrick said he hadn't even met the first-team players.

Arsène wasn't impressed. Reserve team manager Geordie Armstrong suggested to Pat Rice that as the new boss had signed Vieira, Patrick ought at least to train with the first team.

A few weeks later Patrick made his debut at home to Sheffield Wednesday and instantly reinvented the role of the box-to-box midfielder. From his first touch of the ball we all knew he was special.

In front of the midfield was Dennis, the maestro, dropping deep to receive the ball on the half turn, a player with everything in his game: vision, technique, pace and fire in his belly. He played the game to perfection.

To the left was Marc Overmars, who travelled so quickly

you almost couldn't see him move. He was an immensely clever and elusive opponent, who was ruthless with his finishing.

Marc is not talked about nearly enough for what he achieved in such a short space of time. His opposing defenders were delighted to see the back of him when we lost him to Barcelona.

To the right, and also never getting enough praise, was Ray Parlour. Ray could drop into midfield to form a three or stay out wide to roast his full-back. He was tough too.

Up front was the flying Frenchman, Nicolas Anelka, the best young talent I ever saw. He destroyed everyone, from Jaap Stam to Rio Ferdinand, and left a trail of destruction throughout Premier League defences.

Ah, Anelka. In the early days I was giggling on the pitch because he was that good it was unbelievable. In training he made us all look like fools, to the extent that poor Tony was spitting feathers one time because Anelka was destroying him. Tony was kicking the goal in anger, so the boss sent him in. Anelka was so quick, and he just sort of arrived out of nowhere, another incredible Wenger discovery.

We played Derby at the end of the 1996/97 season, and that was the day Anelka announced himself to the world – but he almost didn't make it on to the pitch after packing his suitcase the night before, frustrated at his lack of first-team opportunities. Wenger calmed him down, talked him round, and the next day he came off the bench with our unsuspecting opponents not realizing what was about to happen to them. He absolutely destroyed them, despite the fact we only had ten men.

Derby's players were running around saying, 'Who the hell is this? Where did they get him from?'

He actually replaced Paul Merson that day, and that was the end for Merse, who had been a schoolboy in my youth team and had been immense for Arsenal. He was now being shown the door.

So the Anelka secret was out of the bag.

I often felt that Nicolas was misunderstood. I didn't think he was in any way, shape or form arrogant. I thought that he was just a shy young lad, living in a foreign country.

I had the utmost respect for him but I was shocked and surprised when he left Arsenal when he did.

I had done the same, of course, and I felt it would be a mistake for him too. Years later, when I was working on the staff with Wenger and he became available, I urged Wenger to take him back, but he decided not to, having seen him struggle to gel on the pitch with Thierry Henry in the France youth system.

But just like the rest of the team, Anelka got off to a pretty slow start in the Double-winning season. Despite scoring in a 3–2 win over Manchester United, he only found the net once in the first half of the season and later did an interview where he accused Dennis and Marc of passing to each other and not to him.

But even if he didn't score a crazy amount that season, his pace terrorized and terrified defences and he still managed crucial goals against West Ham and Newcastle, in the FA Cup quarter-final replay and final.

The other thing the French lads brought with them was real fight and steel, and a truly bizarre game against Wimbledon brought that home to me.

We originally played at Selhurst Park three days before Christmas and just after that disastrous Blackburn defeat.

But then, at 0–0 and thirteen seconds into the second half,

the floodlights went out. We all trotted off, they got them working, and then it happened again, at which point the referee called the game off. It later turned out the floodlight failure was suspected to be part of a ploy by a Malaysian betting syndicate.

The incident finally led to the boss realizing that Ray Parlour had been affectionately taking the mickey out of him for the last fourteen months, comparing him to Inspector Clouseau from *The Pink Panther*, whose catchphrase was 'Is it a bomb?'

Ray had been convinced the boss was like Clouseau and had been playing Pink Panther movies on the team bus TV on every away trip as a joke. But the boss had no idea why.

So, that night, Wenger was giving a team talk during the wait to go back on the pitch and said, 'I don't know what is wrong, what's happened?' and then Ray, in his best French accent, said: 'It's a bomb.'

The boss had a Clouseau moment, replying, 'A bomb?', and we all fell about laughing. At last, the penny dropped for the gaffer – Ray had been rumbled.

Anyway, the floodlight farce did us a favour because we didn't have Vieira and Petit in the team that day, but we did in March when the game was rescheduled. Wimbledon was a tough place to go and their team was full of so-called hard men such as Vinnie Jones and Ben Thatcher, who still channelled the days of the early nineties, when John Fashanu and others were in the team. And when you go down the tunnel and out on to the pitch, you have to go past the home dressing room.

We were in the tunnel, and we stopped parallel to Wimbledon's dressing-room door, Manu in front of me (I always went out behind him), and we could see Vinnie headbutting the toilet door. The noise in their dressing room was ridiculous and they looked like a bunch of hooligans. Manu looked at them, then turned to me and said, 'I am going to fucking kill them. Yeah?' There was no fear. Manu was driven to win every game in honour of his brother, who he tragically lost playing football. Before every game, he would go to the edge of the box, where his brother's accident happened, pick up some grass and let it go into the wind as a tribute to him.

And typical of Manu, he won the battle at Wimbledon, us winning 1–0, thanks to a Christopher Wreh goal.

By that point we were deep in the middle of our unbeaten league run, which stretched for eighteen games – until we won the title. Tony and I were barely conceding a goal – just two in thirteen matches. Our games complemented each other perfectly. I was more mobile, he was better in the air – we were so linked it was as if we didn't even have to think. We were the two remaining members of that Class of '83, we were steeped in the club, and we were representing all those people we came through the ranks with.

Those victories were when I really saw the value of Tony having won the title previously. That support next to me was invaluable in the run-in, and we managed twelve clean sheets in fourteen games to win the league with two games to go. Suddenly everything was falling into place.

But not everyone was convinced by our form, with bookmakers Betfred paying out on Manchester United to be champions with us twelve points behind. That's how much it looked like it was in the bag.

Old Trafford, of course, changed all that.

While we had been finding our feet, United had stumbled, winning just four of their previous ten games. The gap was closing, and we went there nine points behind United but with three games in hand. It was in our hands, but we were still an outside bet.

The game was a morning kick-off (at 11.15 a.m), which is always a bit odd. We'd have a similar routine but everything happened a few hours earlier than a 3 p.m kick-off.

You'd go in for breakfast and they'd have spaghetti Bolognese and chicken and all sorts laid out at eight o'clock in the morning. I couldn't stomach dinner at that time of day, so I stuck to breakfast foods. But a lot of the guys would just carry on like it was normal, and the boss liked that, as he was all about routine.

The team that day was pretty much our strongest XI but with two glaring omissions. David Seaman was injured, so Alex Manninger was playing. But that wasn't an issue, as the young Austrian had been in the team a few months by that point and was keeping plenty of clean sheets.

And Anelka, recovering from injury, was on the bench.

So out we went on that historic day, with Manninger; Dixon, Keown, Adams, Winterburn; Parlour, Petit, Vieira, Overmars; Wreh, Bergkamp.

I never approached big games with fear. I would look around the dressing room, see the quality and think, 'We can win anything with this group.'

United struggled that day. They had some early energy, but we were in control of the game after that, really. Tony and I largely kept Andy Cole and Teddy Sheringham quiet, and Overmars was at his brilliant best, giving Gary Neville and a young player called John Curtis a torrid time. He should have scored earlier than he did, missing a couple of good chances.

Anelka came on for Wreh on sixty-six minutes, and then, just when it looked like the breakthrough wouldn't come, it did, and I can still see that magical goal now if I close my eyes. And it wasn't only a special goal because it won us the three points and set us on our way to the title – it was also Arsenal's first goal at Old Trafford since the formation of the Premier League in 1992.

I had the ball about halfway in our own half, with a decent amount of time. And it's funny because after all the talk of beautiful football and learning to pass out from the back, this goal was a bit more direct. I pinged a long ball towards Dennis, who beat Neville in the air. Boro, our coach, later claimed my pass was a clearance. The ball hung in the air again, and Anelka beat his man to it and brilliantly managed to flick a header on to Overmars. And this time that was it, he hared into the box and slid a perfect finish past Peter Schmeichel. Cue delirium. And it got worse for Schmeichel, who pulled his hamstring coming up for a late corner, meaning he missed the Champions League tie against Monaco later that week in which United went out.

We could see the light now – we could see that league title. We just had to keep winning – and we did. We entered into a tunnel where we ate, slept and drank football and nothing else mattered. The gaps in between the games were agonizing, and you needed to rest, but really all you wanted was to get out there and play.

There were no real scares in the last part of the run-in, despite a couple of tight 1–0 wins. There was some personal frustration, though, as I was sent off at Bolton and then broke my eye socket and suffered a detached retina in the FA Cup semi-final against Wolves. But I was back for the three matches that led up to us winning the league, the crowning moment of course being the famous 4–0 win over Everton.

Now, before you say that I can't have been playing as the famous final goal was Bouldie playing in Tony to score, I was! I started alongside Tony that day, and Bouldie came on with ten minutes to go and with the game and the title in the bag. It was the boss's way of showing him how important he'd been to him.

For that moment, Tony read the script perfectly. I thought, 'Where is he going?', but then the ball to him was so well weighted and it was an unbelievable finish. I would just like to mention that I had some fun of my own in those closing moments too, throwing in a few stepovers and going on a few runs because the party hat was on.

Those moments as we celebrated were just wonderful. I enjoyed every second of it, milking it, drinking in all the success. As Queen's 'We are the Champions' played at the final whistle, I let it all soak in. Whenever I hear that song now, it takes me back to Highbury.

We were indeed The Champions.

All that season my friend Chris Jones, and my brother William came to every home game, and I enjoyed their support and banter as we travelled to and from London for the games. So, after the joy of that Everton win, the big question was where were we going to celebrate, as the party and bus parade were scheduled for after the FA Cup final.

We headed to Camden, as my brother and Chris wanted a beer. We went into a Chinese restaurant and they said, 'What are you drinking?'

We replied, 'Well, it's obvious what we're drinking, isn't it? I've got my Arsenal tracksuit on, you know we only drink Carling now, because we're the Carling Premiership champions.' I thought it was a good line, but the waitress didn't know what we were talking about. So she brought a

Chinese beer and the guys drank that. Lots of it. Not me, I was driving.

Of course, we weren't done yet. There was an FA Cup final against Newcastle to play.

We'd had a pretty kind draw in the cup, but boy did we make it hard for ourselves. We drew 0–0 at home to Port Vale in the third round, then we won away on penalties in the replay, playing on a pudding of a pitch, and just ground out the result; we won 2–1 at Middlesbrough in round four, with Paul Merson scoring the goal for Boro; then we drew 0–0 at home again in round five, needing a replay to beat Crystal Palace.

Then we drew 1–1 at home to West Ham in the quarter-final. In an unusual turn of events, I was through on goal and was brought down for a penalty that we scored.

It sent us on our way to Upton Park under the lights for another replay. It was never an easy task there and, after half an hour, we lost Dennis to a red card. It has to be one of the best performances I've ever been involved with in an Arsenal team with only ten men. We went in front, but they levelled in the eighty-fourth minute (through another old boy, John Hartson) to take it to extra time and penalties.

It was definitely an over-our-dead-body performance.

So we scraped through to the semi-final against second-tier Wolves, which was a case of getting the job done, which we did thanks to a Wreh goal.

I remember after the game sitting in the dressing room at Villa Park feeling very emotional. I had finally made it to an FA Cup final, which is pretty well the reason I wanted to be a professional footballer all those years ago.

But at the same time, I couldn't see out of my right eye . . .

During the game, I'd suffered a serious injury, breaking my

right eye socket. I had a detached retina and had damaged the optic nerve.

The surgeon told me I had been close to losing the sight in that eye, and I still see that same eye specialist, Paul Rosen, every three months as the detached retina has now developed into glaucoma.

I remain indebted to Paul for getting me back, fit to play the remainder of that season so quickly.

I told Wenger everything was OK, but when I went back to see the specialist for a routine appointment, it turned into a full-scale second operation to repair another hole in the retina.

You are normally advised not to play any sport for at least two weeks, but the next day I was due back at Arsenal for training, so I persuaded the specialist to agree that I should take the risk and hopefully all would be well.

If I had not got back for that Barnsley away game, Wenger would not have picked me, I'm sure, and I couldn't face sitting and watching more games from the sideline. So I was prepared to put my eyesight at risk and, thankfully, everything came off. Not that I told Nicola – she would have tried to stop me.

Another one for the list of things I've broken in my career!

With the final in mind, after securing the Premier League trophy, the boss gave a lot of us a rest away at Liverpool in the game after we'd won the league. A team with no Seaman, Keown, Adams, Winterburn, Petit, Vieira, Overmars, Bergkamp and Anelka got well beaten; the result was 4–0. It didn't really matter.

Then, on the last day of the league season, six days before the cup final, we played at Aston Villa. I can't say I gave it my all – it was the first time I'd played a game to make sure I didn't miss a final. I'd missed so many in the past.

I even said to the boss that I wasn't sure I wanted to play, but I did, and I survived – and we lost 1–0.

The build-up to an FA Cup final is a really sweet occasion.

Everyone else's season is pretty well finished (unless you're playing international football), but you have a nice week training in the sun.

Looking forward to a day out at Wembley, I remember doing extra training on the Friday and Wenger tapping me on the shoulder to tell me I was ready and to go in and rest.

Stephen Hughes was my roommate, and that person was always so important to me because you're spending so much time with them. When you sleep, they need to sleep; you need to share a routine. You need the same interests and sense of humour.

Me being the organized older one, I suggested on the Friday night that we did a mini dress rehearsal. We'd gone to games that season in tracksuits, but for this we were going in a traditional FA Cup final suit, so we did a quick check to make sure everything fitted.

We were fantastic in the final, a 2–0 win never in doubt. Ray Parlour got Man of the Match – he, like me, had come so far under Wenger – with Overmars and Anelka scoring the goals. Tony and I kept Alan Shearer quiet enough until I trod on the ball and presented an opportunity for him which he did not take. The feeling afterwards was pure pleasure.

So it hadn't been easy, but a first Double for the club since 1971 was a huge prize, especially as it was only Wenger's first full season.

Missing out on playing and winning in so many finals was forgotten as I climbed the Wembley steps to the trophy. I can still remember the feeling of success. As I made my way off the pitch, Geordie Armstrong, who was part of bringing me back to the club (it was his scouting mission in '93) dragged me back out on to the pitch and into the goalmouth to suck it all in again. He told me that as one of the 1971 Double side, he hadn't taken in the enormity of the success and he wasn't going to let me do the same. I really appreciate him doing that.

It was a very rewarding day, but when I sat in the dressing room, I felt a bit hollow.

I was a confirmed winner, but it didn't make me feel any different.

I always knew I was a winner, but now these medals were there to keep people quiet rather than change me in any way. They just reaffirmed the belief I already had in myself.

It was such a huge season for us English players. Despite the quality around us, we had survived, we were still being picked, our reputation was growing, playing alongside these foreign geniuses.

The parade after the cup final was amazing.

We were all on the bus with our kids, and the bus was hardly able to move, such was the sea of people. Callum was old enough to appreciate football by then, just about, and his first three games watching me were winning the league against Everton, the FA Cup final and then our Charity Shield victory the season after. So when he got to his fourth match, a regular league game, he turned around and said, 'When are they bringing out the trophy?'

Our Double team were mould-breakers, pioneers, the men that allowed modern Arsenal to be what it became. No longer were we 'Boring, boring Arsenal.'

When I was a kid coming through, people at the club used to keep beating this drum about the '71 Double-winning team. So to think that I ended up with two Doubles is incredible. And, to be honest, we could have had four, because in '99 we lost the league by a point and went out of the cup by a whisker in the semi-final, while in 2003 we won the cup and imploded in the league.

In 1998 we won the title with seventy-eight points. Of course, these days, ninety or even a hundred points isn't unheard of, but I'm not sure that means our achievement was any less. Back then there were more teams who could take points off the top clubs. And top teams these days don't have to do battle on cabbage-patch pitches. Now every Premier League ground is like a snooker table, so there is less differentiation and quality tends to shine through more often.

Also, very few sides are purely physical, like Wimbledon used to be. In the modern game, most sides are trying to pass the ball intelligently, keeping it on the ground as much as they can – all copying the style we pioneered under Arsène. But you've got to be really good to play like that consistently, and so the cream usually rises to the top.

But if you'd have told me as we went off on our holidays that summer that we wouldn't lift another major trophy for four years (no, I'm not counting Charity Shields), I'd have thought you were mad or a Spurs fan.

It's Fergietime!

The 1998/99 season in English football will forever be remembered for Manchester United's Treble, and I suppose for our rivalry with them. When I look back now, the side we had was probably better than the one that won the Double the year before.

We conceded just seventeen goals all season, we got the same number of points (seventy-eight) as the year before and we played some fantastic football again.

What let us down was a lack of goals and squad depth up front. Ian Wright had gone because he knew he wasn't going to be number one striker any longer, which really left us only with Christopher Wreh as back-up to Anelka. Compare that to United's four options of Dwight Yorke, Andy Cole, Teddy Sheringham and Ole Gunnar Solskjær.

Ian was a real loss to the dressing room. He was a larger-than-life guy with a fantastic sense of humour, a real presence. If he had stuck around another season and chipped let's say a dozen goals to supplement Anelka, I'm sure we would have retained our league title.

The end of that season, particularly the famous FA Cup semi-final at Villa Park, was when the Arsenal–United, Wenger–Fergie rivalry really started to develop. When it felt like the whole world was watching those games.

We'll come to that game in a bit, but first let me explain some of the things going on in the background as the tension rose between the two clubs.

One of the sore points was around England camps. Sir Alex Ferguson wasn't happy about England players returning to Luton airport from away trips as he thought it gave the London-based players an advantage. So Fergie being Fergie, he had a word and we suddenly started landing in Manchester. Wenger was annoyed, but Ferguson was saying there were more players from the north than the south. So every time we landed, the boss asked, 'Where did you land this time?' Because he didn't want players doing another thirty-five minutes on a plane. That's how much of a rivalry it became.

These days the squad lands in Birmingham, halfway between the two.

At the peak of our rivalry, our physio, Gary Lewin, was also the England physio. And he bore the brunt of the paranoia between the boss and Fergie.

I fractured my shoulder against Italy in 1997 at a pre-World Cup tournament, but we didn't know it at the time. After a challenge in the air, as I landed, Casiraghi, my Italian opponent, pushed me to the ground in a press-up position and I felt something crack in my right shoulder.

There was a soreness and stiffness, but I didn't think it was anything serious, and six days later we were due to play Brazil, so I rested up, missing the France game, and joined in training after a fitness test without any real issues.

After twenty minutes against Brazil I went for a header and Leonardo backed into me so I fell over the top of him. I went to put my right arm out and my right shoulder completely snapped. It was a clean break. I was in agony.

We only knew later on, after X-rays showed the extent of the damage, and I was out for five months (which is why I missed the start of our 1998 Double-winning season).

The boss, being a meticulous man, went through the list of players who had X-rays immediately after the game against Italy (I hadn't) and asked Gary why it was that David Beckham, a Man United player, got an X-ray for a dislocated finger while an Arsenal player with a fractured shoulder didn't get one. (Maybe David has particularly sensitive fingers?) Arsène was fuming. I never held it against Gary. He couldn't have known how bad I was, and it was never mentioned again.

I want to say something more here about Gary. He's a great guy, Arsenal through and through. He was the goalkeeper in my very first Arsenal youth game, but the club thought he wasn't quite good enough. They really liked his character, though, and as he was interested in a career in physiotherapy, the club supported him.

When I returned to Arsenal, Gary was an important member of the Arsenal staff, doubling as the physio for the England squad. Over the years at Arsenal his role developed considerably. He was admirably adaptable. When Wenger arrived, Gary was happy for Dutch physios to work with Dennis Bergkamp. He also welcomed the nutritionists Arsène brought over from France. Ultimately he became much more than just the club physio, involved in making the whole machine of Arsenal tick along efficiently.

As I said earlier, I only played in the French national stadium Parc des Princes twice. The first time, I was stretchered off in the Cup Winners' Cup final, and here I was, stretchered off again. I felt as if I was cursed on that pitch.

Amid all this, Gary got himself right in the middle of the Wenger–Ferguson politics.

Fergie was so good at influencing power, and referees were no different. I got a bee in my bonnet about that after the FA Cup semi-final replay because he practically attacked the referee at half-time.

After that match I decided that whenever we played them, I was going to make sure I was man-marking Ferguson at the break, following him down the tunnel, close to him in case there was any funny business. It was a game within a game with them; they'd surround the referee and we knew we had to do all of these things to match them everywhere. So if they were around the referee, we were around the referee.

Another tactic we adopted was that we would never walk on to the pitch first.

We weren't waiting for anyone. Let's make our opponents wait for us.

Let them stand in the tunnel and think about how good we are.

But whenever we played Manchester United they tried to play the same waiting game and, once, referee Graham Poll came to our dressing room to tell us to come out.

We said we wouldn't until they came out.

He said, 'They're saying the same thing. Someone's going to get fined if you don't come out because we've got a kick-off time to make.'

This wasn't a Wenger rule, it was the players. We needed to fight for every ball, every decision, because Man United were running English football. And when you're in a rivalry like that, you have to fight every inch of the way to be champions.

Then players come together on international duty and you're expected to be teammates. In the build-up to France '98, Gary Neville was asking me questions about how we pressed as a defence at Arsenal. He didn't seem to know when we squeezed, when we dropped off, and he was asking me basic questions which I answered, because I thought it might be necessary for England when I played with him.

Neville was obviously a very good player, but I saw Roy Keane, David Beckham, Paul Scholes and Ryan Giggs as the most important in that United team. Beckham always made an impact in the big games and his crosses were very difficult to deal with because they were virtually on a sixpence for a striker. They were always dipping away from you as the defender.

The other challenge was those four rotating strikers with such different styles and strengths. They'd bring them on and off in pairs quite often.

What were they like to play against? Well, Solskjær was nicknamed The Baby-faced Assassin by the media, and he had a real edge to him. If he could do you, he would. He was physical, a player with a bit of a nasty streak.

Sheringham and I had played against and with each other from the age of seventeen, and so there was always an edge and I never had to work hard to get up for that. There was a semi-dislike between us.

He was a tough opponent because of his intelligence. He often stopped and stood still when everyone else was moving around him, which made him the most difficult person to pick up. Cole was the quickest, and Yorke was more of an all-rounder. They all had so much talent and an eye for goal.

Keane was, to borrow Paul Ince's nickname, United's 'guv'nor'. Everything went through him – he had to have the ball. Vieira was that for us. If you didn't give Patrick the ball, he went berserk, and Roy Keane did the same. They were the two stags in midfield. Hard to imagine that during the week, in training, Patrick could be like a dreamy teenager who needed gee-ing up. On matchdays, he was a lion.

As painful as it is, I suppose we'd better talk about that semi-final replay properly, and in particular the Giggs goal that went into folklore – and which I try to avoid looking at when it gets replayed what seems like a hundred times a year.

To set the scene, the first game had finished 0–0. It was a tense game, with Keane having a goal questionably disallowed for offside, and then Anelka squandered a late one-on-one with Peter Schmeichel, and then extra time became tough for us when Nelson Vivas was sent off for a second yellow card.

The replay, under the lights, took place in between United's Champions League semi-final ties against Juventus in mid-April. It was a meeting of two incredible sides. Neither of us had lost a game in any competition since December.

United rotated some players with Giggs, Paul Scholes and Yorke on the bench, but we were virtually full strength, with Freddie Ljungberg getting the nod ahead of Marc Overmars. You could see things hadn't become nasty between the two clubs yet, with both teams laughing a bit in the tunnel ahead of kick-off. There was respect, although also a bit of suspicion but things hadn't boiled over. Yet.

United took the lead through a beautiful Beckham goal. They could have had more, with Solskjær and Swedish left-midfielder Jesper Blomqvist missing really good chances.

Then midway through the second half, things heated up. First Bergkamp equalized, his shot deflecting past Schmeichel, and then we thought we were ahead when the Dane spilled a shot and Anelka rounded the keeper to score. The goal was ruled out for offside. But you could start to feel the tension, and that is when Keane almost cost them the Treble. He lunged in on Overmars and got himself a second yellow card. We had an extra man, and momentum.

And then came the two moments that defined the game. First, Phil Neville brought down Ray Parlour for an extra-time penalty.

Bergkamp stepped up and, at that moment, I was thinking Dennis shouldn't have been taking it. Why? Because he missed the cup final the year before and so it had extra significance to him. I felt he was under more pressure than anybody else. He desperately wanted to get back to Wembley.

I guess the issue was there wasn't a long list of people who could take a penalty. Anelka hadn't taken penalties at that point in his career, Overmars had only taken the one, and Dennis was on a run of scoring seven in a row and hadn't missed one in four years.

But of course this time he did miss, or Schmeichel saved anyway, and we just started to get the feeling that fate was against us.

For the Giggs goal, one thing that people haven't mentioned is the possible reason behind Patrick's wayward pass. That pass he played was one he'd made a thousand times, always out to Parlour, who had gone off just four minutes earlier. And it's like Patrick was still expecting him to be there as he played the pass that Giggs intercepted.

Before I dissect my role in the goal, let's just say it was a fantastic piece of magic and one of the greatest ever FA Cup strikes. But looking back, I feel like I could and should have stopped him.

My downfall was that I reacted to Dwight Yorke when he made a run off the ball and that changed the line and angle of my approach towards Giggs. Instead of showing him to the touchline, I was forced to show him inside, trying to make a tackle, which I missed. If Yorke hadn't made that run, I would have stopped Giggs. I thought Giggs was going to pass to Yorke, but he, of course, didn't, and by that point my body shape was wrong and I'd lost my balance trying to stick a leg out. Then he skipped past Lee Dixon, Tony couldn't get across in time and he fired a brilliant finish past David Seaman.

If I could live that moment again, I would just go straight to Giggs and not change my path for Yorke's run. I probably would have brought him down. Keane took out Overmars, who had run in to score ten minutes earlier, and maybe I was just too honest. Easy to say with hindsight.

Years later, some statisticians watched that match back and worked out the expected goals for it. We had 2.51, and they had 1.62. Or, in non-football-stat speak, we had chances good enough to score two and a half goals and United a lot fewer. You can see we edged in lots of the stats from that night: 27 shots to 16, 9 on target to 4, 56 per cent to 44 per cent possession. But to use a classic football cliché, there is only one statistic that really matters and that was Arsenal 1–2 Manchester United.

I made the mistake of stepping into the Manchester United dressing room after the game to congratulate them. Gary Neville's celebration was so outlandish – he was jumping around like a lunatic – I just turned around and went back out. I was recently working at a United–Arsenal game and had a chance to reminisce with Gary and Roy Keane, and it was nice to share some memories, obviously with the undertones of trying to wind each other up along the way.

To be fair to us, we did not crumble after that. We won our next games convincingly: 5–1 at home to Wimbledon, 6–1 at Middlesbrough, 1–0 at home to Derby and 3–1 at Spurs, who were desperate to ruin our title bid. Kanu, the Nigerian international, who had joined us from Inter Milan to boost our attack in January, was coming into his own, scoring four goals in those matches. And United, no doubt with a lot of focus on their Champions League semi-final against Juventus, were opening the door for us. They drew at Leeds and Liverpool, which meant we were three points ahead of them going into our final two games, albeit they had a game in hand.

United won their game in hand at Middlesbrough to go top of the table on goals scored. Things were tantalizingly close with two games each to go. And then we were facing Leeds away, a tough game against a top team — managed by my former Arsenal teammate David O'Leary. We had the advantage of playing a day before United too, the chance to go back on top.

We finally lost our unbeaten league run that night against a team going for the top four. Ian Harte missed a penalty for Leeds, but Jimmy Floyd Hasselbaink's goal made the difference. I remember having to have eight stitches in a leg wound from Hasselbaink, who was always tough, but this time not so fair.

One of Wenger's less successful attacking signings, Kaba Diawara, came off the bench and missed some gilt-edged chances. It all meant United needed just four points from their final two games to win the title. And one of those was against Tottenham, whose fans were desperate to not see us defend our crown.

I thought O'Leary acted completely over the top in the Leeds game. He was celebrating the result against us a bit too much and I was told their players were promised that if they won that game, they didn't have to play in the last match of the season. And sure enough, their team contained a lot of changes on the final day.

I just didn't understand why a man steeped in so much of Arsenal's history was hell bent on behaving in such an undignified manner. Of course he wanted to win for himself, but there are ways for managers to behave in public. He crossed the line. Leeds's Alan Smith told us afterwards on England duty that his team talk was so animated before that game.

That was not the end of my issues with Leeds. While on international duty at the end of the 2001 season two years later, Adam Crozier, the chairman of the FA, asked to speak to me about an incident that had happened a few weeks earlier.

Leeds had missed out on Champions League football after losing a crucial game to us and a rather disgruntled chairman, Peter Ridsdale, had asked the disciplinary committee to look at video footage and press charges against me for an incident involving Mark Viduka.

I was accused of elbowing him and stamping on Lee Bowyer, both of which were just not true.

Crozier told me that the investigation would probably drag on, but in the meantime I was clear to play for England in the two summer internationals.

But it seems Ridsdale wouldn't let it go and there ended up being a hearing, for some reason in Sheffield. My legal representatives showed footage that supported my innocence, but halfway through there was a power cut and I never felt I had a chance to put my own case.

The Lee Bowyer stamp ended up being unproven, but I was found guilty of elbowing Viduka, which was absolute rubbish. I received a £10,000 fine and one-match ban.

The next season, a tribunal cleared Viduka of elbowing me, despite the offence being shown clearly on television.

Later, when I was on England duty, Rio Ferdinand, Viduka's clubmate, told me Viduka had admitted to him that he'd elbowed me. 'I caught him a fucking peach,' was how Viduka had put it.

Anyway, back to the race for the 1999 title. We had a glimmer of hope as United drew their next game with Blackburn, but they weren't going to make the same mistake twice – they just had to win their final match. Even though Spurs went 1–0 up at Old Trafford, United ended up clinching their fifth Premier League title.

We just felt hollow, and then came their crazy last-minute Champions League win against Bayern Munich, when they scored twice in injury time to come from behind and win.

I laughed, because we'd been on the receiving end of something similar with them. I think we probably helped them to achieve that trophy because we had raised the bar of competition over the previous years. When we won the league in 1998, they went and bought Jaap Stam and Dwight Yorke and we just couldn't match them financially because of the cost of building the new stadium.

But when I look back at that season, I think we were a better team than them, truly. We had that fantastic defensive record, we had the huge disadvantage of playing our Champions League home games at Wembley (for financial reasons – the players were not consulted) and you have to wonder if there was some greater force at play to get them over the line that season.

One of the strangest parts of that rivalry was that there were so many England players from the two squads.

You were major sporting enemies and then would have to teach yourself to be teammates for your country.

At the end of that season, for example, Dave Seaman, Ray Parlour, Phil Neville, David Beckham, Paul Scholes and I were all involved in the Euro 2000 qualifiers against Bulgaria and Sweden.

At the England camp, all the Man United players would sit together and they'd come down early for their food, so they often didn't feel fully integrated with the rest of us.

It was strange to have to play together, because we were bitter rivals. Arsenal are normally expected to have their main rivalry with Spurs, due to them being just down the road. But United were the ones winning everything.

It would be like a tug of war. If we saw their game before us and they dropped a point, the rope would come our way, and if they won their game the rope would go the other way. But we loved it when we played head to head because all the bullshit stopped.

But then, for a while, so did those big games between us and the epic title races. For the next two seasons United won the league pretty comfortably, even if we did finish second. There were no big cup clashes between the two sides, just the sight of United lifting trophies.

We lost key players in those summers too, first Anelka leaving for Real Madrid and then Overmars and Petit going to Barcelona. Money was talking, and we didn't have enough.

It was devastating when Petit and Overmars left. I found out about it the same way as everyone else – through the media. Overmars was with us pre-season, but he was restless, a cat on hot bricks. We knew he was going, but Petit was more of a surprise.

It was a double horror.

People shouldn't underestimate what an amazing signing Overmars had been. When the boss bought him, nobody across Europe would touch him because he'd been out with a cruciate ligament. His good leg was twice the size of the injured one, and he still ran like the wind. Petit was phenomenal in '98 especially, and went on to win the World Cup and Euros.

The bigger picture was the development of the new stadium because it made us wonder if we could still be successful. We were losing all these players and had to use the money to put down a deposit on a new ground.

We were trusting the manager to guide us through this period, and at least we saw incredible quality coming through the door, with Robert Pires, Gilberto Silva and Cameroonian right-back Lauren, to name but a few.

The pinnacle of that, of course, was Thierry Henry.

Thierry was an immense talent from the minute he arrived. I'd seen him play for Monaco on the wing, a flying machine.

At first he was just lacking a little bit of confidence, especially after struggling at Juventus.

What struck me, much like Patrick Vieira, was how quickly he picked things up. Within weeks he was speaking perfect English. That was quite the contrast to some players we played with. The Brazilian left-back Sylvinho could only ever say 'OK', no matter what the conversation, though he was a lovely lad with a big smile on his face.

The Swiss centre-back Philippe Senderos was another who could speak multiple languages – he was so impressive – but despite that intelligence, he didn't always speak the language of football, often standing in the wrong place at the wrong time.

Henry had no such problem, especially once the boss moved him into a central area. He studied clips of how Ian

Wright used to pull off the defender's shoulder and picked it up within no time. Whereas, at the beginning, it was pure pace, then he created a rhythm and a swagger. Everything became calculated — every change of pace, every foot he planted was precision. It was amazing to see him put all his skills together and then launch them at our opposition.

I took a lot of pride in training flat out throughout my career but, at his peak, Henry was becoming more and more difficult to play against. If he could embarrass you in training, he would. People were bouncing off him by the end because he was probably the strongest person in the gym.

Jens Lehmann used to try to touch the gym ceiling, and Thierry watched him get closer and closer for weeks but without quite getting there. Then Thierry came in one day, took off his flip-flops, said he'd seen enough and would show Jens how to do it. He jumped in the air and put the palm of his hand on the ceiling. Jens was pretty pissed off.

So when Henry scored his first goal for us — a beautiful turn and strike at Southampton after receiving the ball from Tony Adams — I ran to him to say, 'I'll tell my grandson that I played with you if I have one.' He replied, 'What are you on about? Are you taking the piss?' And I said, 'No, that's how good you are. You need to know this.'

I needed him to know, because it wasn't happening quick enough for Henry at first and I needed to tell him something that was going to really stick in his mind. It happened to me as a young player when the great Pat Jennings came up to me at half-time when I was playing in front of him and said, 'How the hell did you block that? I thought it was in the back of the net.' So I understood the power of the words of a senior player.

I was one of the most senior players by this point and

realizing I had a role to play in the dressing room. Tony used to say, 'Right, get them going,' and I'd tell them there wasn't a group of players I'd rather be sitting with and that we'd spent a lifetime waiting for players this good. And I meant it.

It didn't mean we weren't any good in those two trophy-less seasons. We came so close to two cup successes: the UEFA Cup in 2000 and the FA Cup a year later.

It became painful because we should have won them, especially the cup final against Liverpool.

In the UEFA Cup final, we lost to Galatasaray on penalties, and I should have scored the winning goal. The ball came across the box and I had a chance, but I snatched at it. If I had taken another step I could have actually put it in the back of the net. Henry missed a good chance as well.

They went down to ten men in extra time when Gheorghe Hagi was sent off, but it became a really difficult night for us. The penalties were all taken in front of the Turkish fans, and then Davor Šuker, who scored every one of his thirty-seven normal-time penalties in his career, missed the first one for us. From then on, there was no way back. I really didn't want to take a penalty, and I admire every player that does. These days players are so drilled, everyone is coached to take a penalty, pick a spot, so now I'd have a plan. But then we hadn't even practised, I don't think.

And in 2001 – or what is now annoyingly called the Michael Owen cup final – we really should have won it. For starters, Liverpool's Swiss centre-back Stéphane Henchoz handled the ball twice on the line, but nothing was given. If VAR had existed then, we'd have won that game.

At 1–0 up, we lost that game trying to win it. And the boss still blames me because I went up for the free kick that led to

Owen's winner. After the game he asked me, 'Martin, what were you doing with the goal?'

Decades later Arsène admitted he'd been wrong to rest most of the team for the last league game of the season. He wanted to keep them fresh, but realized some of them had switched off psychologically.

On a personal level, things had started to change a bit with the boss, as that criticism for the goal shows.

I started getting a lot of injuries and, as I was getting older, I felt there was less support. The club had finally given me a two-year deal during that 2000/01 season that put me on better money, but I was injured when we went to Old Trafford and lost 6–1. It was humiliating. I'd rarely heard the boss swear, but he said to me the day after that game, 'Fucking when are you going to be fit again? Ever since I gave you that contract you've been injured.'

I replied, 'Are you paying me too much then?' And he said, 'Well, yes.' And I said, 'Well, it's about time you paid me too much, if that's the case.'

It was his anger and frustration with losing to that team in that fashion.

We were more honest with each other by that point and could say what we wanted, within reason. Having a go, I didn't mind that, because we had a bond – he had given me the best years of my career. But he was wrong on that. Arsenal struggling had nothing to do with me taking his money – I wanted to be out there too. And it wasn't just me. Our back four that day was Sylvinho, Oleh Luzhnyi, Igors Stepanovs and a young Ashley Cole. It was always going to be a struggle.

So what really happened with those Owen cup final goals against Liverpool? For the first one, Ashley, playing in his first final, lost contact with Owen, which allowed him to score. I told Ashley afterwards that he'd learned a valuable lesson: you can't lose your man in a cup final, or it's over. Ashley was a quick learner and went on to win seven FA Cups, and become the finest left-back I've ever played with.

For the second goal, I looked at Tony Adams and Lee Dixon staying back for our free kick and thought that two defenders would be fine. So I went up as normal. But then we hit a poor free kick, they broke fast and Owen shoved off Lee, sped past Tony and fired across Dave Seaman to win the game. Owen, when I spoke to him recently, said that if I had stayed back he might not have scored, because he knew I could match him for pace.

I remember being on the pitch afterwards with some of the players and saying, 'This can't happen again.'

We had thrown away another golden opportunity. It would've been easy to have felt so deflated that we never bounced back – a different group of people would have crumbled. Instead, this defeat gave us the oxygen and desire to rise up like a phoenix from the ashes the following season.

Dreams Can Come True

So it had been three agonizing seasons without a trophy, we'd had two near misses in cup finals and there we were, sat in a room watching a video about geese.

Yes, you read that right. Geese. Flying in formation in a V-shape with one at the front and then, when the leader got tired, he or she went to the back and another bird took over.

Why? Because Wenger, in his determination to get that bit more out of us and return us to winning ways, had brought in a psychologist. And that man, Dave Elliott, who not everyone in the squad loved or bought into, thought the geese video was a good way of drumming home some messages.

Dave and I have differing memories on what happened when he first turned up at the club. He always reminded me of Del Boy from the TV show *Only Fools and Horses*, he had a successful personality, had done well in business, wore rings, drove a posh car and came with a flip chart. He intrigued me – he looked more like a salesman than a psychologist.

So the contentious bit is I am sure he arrived in October 2001 and said to us, 'Guys, great to see you. Lots of winners in here, but you're all second best.' When I once told that story on the radio he got in touch to insist that was not the case. But I'm pretty sure, and the point stands. He was telling us we were continually coming second to Man United.

Then he drew a circle and said this was the area where we could get maximum performances. Then he drew another circle inside of that one and said the area in between was the comfort area. 'You don't really believe it now,' he said, 'but that's where you're sat, and to get to boiling point we need to get to the outer circle, as that's where we'll get the best results.'

The boss clearly felt that he needed someone else to come in, a different voice. That was a big strength of Wenger because he recognized the issue and brought someone in. If you can't do something yourself, don't pretend you can, bring in someone who can.

Not all the players and staff took to Dave, as they felt he tried to take too much credit for our success, but despite that, I do think it was thought-provoking, and it worked. It helped to give us some direction and to wake up a few of us. He got a reaction.

We also became a better squad in the summer of 2001 with the surprising and controversial arrival of Tottenham captain Sol Campbell on a free transfer, a move that stunned the Premier League. It also provided a match I will remember for the rest of my life.

I was on a family holiday in Barcelona, where Marc Overmars was now playing. Their season was still running so I called Marc to tell him I was in town and he asked if the boys fancied watching a training session.

He sent someone to pick us up and, when I went into their dressing room with the boys, they greeted me like I was one of their players. Petit and Overmars were both there, Petit got a signed shirt for me and Patrick Kluivert was saying, 'Keown's here, Keown's here!' I was really humbled. So we watched the training in the sun, then their manager, Carles Rexach, offered us tickets to the game.

And it was no normal game. Barca were having a difficult season and, going into the final match, they were fifth, needing to beat fourth-placed Valencia to get into the Champions

League. So there we were in the stands, and Rivaldo scored a hat-trick, the winning goal in a 3–2 victory coming in the eighty-eighth minute. The whole stadium, including us, was singing, 'Rivaldo, Rivaldo.' I went down to the tunnel after the game, went in to see the manager to say thank you, and he was jumping up and down, calling me his lucky mascot.

Anyway, the reason I bring this up is that Sky TV found out I was there and Steve Archibald came up to me with a microphone and said, 'Apparently, Sol Campbell may be coming to Barcelona.' So I said, 'Why wouldn't Sol Campbell come here? It's an incredible club. The Camp Nou is an amazing stadium, the team is fantastic, a great set of people. I can fully understand why Sol Campbell might want to come here.'

The next thing I knew, he had signed for Arsenal and the press were saying, 'Sol Campbell has come to take your place.' On England duty I, of course, said I wasn't worried and was excited to have such a good player coming to the club, and I meant it.

I was just thinking we'd be lucky to have him. I was, in my strange way, thinking, 'OK, Tony, let's see who's good enough now to play with Sol Campbell.'

Of course, when I went back to training in the summer, our coach, Boro Primorac, was teasing me, saying I'd told Sol to go to Barcelona as I was worried I wouldn't get to play any more.

The first day of pre-season, the boss had a brief chat with me and Tony and told us we were going to share the role now with Sol, so he was going to play and one of us would be alongside him. Then we went for a run around the training ground, and we'd gone about 800 metres, and Sol, despite being eight years younger than Tony and me, was 300 metres behind everyone else. So the boss came up to me and Tony and said, 'For fuck's sake, I maybe got it wrong because Sol, he cannot run.' And we were laughing.

He just wasn't fit. But Wenger told him he had to play him to get him fit. And so he did.

I spent a lot of time with Sol and became big buddies with him. He's a very private guy, but once you become a friend, you're a friend for life.

He was a superb player. He was rapid, though he struggled when turning sometimes. He was like a train. He was hard to get going but, once you got him out of the station, nobody could stop him.

It was a high-profile, brave move, switching from Spurs on a free, and it takes such strength of character to do that – he could have easily gone to Barcelona or Man United. Most footballers wouldn't have done it.

The hatred Spurs fans had for Sol came to the surface on his first trip back to White Hart Lane on Saturday, 17 November 2001. That day, the Spurs fans bombarded our coach with bottles. We wanted to have it out with the fans, to fight them. When they're throwing things at you and you're a target, you want to retaliate. Though we of course knew that wasn't a good idea.

When I walked out on to the pitch that day, I had never seen hatred like it. There were effigies of him, and the Spurs fans released balloons with 'Judas' written on them. But that match was the making of Sol. We were both like lions, trying to keep Spurs out that day, and we thought we'd won the game with ten minutes to go when Robert Pires scored. But then our goalkeeper that day, Richard Wright, let in a very saveable shot from Gus Poyet at the death and the game ended in a draw. But we bonded massively, being on the pitch together.

Sol was fantastic for us that season, and I think people have a point when they say Sol should have captained England more than three times. Sol certainly thinks so too, but the fact he was a private person probably worked against him, as he gave the incorrect impression that he wasn't part of the group.

As for Spurs, as I said earlier in the book, Manchester United were our main rivals because they were competing with us for trophies. But Spurs were still very important to our fans and, luckily for me, I rarely lost to them (we only lost one of twenty-nine games to them during a period in the late nineties and early noughties) and in 2004 had the joy of clinching the league title at White Hart Lane, just as the first Arsenal Double team had done in 1971.

For me that rivalry started when I was in digs with Dot and Charlie, as Charlie was a Spurs fan and he never stopped talking about Danny Blanchflower's 1961 Double-winning team and how they played pretty football. But even in the early days, we Arsenal trainees had our big wins – one was 10–1 in an important big youth team game, and later we beat their reserve side 6–0, with me and Tony Adams in the team together. That made a lot of people at Arsenal sit up and take notice. Beating Spurs mattered a lot to the fans, and people like Pat Rice would hammer home how much we had to win that derby. I just thought we had to win every game, regardless of whether it was Spurs.

But, as a footballer, your job dictates other people's happiness, and so Coventry at home is not the same as Tottenham away.

Anyway, enough about that lot.

We actually had a pretty mixed start to the 2001/02 season, winning only eight of our first seventeen games. We were fifth but unbeaten away from home in the league and, luckily, most teams around us were stuttering too. Manchester United had lost three games in the league and six overall.

I was injured for the start of the season, having collided with David James when playing for England. He hurt his posterior ligament and I severely damaged my ACL, not that I knew the extent of the damage for a couple of years.

I returned in September.

Then – after a bizarre night at Highbury when Ray Parlour was sent off early, Newcastle were given a ridiculous penalty with five minutes to go and Bobby Robson's side won in London for the first time in four years – things changed.

Robson told the media that our team needed to learn how to lose, questioning our behaviour afterwards. His remark had a galvanising effect on the squad. We decided we weren't going to learn how to lose – we just weren't ever going to lose again.

We found our rhythm, not losing another league game all season and going on an incredible run which saw us win thirteen league matches in a row. And in the first twelve of those (when the title was still live) we only let in three goals, which is quite extraordinary. And what is more, we were doing it without a consistent defence. Tony, Sol and I were all injured at different times of the season, but whatever combination of central defenders the boss put out, we did the business.

There was a fourth musketeer, too, the underrated Matthew Upson. He became my roommate, and was, and remains, an all-round great guy. Matthew broke his ankle too, that season, but still made twenty-two appearances, playing a crucial role in our fabulous campaign. He went on to thrive under Fabio Capello for England, collecting 21 caps.

It was at Blackburn in late January that I broke my leg, just as our run was starting to gain momentum. (It was a bad few days, as I had been sent off in the FA Cup against Liverpool three days earlier; learning from Giggs's 1999 slalom through our defence, I took out Michael Owen when he was through on goal).

The break happened when I landed heavily after winning a header. I played on for another five or ten minutes, in agonizing pain, until my good friend and physio Colin Lewin told me to come off. I'd been telling him it was broken, and he said 'Are you a fucking doctor now?' He thought there was no way I could walk off the pitch under my own steam if I really had a broken leg.

The next day, Colin took me in for an X-ray, and said, 'If that's broken, I will show my backside in Sainsbury's.'

As it turned out, I had a spiral fracture of the fibula, and I still get pain in it now. It's amazing what you can get away with when the adrenaline is pumping. (Needless to say, Colin never did drop his pants in the five items or less checkout queue)

But before too long I had the boss saying to me, 'I need you back.'

So I came back, though I had to pop painkillers and anti-inflammatories just to get on the pitch.

I made my comeback on 1 April at Charlton and we didn't concede another goal for the rest of a league season which culminated in another memorable trip to Old Trafford. More of that later, because though usually the FA Cup Final takes place after the end of the league season, in 2002 the Final was on 4 May, 4 days before we were due to play at Old Trafford. God only knows why the powers that be thought that was a good arrangement.

But for me, the 2002 final was another disappointment.

I had been so frustrated by those cup final losses to Galatasaray and Liverpool, so you can imagine how I felt when the boss called me into his office ahead of the 2002 final against Chelsea and told me I wasn't going to be playing, as he needed me for the league game at Old Trafford in midweek.

Anyway, happily, we won the cup final, a match best remembered for Ray Parlour's stunning opening goal. I made a cameo appearance with a couple of minutes left, but I doubt anyone outside of my immediate family remembers that.

Then, a few days later, came our crowning glory.

Whenever we turned up at Old Trafford, we used to stay in the Lowry Hotel and the United fans would always try something. One year we were there, they set all the fire alarms off and the boss came down in his slippers and pyjamas and everyone was taking the piss. He looked a funny sight in the middle of the night.

Another year, a crane was repositioned next to our hotel and all we heard was boom, boom from five o'clock in the morning.

The fun and games started the second you arrived in the city, so you were on red alert. We went for a walk that afternoon and some clown jumped in front of us, asking us how we dared step foot on their sacred Manchester pavement.

To set the scene for that game in 2002, it was the penultimate game of the season and we went there needing a draw to be champions, on eighty-one points to United's seventy-six.

That day, we didn't go there thinking about the league title, it was about us and them; it was personal. It was a case of making sure we didn't lose – and Thierry Henry and Tony weren't in the squad, with Dennis on the bench. When the game started, they tried to kick us off the park and I thought, 'Happy days,' because it wasn't going to work against our team. They couldn't match us playing football, so they tried to kick us. It was a compliment.

I have such a very vivid memory of the match. Above all the games I've ever been involved in, this is the one I can replay back in my mind as if it had just taken place. We worked incredibly hard out of possession, stopping United from developing any play and dominating the ball, waiting for our chance to come.

It was of course French striker Sylvain Wiltord who pounced to score the winner after Fabien Barthez parried Freddie Ljungberg's shot. It maintained our record of scoring in every game that season, something we didn't even manage with the Invincibles.

It makes me smile even now to think of Sylvain 'pouncing'. He was such a lovely, laid back guy off the field. Once, when the boss called a meeting to have a go at us for poor timekeeping, Sylvain sauntered in ten minutes late. Arsène was outraged. 'Fuck's sake Sylvain, you are even late to a meeting about lateness. I fine you £10,000!' Sylvain shrugged a very French shrug, and the rest of us all just laughed.

I've never seen a stadium empty out so fast as we celebrated winning the Double at the home of our rivals. After those three second-placed finishes, here we were again – champions of England and Double winners – and it felt incredible.

Then we caught sight of Dave Elliott, our psychologist, alone in the empty stand, and we all acted like geese running towards him, flapping our arms, remembering the video.

Afterwards everyone in the media was saying how gracious Manchester United were, and Sir Alex Ferguson did pop into our dressing room to say 'well done', but it was very quick and didn't feel heartfelt. Of course not. He hated to lose as much as we did. I read that their fans applauded us off the pitch, but there weren't any in the stadium when the game finished, so I'm not so sure. To win it there, to conquer Old Trafford again and wrestle back power as the top team in the league was perfect.

That 2002 squad was stocked with quality players. As in '97/'98, there were two groups, some coming towards the end of their Arsenal careers, like Tony and Lee, playing their last seasons.

Lauren was in place – another great find of Arsène's – convert from a winger to a full back, and quickly imbued with our fighting spirit. Sol Campbell had arrived of course, and Matty Upson was coming through – all natural successors.

Plus, we had four great strikers in 2002: Bergkamp, Henry, Wiltord and Kanu. Kanu radiated natural authority in the dressing room. Even though he only spoke on very few occasions, when he did, everyone listened.

Sylvain Wiltord was great fun to work with and won everything in the game. Brazilian midfielder Edu had such wonderful talent and would have started in any other team regularly.

However, once again, despite all the joy, there was a contract stand-off going on in the background.

I was now thirty-five years old, a double Double winner, and Sven-Göran Eriksson had selected me for the 2002 World Cup in Japan and Korea. Yet Wenger hadn't come near me for weeks to discuss what would happen next, which would have been nice when I was struggling with my broken leg.

Then, the day before we were due to parade our two Double trophies through the streets of Islington, and only two days before I was due to leave for Japan, Arsène said we needed to get me signed and was I free to talk the next day? I couldn't believe he was saying this now.

I said, 'Boss, are you taking the piss? Tomorrow is my last day with the family for five or six weeks!' So no, I couldn't sort out my contract right now.

To my surprise, he said, 'In that case, I will fly to Japan.'

Out in Japan, Wenger offered me a one-year deal, because Arsenal's policy was that if you were over the age of thirty, you didn't get any longer. The only thing was that I was going to be a free agent in July, and Bobby Robson at Newcastle had already offered a two year deal at about ten grand a week more than Arsenal.

It may seem that I'm always banging on about money, but players of my generation only really began earning once Sky TV started paying big bucks for the rights to the Premier League. My pay for one year in the early 2000s was equivalent to ten years' salary back when I was starting out. That sort of money was life changing, it meant long term security for my wife and sons. And Nicola had to put up with a hell of lot as a footballer's other half. No wonder I, and many other players, were unwilling to hang up our boots.

I have to admit I was tempted by Newcastle's offer, but my son Callum, who was all of nine, said to me, 'Dad, you're playing for the best team. Why would you go to Newcastle?' Kids have a brilliant way of seeing things more clearly than adults sometimes.

I knew deep down that I didn't want to leave Arsenal. I was still playing at a really high level, we'd just won the league at Old Trafford and I was off to the World Cup in Japan. And looking back it makes me shudder to think that if I'd left North London, I wouldn't have been part of that Invincibles side, or won an FA Cup medal in 2003.

I told Wenger the situation, and that we needed to be imaginative.

He asked what I wanted, and I asked him, 'If I play more than twenty-five to thirty games next season, would you be giving me another new contract the following year?'

And he said, 'Yes, I probably would.'

So I suggested he give me a two year deal now, based on the number of games I had played in the season just ended. And we agreed that in that second year I would earn far less if I wasn't in the team. But if I did play, I wanted big bonuses instead. Arsenal agreed, and Wenger went one step further by agreeing to pay me the appearance money even if I was an unused substitute, the logic being that if I was on the bench, I was at the level he needed me.

For once, I came up with the solution rather than getting angry at Wenger and David Dein.

I didn't have a crystal ball, but I just knew this team was good, and that Arsenal was the best place for me. So I signed a two-year deal with that novel clause in it. And boy, I'm glad I did.

My Rival, My Partner, My Friend

Tony Adams.

There is no player I associate my career with more than Tony. We came through the youth team together, we jockeyed for starting positions and in the glory years we were so often alongside each other, lifting trophies.

When I left Arsenal for the first time, Tony's dad wrote a lovely letter to my dad saying what a shame it was I was leaving. There was a closeness and respect.

In my years away from the club, Tony was a constant reminder to me of what could have been. When he was winning things and I wasn't at Arsenal, that was tough.

Tony and I are very different characters, but we both have a burning love for Arsenal. We were there with each other at so many key moments in our careers. So I invited him round to my house recently so we could catch up and try to understand each other better all these years later. What did we really think of each other and what we achieved together?

This is that chat from what was a pretty revelatory afternoon for me. I hope you enjoy it as much as I did.

Tony: When was the first time we met?

Martin: It was evening training at Arsenal. I was doing a 6.30 p.m. session on a Thursday, coming in from Oxford, and you were coming in from Dagenham. You were the year below me in school years but we're actually only three months apart in age.

Tony: I don't know about you, Martin, but I came from schooling that wasn't for me. You were more educated than I ever was. I didn't sit an exam.

Martin: I actually had a lot of issues, especially with reading and writing. I can't spell out words, really, even. I have to do everything from memory. It still causes me problems now in commentary and I have to work so hard to get my head around certain pronunciations.

Tony: It's amazing how you look back. We all presumed that you were educated and more clever. Maybe because you were from outside London and sounded different. We were still mates, though. I remember us going to Ilford Palace for a night out in those early days.

Martin: I went to discos, and I'd dance. So there I was, dancing stupidly, and you guys were all watching, going, 'He's a lunatic, you're not supposed to dance, you're supposed to look cool.'

Tony: Your socks were the same colour as your shirt . . .

Martin: Did we have an early rivalry, do you think? Back then I thought the club pitched us against each other a little bit.

Tony: I was definitely feeling a rivalry, but I think that's normal when two great players are in the same club.

Martin: They were saying us two were the future.

Tony: Yeah, but it's how you balance that, and we didn't have the coaches to make it work. Maybe if we had Arsène

Wenger he would have done it naturally and it would have been OK. We came into a club that had three managers in three months. It was carnage. They didn't know who you were and, apart from George Graham, they didn't know who I was. I had a history with George. Before he came to the club, he was big friends with Terry Venables and they both knew me intimately from when I was England captain for Under 15s.

Martin: It was tough even before that. I was supposed to sign pro forms and couldn't do it because Terry Neill was sacked and they put everything on hold.

Tony: Exactly, and I'd already signed. But you'd take it personally every time, you'd think it was somebody out to get you.

Martin: Yeah, I knew that you'd signed and thought, 'What am I doing, sitting here?'

Tony: I don't think they went out of their way to pitch me against you. I really don't think they did. It was just circumstantial.

Martin: I'm not so sure. They used to say things like, 'Two good young centre-halves, we can't put them together.'

Tony: Liam Brady said to me once that you and I were the future of the club. He said that to me in the marble hall. And we had David O'Leary.

Martin: I probably shouldn't have asked David's advice about whether I should turn down Arsenal's contract offer. After all, I was a rival for his position.

Tony: It certainly worked in his favour. It was a tough time. I was full of insecurities at that age. I think most kids are.

We were trying to do a man's job when we were just teenagers. We'd been given this talent and inner drive and wanted to be professional footballers more than anything else. We both drove each other on in that respect. And it was perfect for me, and maybe perfect for you too, that we had this kind of healthy rivalry, because it pushed us both to the top. But we were in an industry of dog eat dog and you weren't really that streetwise. There were a lot of Londoners in the camp, a lot of prima donnas, razzmatazz superstars.

Martin: Do you think people targeted you, Tony? Tony Murtagh told me that because I was doing things a bit quicker than other people, I got picked on. So you were the London centre-half and I was the out-of-area centre-half, the only player in that team from outside of London. I felt for years like an outsider. I'd open my mouth and it was like, 'You're a country bumpkin, where's your combine harvester?' They said it was banter. But it was just rude.

Tony: In that era and culture people would take the piss out of you whether you had a big nose or you lived in Oxford or you were a bit more clever than everyone else. It was seen as a weakness if you couldn't take it. I didn't feel this at the time but, looking back, I'm full of admiration for you because you stood up for what you believed and took no shit. But I knew the run-ins you had with everyone, Martin. And I had to eventually pick up the pieces. They're fucking bastards, Martin.

Martin: Yet in all those fights that I got involved with, there was never one between me and you because I liked the way you went about your job.

Tony: I did mediate a lot for us as well, because I respected you. You were determined, and some people don't like that. You tell it like it is, Martin. You don't tolerate idiots. A great example is the Charlie Nicholas story . . .

Martin: I didn't know you would even remember that.

Tony: I headed a lot of balls, but I remember it all, mate . . .

Martin: I remember smelling alcohol on him in training. Then one day he was pissed and threw a punch. So I said to our assistant, John Cartwright, 'As a young player, am I allowed to hit back?' And he said, 'Absolutely.' And Charlie shit himself.

Tony: That is when I'd mediate. Because we still needed Charlie to be successful. I'd go to Charlie behind the scenes and tell him to give you a break, tell him that you're not a complete lunatic.

Martin: But you were young then, Tony . . .

Tony: Yeah, but I always had that kind of leadership and I knew how to get the best out of you and other people to make me look good. It was no good you ripping all their heads off when we had to play together on a Saturday. So that was my development as a future captain, I suppose. It was very fractious back then. There were all these brilliant kids coming through. And you've got these superstars that are actually a bit fearful of all these kids.

Martin: You were smart enough to see it – I just saw people attacking me. When I left Arsenal the first time, did you think I was mad?

Tony: I admired you for standing up to George. I never did that. I knew it was a finance issue and you had principles, which I probably didn't have at that moment in time. I wasn't a man. You were more of a man at that stage than I was, which I suppose worked against you.

Martin: I think it was a fatal mistake. The suffering, watching my mates, you included, winning those trophies. And then our lives took these disparate paths for a bit. I don't think people understood how good the team I left behind was.

Tony: Six internationals came out of that group – there's a book to be done on the class of '83. When we won the league in 1991, I know you'd moved on and were very sad around that, but you were definitely instrumental in pushing us forward.

Martin: Mickey Thomas said to me recently that I did you all a massive favour because when I went, everyone got new deals. They realized they couldn't take the piss any more. Is that true?

Tony: We got OK deals, but it wasn't until the money came to the club when the Premier League really took off that everyone got bigger bumps.

Martin: I felt so stupid. I caused myself so much aggravation trying to stick to my principles.

Tony: Yeah, but you are who you are and it's made you who you are today, and you're still here fighting and it's great.

Martin: Who do you think was better at what on the pitch?

Tony: You are one of the best man-markers I ever played with. People called you The Rash for a reason.

Martin: I used to see that reputation as taking something away from me because I wanted to play in a four and man-marking meant I often wasn't.

Tony: But you were no good at playing in a four at the start. It took me a long time too. Your distribution improved so much. At the end of your career you were absolutely fantastic. At the beginning they used to laugh at my left foot, Alex Ferguson screaming from the dugout going, 'Shove him on his left!' But then you learn. And that's why we had long careers.

Martin: I think you were better in the air than me. I know you could see the game before I could. When I came back to the club after Everton, I didn't have the early schooling that you had under George, and I really needed that. I soon learned that you either come up together or you drop together. And I was determined to prove to George that I could do it. It felt different between us when I returned. We should have had a sit-down chat when I came back.

Tony: I don't think I was in the right place. I was in the height of my using from 1992 to 1996. I was not present off the pitch. I could get up for cup games, European games, the cup Doubles, but I couldn't do the whole season, no matter what.

Martin: And also I felt like I wasn't really wanted. This was not the prodigal son coming home. I thought the strength of the group was the four. Maybe not for you because you'd played for England sixty-six times separately, but I think the others were reliant on being that famous back four.

Tony: Yeah, they were. I always say, individually, yourself and Sol Campbell were much better players, but as a four it really worked.

Martin: I was coming in, having to break down this back four if there was going to be change. You'd grown from this young kid. When I arrived back, you (and Paul Merson, really) were now massive figures in the game. You'd won a lot of stuff and were not just known in England but in Europe. And you were different, distant.

Tony: I was very isolated.

Martin: I got the feeling you didn't want to play with me.

Tony: Oh, no. I just didn't want to play football at that stage. My private life was so messed up, my head was so scrambled. I was detached because I was full of fear and doing some shit that I'm not too proud of.

Martin: So the success had wounded you, not made you grow?

Tony: It really did. You were different from us, Martin.

Martin: But I didn't want to be different, I wanted to be the same, to be part of the gang.

Tony: I admire you now for being like that. You've been principled and come through all that stuff. So maybe it affected you on the football pitch, but my God your principles were sound. I didn't have the power to say no.

Martin: Did you feel I was aware of what you had been through?

Tony: I'll be honest with you, I don't think you were because you weren't there during the madness.

Martin: I wish I was a bit more aware. I wish I had been able to help, talk, listen. I feel like I know you better now, listening to this, than I have at any point. I think there's a shift in your ego now. Back then, maybe that was part of the look . . .

Tony: It was fear, all that bravado and front. But really I just wanted to be hugged.

Martin: And is that what Wenger brought in some ways?

Tony: Not really, because I'd sobered up by then, but Wenger and I had lovely conversations, spiritual ones, because his mum and dad ran a pub, so he saw how alcohol changed people. I told him about a few things that we used to get up to and he just couldn't believe it, going to Marbella just to get shit-faced for a week.

Martin: It was hard being on the outside of that. When you were sat on the bus, did you think there were certain places for certain people? I felt that the establishment sat at the back.

Tony: Martin, I think that they almost feared you and couldn't understand why George had brought you back.

Martin: When you say 'they', do you mean Bouldy?

Tony: Yeah, and a few of the lads.

Martin: Bouldy pulled me aside one day and said, 'Make no mistake about it, you won't be my mate because you're here to nick my place.'

Tony: And they may have judged you as you were when you left the club and not when you were bought. These are just my memories — it could be a load of shit because my head was up my ass at that time. It was really difficult, when my wife was taking crack cocaine and I was on the piss all the time, to get any kind of comprehension. I didn't give a shit about you coming back to the club, I was more concerned with saving my life. But we had all lost control at that point. Did you play against AC Milan in the Super Cup in 1995?

Martin: Yes, the one we lost 2–0 on aggregate.

Tony: George was in the dressing room, and he was a broken man. He just didn't want to be in the job any more, and it was the first time I'd ever seen him like that.

Martin: It all turned into quite a crisis, didn't it, because we lost George, Merson had come out with the gambling addiction just before, then Bruce Rioch didn't work out as manager and then you came out with your alcoholism just before Wenger arrived.

Tony: Yes, I didn't report back to pre-season training in '96 after the Euros. Can you imagine that? Harry Kane or someone just not going back to training? I turned up on the Monday after the first game against West Ham. But once Arsène came in shortly after, things got better. Ah, '97/'98. I mean, we've spoken a lot about the shit . . .

Martin: So there was the Blackburn game in December, after which you needed to go away for a bit because of your problems, and then there was one last game we lost together as a pair, against Villa, that season.

Tony: That's right.

Martin: As a partnership, we had nine clean sheets. We'd both grown as players so much.

Tony: Wenger said to me he was surprised how good we were.

Martin: I read something the other day saying that the youth team partnership finally came back together. I broke my shoulder, so I missed the start of the season, came back ready to go, and you went off for a month and then bang, it was win, win, win. To be honest, I thought this stuff about Tony Adams was mythical until then. That's when I saw the real Tony Adams: focused, properly wanting to win over our dead bodies.

Tony: Yeah, that's exactly what it was.

Martin: What happened in that month when you went away to France?

Tony: I had an ankle injury. And I wrote my autobiography *Addicted* there as well. And then I felt alive again.

Martin: I thought I really needed you then, because I hadn't really won anything. When you're on a journey, you need people there who have done it. We had so many clean sheets, and we were just ticking them off. And in 2002 we did it again, despite a season of awful injuries, we went back into '97/'98 mode.

Something I've always wanted to ask you is about that 2002 FA Cup final.

Tony: Go on . . .

Martin: At the start of the season the boss pulled us in and said that Sol was going to play and one of us would play alongside him. I had an injury at the start of the season with my knee and I was in and out, and then you had problems, so it kind of worked all the way through the season, with Matthew Upson featuring too. And then we had to play together because Sol had some issue at the end. Then we got to the cup final and the boss said to me, 'You're not playing tomorrow, but you'll play on Tuesday against Man United as it's a much bigger game.' I'm assuming he said the same to you?

Tony: He said nothing, and then when we won the final he said, 'Don't worry about the Man United game. The most important match is Everton, because we don't think we're going to win at United. So you're not playing at Old Trafford.'

Martin: He didn't want you to go to Manchester?

Tony: No, I stayed at home. He told me to rest.

Martin: I assumed you just didn't want to go.

Tony: No, no.

Martin: I'm glad you cleared that up, because I assumed you just didn't want to be on the bench.

Tony: Wenger said there was a good chance, even if he put out his strongest team, that we weren't going to win. And then you boys went and did the bollocks for us – job done, title won.

Martin: It's a shame you weren't there.

Tony: I would have liked to have been there, but I was at home watching it on television.

Martin: It's so nice hearing all this and understanding it properly. Why do you think we've only seen each other a handful of times in ten years? Is that just life?

Tony: I think football is transient and people's lives go in many ways. I've got six kids and grandchildren, a house here, a house there, a business, two charities. You've got your stuff going on. How many players played for the Arsenal, and how many am I even having this conversation with? Lee Dixon and Dave Seaman are the two that I have some contact with, really.

Martin: Thanks so much for the chat, Tony. It's been special.

Tony: My pleasure.

I found that meeting so illuminating.

Tony and I were side by side for so long, but we never had a proper chat about ourselves. We were quite similar really, but didn't share our insecurities with each other.

I was surprised when Tony started describing us as two great players; he put me in the same bracket as him. I previously didn't think he thought that, but it was very powerful to hear it.

The conversation provided a little bit of closure. Weirdly, it's almost like I can sleep easier now I've got Tony's approval.

Winning the Battle

It's FA Cup final day, 17 May 2003. Kick-off was moments away and, as we got up off our seats in the changing room to head out on to the pitch at the Millennium Stadium, my right leg almost buckled underneath me.

'Help me,' I said to Ray Parlour, 'I can't even stand.' He gave me a confused look. I was staggering across the dressing room. The top of my leg was numb and I was in trouble. I went to kick a few balls while the captains tossed the coin and I couldn't really feel anything.

The game started, and I couldn't run properly. It's probably undetectable on the video, but I was a mess.

My hip flexor muscle had literally shut down, but if I told myself to do it with my body I could swing my leg into action, but with a slight delay.

It cost me a booking as I tried to win a ball that normally I would've won comfortably.

I remember running forward was fine, but when I tried to run backwards it was hard to coordinate my movement. At one point, I was right in front of the dugout, running backwards, tripped and fell over.

I looked over to the bench, and I could see the club doctor, Leonard Sash, and physio, Gary Lewin, head in hands. I thought this was going to be the longest ninety minutes of my career. And all because I'd hidden something from the gaffer – something stupid and dangerous.

In the 2002/03 season, it was becoming pretty clear to me and the boss that my age was catching up with me.

My body was letting me down and we got to the point – understandably – where the boss wasn't sure he could trust me any more in terms of fitness.

I played in the Community Shield at the start of that season and was Man of the Match as we kept a clean sheet in a 1–0 win over Liverpool. No goals in Cardiff for Michael Owen this time, and all the more remarkable as I was wearing odd boots that day; my deal with Puma had run out so I found an odd boot in the kit bag and borrowed a spare from reserve goalkeeper Stuart Taylor.

For years, I'd been, perhaps surprisingly for a player perceived as a hard man, wearing red boots – and not because I wanted to be flashy. The reason was that my feet are different sizes and the only colour Puma had left of my sizes when I signed with them was red!

In fact, the season started really well. I was in the team alongside Sol, and we were unbeaten for the first few weeks, including winning our opening Champions League game against Dortmund and getting a decent draw at Chelsea, despite Patrick Vieira being sent off.

At this point technology was coming into the game in a big way, and teams were keeping tabs on how much running each player did in a match. The boss thought my average was a bit low. My argument was that with good positioning an experienced defender doesn't have to dash all over the park. But to boost my stats, every time one of our players scored a goal, I made sure to sprint across the pitch to join in the celebrations.

Things were good.

But then it started. After nine minutes in our second Champions League game (a 4–0 win away to PSV), I had to come off with a hamstring injury, which kept me out for two months. In that time, the team lost three league games, two Champions League matches and were knocked out of the League Cup.

We found form again in the league (despite a loss at Old Trafford), but the second group stage of the Champions League was pretty disastrous. We drew all of our home games (against Roma, Ajax and Valencia) and went out before the knock-out stages.

I started to get a lot of little injuries and had to miss the odd game here and there but still managed thirty-two starts in total, with three more appearances off the bench. So I comfortably exceeded the target Arsène had set that day in Japan. In hindsight, that's not bad, considering the next season was my last at the club, but at the time it felt frustrating and I realized my time at the very top might be coming to an end.

It didn't help that Dennis and I were the only outfield players over the age of thirty. Previously, when there had been several older guys in the squad, we'd train together and be allowed to pace ourselves. But now, at thirty-six, I was doing every minute of every session with 'the youngsters', when really my training should have been tailored, with more rest built in. And each time I picked up an injury, I felt the boss was losing faith in me.

We lost out on another Premiership title by losing at home to struggling Leeds United, then drawing at Bolton, where I scored an own goal. I was having problems with my hip flexor, a new injury to me, and was starting to wonder what else was left on my body to damage. I knew I had to get fit for the Cup Final against Southampton, because it was surely going to be my last one.

To try and protect myself, I told the boss I didn't think I could train all week ahead of the game and be fit, that maybe

I needed to leave it for a few days to avoid a recurrence of the problem.

He was not impressed and told me that if I wanted to play, I had to train. I was in a difficult position. His approach had changed from how he was when I was younger. In fact, there had been times he pulled me out of training and said I was doing too much. I could sense this time that he wasn't convinced I was fit. So I had to spend that week proving it. And it had gone well until the Friday morning, when I went for a header and the hip flexor felt sore. The boss looked worried, and my cup final was in huge doubt.

I had missed so many finals in my career and I was determined not to miss this last one. So on the Friday when I felt that pain in my hip flexor, I asked Gary Lewin if it might feel better with an injection. It was something I'd never considered before. I once had injections in a toenail when somebody stamped on my foot, but never into a muscle and just before a game.

I decided before having the jab I'd go back out on the pitch and give it one last try. See how it felt with the adrenaline flowing. Gary threw a ball at me to head, and as soon as I jumped, it hurt. I was going to need that injection, especially as I was up against their danger man James Beattie, a tall, strong striker, which would mean a lot of aerial duels.

The painkillers went into my hip and I felt fine. The gaffer did the team talk and, as he finished, I got up and staggered across the dressing room. In a panic I asked the doctor how much he had given me. I was going on to the pitch for one of the biggest occasions of the season and I was wobbling all over the place. The drugs had worked too well.

It was lucky for me the Arsenal were by far the better side that day. We'd had a tough route to the final, but I had enjoyed the games, beating Manchester United in the game that became famous when Fergie kicked a boot across the changing room and hit David Beckham in the face. In the semi-final against Sheffield United, David Seaman pulled off what many people have called one of the greatest saves of all time, scooping the ball off the line when it seemed destined to go in. I like David Seaman but I don't think it was that special. (My tongue's in my cheek though.)

In the final, Southampton were decent enough – they had finished eighth in the league that season – but I'm not sure I'd have got away with the state I was in if we had been playing Manchester United or Liverpool.

But apart from a couple of late scares, the Saints didn't really trouble us that day and Robert Pires's goal was the difference.

Our third FA Cup final in a row, our second victory on the trot and the third time lifting that famous trophy in my career.

I tried to enjoy the summer break, but my injuries were starting to catch up with me and I wondered how much longer I could go on at this level. At the start of the 2003/04 season, I wasn't even in the squad for the Community Shield – a lot had changed since I was Man of the Match the year before. Twelve months earlier, people had been saying about me, 'He's going to go on for ever.' But I wasn't.

Wenger wanted to try Kolo Touré out in central defence. The boss asked my opinion and I was all for it. Kolo was quick, strong and tough – he only needed to learn positional sense, and I intended to give him all the help I could. Ever since I'd been a young player dealing with the hostility of older pros, I'd promised myself that I'd never hold back a promising newcomer.

The boss didn't renew David Seaman's contract that summer, and off he went to Manchester City, with Jens

Lehmann coming in to replace him. Dave's last act for the club was lifting the FA Cup – not a bad way to go.

As the 2003/04 season loomed into focus, I was going to be the last of the Old Guard. I didn't know, how could I, that I was going to play a part in one of the most spectacular campaigns in footballing history, and be part of a side that would go through a whole league season undefeated – the Invincibles.

My involvement – I made ten appearances, just enough to get me a medal – started on the opening day, when Sol was sent off at home to Everton and I was subbed on to help shore things up. I got back in the team for two trips to Manchester: a 2–1 win at City and then the game that I am without a doubt best remembered for, the one that confirmed so many people's perceptions of me and, in my opinion, made the boss feel, after injury issues, that he couldn't rely on me any more.

It's time we talked about Ruud van Nistelrooy.

Ruud Boy

I sometimes wonder whether people would even remember me if I hadn't been involved in the incident with Ruud van Nistelrooy.

It was so many things: a moment of joy, anger, the beginning of the end for me and part of an incredible season for the club.

And it does deserve its own chapter in this book because of everything it stood for.

I'd been on the edge of things and you could say it was a big call for the gaffer to play me at Old Trafford on 21 September 2003.

United were a point behind us coming into that match. It was early in the season – we'd only played five league games – and were, of course, unbeaten – while they had lost one game, against Southampton.

I was playing because Sol had suffered a bereavement – his father had sadly passed away and he was rightly given some time off by the club. So I lined up in a back four alongside Kolo Touré, with Lauren and Ashley Cole as the full-backs. The boss had put Pires and Wiltord on the bench in favour of Ray Parlour and Freddie Ljungberg, and we were a strong team:

Lehmann, Lauren, Keown, Touré, Cole, Parlour, Vieira, Gilberto, Ljungberg, Bergkamp, Henry.

United played a defensive midfield three to try to stem our attacking talent and lined up: Howard, G. Neville, Ferdinand,

Silvestre, O'Shea, Fortune, Keane, P. Neville, Ronaldo, van Nistelrooy, Giggs.

I don't think there was anything wrong with my footballing performance in the game. I was still proving that I was at the level and keeping van Nistelrooy out. Little did I know that things were going to descend into something that now has its own Wikipedia page, called 'The Battle of Old Trafford'.

I'd had some issues with van Nistelrooy the year before. He'd always do this really annoying thing where he'd step back and stamp on your feet. He was trying to provoke a reaction. In my opinion it was quite an unsporting thing to do, but he was good at it.

Eventually, I got fed up and swung my arm at him to get him off me, catching him in the face. He went down as if he'd been punched by Joe Frazier, and the referee, Dermot Gallagher, came running over to find out what had happened.

Around this time, the FA started introducing retrospective banning, so, seeing the bigger picture, I said to Dermot, 'You probably need to book me.' He said he couldn't because he hadn't seen anything. Maybe he'd borrowed the gaffer's glasses.

I explained what had happened and that I deserved a yellow card, and that if he didn't take action, I might get in trouble retrospectively with the FA, and end up with a red. But Dermot stood firm. He wouldn't book me. Referees, eh?

A few days later, I spoke with Dermot again. He confided that the FA had asked if he'd have sent me off if he'd seen it, and he'd said he couldn't say that because he didn't see it, but they were insistent, and he really had to dig in. So the FA couldn't ban me and gave me a £5,000 fine instead.

But back to Old Trafford. Van Nistelrooy had already lodged himself as an annoyance in my head. I thought he was very clever, the way he used the rules to his advantage.

Take what he did when the offside rule changed so you were onside until you touched the ball. He would stand in an offside position knowing his teammates weren't going to pass him the ball. But we still had to be alert to him, because Man United would switch the ball to Ronaldo, he'd run forward, all of a sudden van Nistelrooy wasn't offside any more and we had a 20-yard race to get back to him. Of course, some might say that it was just Ruud being a good player and using the new rules to his advantage. And pretty soon lots of teams were adopting the same tactic.

Mainly, what I didn't like about him was I couldn't trust him. I used to have plenty of physical battles with players like Mark Hughes, who was tough as nails but honest. But van Nistelrooy would just collapse like a pack of cards at the least contact, especially inside the penalty box.

I'm self-aware enough to appreciate that I was no angel. And yes, I learned some techniques over the years that I used to wind up opponents. I've spent the past couple of decades apologizing to all manner of centre-forwards, lovely people like Emile Heskey and Jimmy Floyd Hasselbaink, because I was two characters, really. When I put on my red boots, I became an angry warrior who just had to win.

I don't know how many people thought I was their most difficult opponent, but I used to set out to make sure they'd remember playing me. And I got to know who it was you could intimidate, and who it was you didn't want to wind up.

If you put in a reducer early on, which most defenders did, some players like Mark Hughes would bounce straight back up. Alan Shearer was similar. Van Nistelrooy wasn't.

I've never watched the full game back, but I recall it being a pretty dull match for the most part. I won five games at Old Trafford in my career, and there can't be many who did that in the Alex Ferguson era.

Every game at Old Trafford was hard fought. You were lucky to get a free kick there, never mind a penalty. If you think I'm being paranoid, there was a ten-year period when no penalty was scored in the Premier League by the opposition at Old Trafford. Tell me how that is.

For one of their players to get booked against us, it felt like they'd almost need to commit GBH.

Referees seemed to just turn a blind eye to it. It was absolutely shocking, some of the missed fouls on our players. Their fans would always shout, 'Same old Arsenal, always cheating,' but it certainly wasn't us doing that.

Manchester United dominated the Premier League. Between 1992 and the '97/'98 season, United won every league title except for one. The team that Wenger built had climbed the mountain in 1998 and again in 2002 by beating them to the league title.

Then, in 2003, United wrestled the crown back. So this game was all about superiority and winning again.

Our result at Old Trafford each year was a powerful indicator of what we could achieve. If we got a win, we knew we could be champions. It had become the most important match of the season, and I was feeling the pressure. I didn't want to become the weak link in the team just because I was thirty-seven.

But for most of the game United weren't putting us under any pressure at all. It was a stroll in the park.

But then things got lively and van Nistelrooy's tricks started to wind me up. Patrick Vieira was booked in the seventy-seventh minute and then shown a second yellow card three minutes later, after Van Nistelrooy jumped on to Patrick's back and Patrick kicked out at him on the floor.

Encouraged by the sending-off, United poured forward with wave after wave of attacks. It was like the Alamo. Suddenly the game changed, the volume went up at Old Trafford, they were coming at us from all angles.

So when I gave a penalty away late on, I felt I'd let the team down. And that maybe people would accuse me of not being at the level any more.

And I was still angry with van Nistelrooy because I felt his overreaction had got Patrick sent off and, if Patrick was still on, this wouldn't be happening.

Of course, it had to be van Nistelrooy who took the penalty, though I later found out he'd missed his two previous, so maybe it wasn't such a clever idea. I just stood there on the edge of the penalty area, fuming, praying he'd miss and my blushes would be spared.

Jens was doing his best to put van Nistelrooy off, hopping from side to side on his goal line, trying to plant a seed of doubt as to where he should shoot. And it worked, the ball rebounding off the crossbar from van Nistelrooy's powerful shot down the middle.

I was pumped, relieved and angry. So I got into his face and gave him a little bit of angry chat. I wanted to give him a bit of stick. 'He's a little bit prickly at the best of times,' said my former teammate Andy Gray on the commentary at the time. Thanks, Andy. No wonder Mum and Dad listened to Radio 5 Live instead.

I was just so pleased that he wasn't getting away with it again after getting my mate sent off.

Of course, it wasn't over. United put another ball into the box that Thierry Henry, of all people, cleared. But then, thirty-four seconds after van Nistelrooy had taken that penalty, referee Steve Bennett blew the final whistle – and I lost my head.

You've all seen the pictures and the footage, I'm sure, me with my arms wide open, jumping in the air and down on to van Nistelrooy's back, a look of pure rage in my eyes. Despite everything I won in the game, despite all those games for Arsenal, it seems to be what I've ended up being most known for.

So, I guess you're wondering what I was doing and why.

The truth is, I was so incensed with his gamesmanship that I just wanted to goad him, humiliate him, and try to get him to react to me in the way that he got Patrick to react to him.

And he was right there when the whistle blew – he was hard to avoid. I remember jumping in the air and thinking, 'What should I do? Should I just jump in the air and land next to him? Or should I just brush him a little bit?' So I made that calculated decision straight away.

I just wanted to let him know that his plan hadn't worked. To make him realize who the real devil on the pitch was and that we weren't going to stand by and let him win.

The press had a field day, of course. My dad in particular was outraged at the reputation some football writers were trying to create for me – though you could say I was doing most of the hard lifting for them. *The Daily Mirror* got lucky when a journalist rang my parents' house after all this, and my father went on the attack, telling him what a great upstanding bloke I really was.

In my opinion the press were going well overboard with their reporting, and ringing my parents' house and bringing my family into it was definitely crossing the line. That was my home, my inner sanctuary. I contacted Piers Morgan, the *Mirror*'s editor, and told him I thought his reporters had gone too far. He agreed not to run the story. I've always been grateful, though a bit of me would quite like to have read exactly what my father had said about tabloid journalists intruding into people's private lives.

My father just wanted to defend me, because he felt that Sir Alex Ferguson and the media didn't know me, didn't know the real person. A bit like I was trying to defend Patrick.

Trying to defend Vieira was expensive, but he had to be protected. A few seasons earlier, I had been sent off for holding an irate Paolo Di Canio back from an equally incensed Patrick. That incident ended with Di Canio notoriously pushing over referee Paul Alcock.

Opposition players used to try to target Patrick. We were wise to it and fought back. But at Old Trafford we had all lost our self-control, me in particular, and several teammates waded into battle alongside me.

Amazingly, after the scrapping, the fights didn't carry on into the tunnel. I was being ferried away, probably in enough trouble as it was.

And, to be honest, the biggest feeling after the game was that we got a result, that we'd got through that.

But then I remember being at the back of the coach and the club photographer, Stuart MacFarlane, said, 'Apparently there's some photograph of you somewhere . . .'

I had no idea what he meant.

'Yeah, you jumping up and down on van Nistelrooy.'

But none of us realized it was that big a deal until the pictures were plastered across every television and every newspaper back page the next morning. By then I was public enemy number one, the lunatic who couldn't control himself and needed to be banned for as long as possible.

Luckily, the club and the gaffer did not feel the same.

What was brilliant about Wenger was that he waited. He didn't say anything to me about it straight away.

We spoke briefly about it after training. He didn't say much. I did all the talking. I told him that I thought I'd gone too far, and possibly my actions had led to everybody else reacting to a senior player. He said maybe that was it, but he vowed to support and protect me, and he started me against Newcastle in the next game. I wasn't sure what sort of reception I'd get from the fans. I wasn't expecting a standing ovation from all four stands. It blew me away.

The FA handed out a record £175,000 fine to us for failing to control our players, and Lauren, Patrick, Ray Parlour and I were all suspended. My part in that was three games and £20,000. The cost of the new Wembley Stadium was spiralling at the time. I'm sure we helped fund the roof. Vice Chairman David Dein joked that the club should get me to take all the rap, bans and fines. Luckily that never happened.

I've been asked many times over the years if I regret what happened.

No, I do not.

I can't live my life with regrets. I reacted spontaneously at the time. We were playing with so much emotion and anger and there was such a bond between the players. If playing on the edge brings success and wins you trophies and

Top left: Holding the Premier League trophy in 2002. Tony's last competitive game, and a second double for both of us.

Bottom right: Me and Matthew Upson, roommate and friend, at the opening of the Arsenal topless bar. Must have thrown our shirts to the crowd.

Top: With David Seaman, marking his last Arsenal appearance with yet another cup.

Bottom: Dominating van Nistelrooy at Old Trafford, December 2002.

Right: The Battle of Old Trafford, September 2003. I was fined £20,000 by the FA. Money well spent.

Bottom: May 2004, just after everyone has cottoned on to Ray Parlour's classic wind-up in the last game of the Invincible season.

Left: An Arsenal legend, with Thierry Henry, Highbury, May 2004. Invincibles.

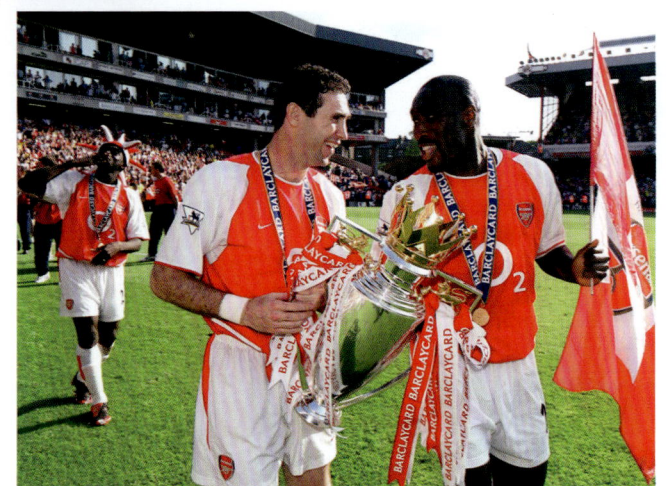

Right: Me, Sol and Kolo, three Invincible centre-backs, with the 2004 Premier League trophy and a silly hat.

Left: Arsenal securing another Premier League title at White Hart Lane, April 2004.

Top: Me, Nicola and the boys – my first choice back four, at Islington Town Hall.

Bottom: Me and my two sons at my testimonial match, 2004.

Top left: Sharing the Premier League trophy with the gaffer, May 2002. You can see he's already thinking about going through a whole season undefeated.

Top right: Coaching alongside Arsène en route to the Champions League final, 2006. A pleasure to work alongside him and my former colleagues.

Top: Enjoying my second career as a pundit, interviewing my former manager, with my pal Dan Walker.

Bottom right: Reunited with Arsène for an Arsenal Legends game against AC Milan in 2016.

Top left: In my last season, at Leicester, 2004 . . .

Top right: . . . and Reading, 2005. Still looking the business, I'd say.

Bottom: Niall signing for Reading in 2015. His mum and I couldn't have been prouder.

Top: An aerial shot of my beloved Highbury, overlooking the Premier League trophy being lifted in 2004.

occasionally boiling over like that is a side effect of that mindset, then so be it.

The only small regret is that my kids were young and had other children trying to mimic what I did on the pitch to my boys in the playground. Though, I later discovered, they were jumping up and down on the sofa at the time, shouting, 'Go on, Dad!'

I didn't always like myself or the person I became in those moments, but I'd learned that you have to be ruthless. Wenger used to say it was like a jungle and you have to survive. George would say to me, 'You're too fucking nice!'

In a funny way, it means people always remember I was there during the Invincibles season. I might have only played ten league games, but people never forget I was there at Old Trafford. It cemented me in a key part of the club's history. I am very proud that, approaching my thirty-eighth birthday, I was still able to make those appearances, although I was annoyed at the time because I wanted to feature more. Injuries and the team's outstanding form cost me that.

And there's no doubt that Arsenal fans generally loved it, me standing up for the team, showing how much I cared, and playing with that raw passion, especially considering the animosity between United and us.

The other side of that is I think there may have been a feeling from high up at the club that was less flattering: 'That's one of our senior players there, and he's taken other players into war when he should be showing a better example.' I hadn't really behaved in a correct and proper manner. I used to repeatedly tell myself as a kid, 'Remember who you are, where you are and who you represent,' from an Arsenal point of view, and here I was, involved in this massive storm.

Maybe on that particular occasion we did go too far. Although, you don't win anything by being nice, and in the years that followed my departure Arsenal were often accused of being too soft by sections of the media and opposing managers. It wasn't lost on me that that period coincided with a trophy drought.

By the time United visited Highbury for the return fixture, I wasn't in the squad. I was injured. I was on the bench for the FA Cup semi-final (back at Villa Park, of course) but I didn't come on, and van Nistelrooy was rested too. I sought him out and shook his hand nonetheless, which took some doing, seeing as we lost 1–0 as they ended our eighteen-match unbeaten run in the FA Cup.

The handshake was to say to him, 'Look, it was nothing personal.' He just sort of leaned back. What else could he do? Because I kind of made him shake my hand.

If I saw him now, I'd like to think there would be a healthy respect for each other, though I can't speak for him. I don't think it's good to carry a grudge. I've never hated anybody. There were people I disliked and I couldn't trust, but I don't carry around any hatred. You're professionals, and if you don't like someone, it's easier to get motivated. And if someone made me angry, I was a much better player. I almost used to try to pick a fight to get angry.

Van Nistelrooy was a top marksman, and you have to respect that.

When I went into the media after playing, I think people were unsure what to make of me. They were expecting this aggressive person and, off the pitch, it's just not who I am. But I still sometimes see that backs-against-the-wall mentality come out. Simon Jordan often provokes me when I appear on talkSPORT because, once I'm bubbling, I'm perhaps a better pundit, more interesting.

At the start of my media work, I didn't think I was very good. I found it awkward talking about Arsenal or former colleagues. But I've separated it now and I feel I'm a whole lot better than I was when I came on board, though I'm not the best person to judge that. I certainly enjoy the media now.

Was I a dirty player? The stats would say yes, I guess, as I had six red cards, and only Richard Dunne, Duncan Ferguson, Patrick, Lee Cattermole, Roy Keane, Vinnie Jones and Alan Smith (who played for Leeds United in 1998–2004 before going to Manchester United, rather than my Arsenal teammate of the same name) had more than me in the Premier League era.

I believe that I was tough but fair, and never, ever the sort to cause anybody any injury on purpose. That's not to say that I couldn't go in hard on a challenge and make myself known to the opposition, physically. There was a toughness to that era, and a lot of hard men.

One particular character I had a few runs in with was Eric Young.

When I was a young player at Brighton, I had a great deal of respect for Danny Wilson. In fact, at my testimonial, he talked about me as a young player who was very inquiring and keen to learn, and clearly someone going to the top. And in my spell there, he came to the rescue for me on the team bus, coming back from a midweek match at Barnsley – which is a bloody long way from Brighton! There was only one seat left. So I went to sit next to Eric Young, who said, 'You can't sit there.'

'There's nowhere else,' I said.

He repeated, 'You ain't fucking sitting there.'

I thought he was joking so I went to sit down and he tried to stop me. It threatened to get nasty until Danny saw it and said, 'Martin, you come and sit here.' He gave me his seat, then went and sat next to Eric.

After that, whenever I played against Eric Young the physicality of the game was always evident, for example, during the 1991 Zenith Data Systems Cup final when I was playing for Everton and he for Crystal Palace.

He came up for a set piece and afterwards, as he was running back to position, all of a sudden I felt him, bang, bang, two blows, his elbow in my face. The first one stunned me, the second put me on the floor. I needed stitches in my mouth and I was lucky I didn't lose my teeth. He didn't even get a yellow card but I'm sure that if it happened today, he'd be sent off.

A couple of weeks later, we played Palace again, this time in the league. Despite my loose teeth I was determined to keep my cool and not get into any tangles with him.

The match was almost over when I went up for a corner and found myself jumping against him. The ball looped up high in the air and seemed to hang there, almost frozen in time, above Eric Young and me.

As I went to head the ball, he saw me coming, and I could see in his eyes he was scared I was going to get one back. I wasn't. But he pulled his head away to try to protect himself, but that made his legs come up underneath him, and he hit the ground hard. I landed heavily on his chest. There was no way of avoiding him. You can't fight gravity.

I came down full force on him, and he yelped in pain. He'd snapped his medial ligament and was out for months.

I was sent off, a bit harshly, in my opinion. I didn't feel sorry for him – I'd needed eighteen stitches in my mouth, and you can still see the scars. Football was a tough, take no prisoners game in those days. And sometimes the consequence of that was injury – to yourself, or to the player you came into contact with.

Invincible

'When Freddie's lost his sting, out comes Daddy on the wing.'

Those were words from the poem my then twelve-year-old son Callum read at my testimonial dinner.

It was an incredible and emotional night, his words — which he wrote himself — being the pinnacle. People came up to me all evening to compliment him, amazed at how composed he was in front of a room of a thousand people. I felt so proud.

I invited everybody to that testimonial game and dinner. It was a celebration, yes, of my career, but also the end of a historic season when we were confirmed as Invincibles, only the second English team ever to achieve that remarkable feat, since Preston North End in 1888/89, in an era when there were only twelve teams in the league.

For anybody who was at that meal, it was a once-in-a-lifetime opportunity, because in that room were all the players from our historic season. That was probably the last time we were all in the same room together, and we never can be again, after the heartbreaking, terrible loss of José Antonio Reyes in a car accident some years later.

We invited close to two hundred staff there from the club, as I wanted people there who hadn't had the chance to come to other testimonials. It was my gesture to say, 'Let's bring the Arsenal family together.'

It was a night I'll remember for the rest of my life. And I even ended up selling the shirt I wore earlier that season in the van Nistelrooy game at Old Trafford after a fan approached me for charity.

The testimonial match had been special too, marked by a particularly lovely gesture by club director Danny Fiszman. Our French internationals had been told they couldn't play in my testimonial because they had to join up with their national squad. Danny stepped in and persuaded the French FA to let their boys play the first half, after which, as a qualified pilot, he would fly them to France in his own private plane.

But to rewind a few months, it had started to sink in, as the 2003/04 season progressed, that this was going to be my last Arsenal campaign. And that was difficult to come to terms with. I'd left Arsenal once before, and I knew how much that hurt me, so I was dreading doing it again.

You want to play for as long as you possibly can. But I was way past the stage most players retire and you're thinking, 'Hold on, how long can I keep defying logic and playing football?'

I've trained really hard my whole career, even in the summer. I never took off more than two weeks (sorry Nicola) because I always said it was easier to retain fitness than regain it. I worked extra hard on my fitness in that last season at Arsenal. But you can't hold back time forever.

I wasn't playing most weekends, but I was still getting niggles, and I had a constant one in my right hamstring that season. And training every day on those really hard pitches didn't help. Tony Adams could hardly train on those pitches at the end of his career because the playing surface had become so firm, the grass laid over compacted sand. It was really hard on the body.

So I was an onlooker for much of that Invincibles season,

and what stood out for me was that my teammates – Arsène's team – were all really good people, smart and intelligent, with many of them reaching their absolute prime.

To highlight just two of them, Dennis Bergkamp was always a class act and great company. He had an edge, too, when required. Thierry Henry had been quite shy at the beginning and lacking in confidence. But he blossomed into an incredible talent. When he arrived, we could all see his potential, and it was a case of, how do we help Henry to be the best he possibly can be? I never knew anyone who learned as fast as he did. He was super-intelligent. You might have been playing tiddlywinks, and he couldn't do it the first time, but by the second time he was unbeatable.

That season we really did feel we had it in us to win the Treble, so it was crushing to be knocked out of the Champions League by Chelsea, then out of the FA Cup by Manchester United. But we always knew we had it in us to win the Premier League, and after the sheer ecstasy of clinching the 2002 title at Old Trafford, this time we had the chance to secure it at White Hart Lane.

That day our title rivals Chelsea lost in the early kick-off to Newcastle, so we went into the North London derby knowing the crown was ours if we didn't lose – and we hadn't lost to Spurs in five years.

We were electric in that first half. Patrick scored after 3 minutes, and Pires made it 2–0 just after the half hour mark. Spurs pulled one back on the hour, and then in added time, some shenanigans between Jens Lehmann and Robbie Keane saw Spurs awarded a penalty and they grabbed a 2–2 draw.

The Spurs crowd went crazy. It was weird how they were

celebrating so wildly when all they did was equalize against us – it kind of showed how far behind us they were.

Jens Lehmann was pretty wild too. Angry wild. For some reason he had thought we needed to win to become champions, and he was berating himself for giving away a penalty until someone explained to him that it was okay, we were champions for the second time in three seasons.

It felt incredible to celebrate on their pitch, in their almost empty stadium, though for me personally, the win at United in 2002 was far more satisfying. But the season wasn't over. We still had to become Invincibles.

In 2002 we'd been unbeaten away from home for the whole season, and Arsène said he felt the natural next step was to go undefeated for a complete league campaign. That was our aim in 2003. Of course we fell short. Years later he commented that I'd been unhappy with that ambition, but that's not right. I was more than happy with that. I love the idea of being undefeated. I just felt he shouldn't have gone public, because that made us sound arrogant and would goad other teams into trying harder to beat us.

But here we were in 2004, the league title in the bag with a handful of games still to play, and Arsène is saying to us, this is the time, this is your opportunity to make history and do something no modern team has ever done.

But once the league was won, the thought of remaining unbeaten became a useful motivation. With the Euros due in the summer, it would have been natural for players to start conserving their energy a little bit. But the boss was pushing to the end. He wanted to make history with us.

It's not easy geeing yourself up to avoid defeat, not once you've won the title. After the Spurs match we scraped a goalless draw at home to Birmingham. Then it was Portsmouth away. It was 1-1 and the big digital clock said there were three minutes to go. I was warming up but the boss didn't seem remotely interested in subbing me on. So I went up to him and said 'Boss, What are you doing? Look at the time?'

Arsène, whose eyesight we know can be variable, said, 'It's only 83 minutes.'

I said, 'Boss, are you taking the piss? It's 88!'

Arsène looked amazed. 'Quick Martin, you get out there!'

I had to beg the linesman to stop the ref blowing full time before I could pull my tracksuit off.

Our next match, 37 out of 38, was at Fulham and we beat them 1–0 with a goal from José Antonio Reyes. I was subbed on at 71 minutes. Much less drama. Maybe Arsène had got his watch fixed.

Then it's Leicester at home, the last game of the season, and I need one more run out to clinch a medal. Once again the clock is running down. Once again the boss doesn't seem to notice. It's a bit of an understatement to say I'm on edge. At least the boss hasn't used up all his substitutes. I start to do my warm-up right in front of him, which the fans seem to find pretty funny.

What isn't so funny is that suddenly I spot Ray Parlour start to sprint up and down the touchline. What the hell's he playing at? As he passes me, he says, 'Gilberto's done his hamstring so I'm going on.'

I dash over to Arsène and say 'What you doing? What about my medal!?' Arsène is totally bemused, the full Clouseau. He hasn't even noticed Ray's warm-up, or should I say wind-up. Meanwhile Ray is doubled over at the success of his piss-take. (What's more he's since built a decent career on the after-dinner circuit at my expense.)

It's all good, I go on for the last couple of minutes, to a generous reception from the fans. It was a wonderful feeling, but mixed with sadness. I knew this was the end of the best and longest chapter in my footballing saga.

I hadn't intended to leave the Arsenal without a struggle, though. I liked to think I had another season in me. Dennis and I always used to try to get a song to spread across the training ground, singing it first in the changing room and then moving from room to room, seeing how long it would take to get everyone literally singing from the same hymn sheet. And in that final season, we were singing 'What's Another Year' by Johnny Logan to try and chivvy the boss into giving us another contract. I still think of Dennis when I hear that song. It didn't work.

That final week of the season, leading up to the last game against Leicester City, I knew the end was coming, even if I didn't want to admit it. With each drive to and from the training ground, I was gradually mourning the end, realizing I was not going to be driving these roads any more, that I was going to have to find a way to let go. I felt powerless, and my worst fears were confirmed when Wenger had his chat with me on the bus.

I was very emotional that last day, especially when it was my turn to hoist the Premier League trophy. I may only have played in dribs and drabs that season, but I was Arsenal to my fingertips. I'd been involved with them for over twenty-five years. Even when I wasn't playing there, I was wishing I was back at Highbury.

That day, I had to stop myself from breaking down. It was all so strange. I knew I couldn't continue playing for Arsenal, but I was devastated to leave.

David Dein told me how fantastic it was to end my career

as part of an unbeaten side, winning the title and getting a testimonial. But all I could think was 'I'm not going to be here next year.'

Was that Invincible team better than the 1998 or 2002 double winning sides? I honestly don't know. I don't want to take anything away from them, because it was an amazing achievement. But the pioneer team for me was the '97/'98 side, because we laid the foundations for how every Wenger team played, and changed the face of English football. Arsène's teams played quick, one- and two-touch passing but with a physical edge, fast and fearless. We went from 'Boring, Boring' to 'Olé' within a year of Arsène's arrival. I was so lucky to be a part of the adventure.

So it's strange to me that Arsenal haven't won the league in the twenty years since. When I left that group in 2004, I just assumed they were going to dominate Europe and win further Premier League titles. But the arrival of oligarchs and oil states, coupled with the costs of building the Emirates Stadium, changed the rules. It didn't help that at times the club lacked leaders on and off the pitch.

But now, with real Arsenal men in the dugout and the boardroom, my club is once again competitive and exciting.

In my final few years at the club, when we went away for pre-season, every 24 July there'd be a birthday cake rolled out for me.

And that last pre-season, I said, 'Guys, I'll tell you now, there's absolutely nowhere on earth I'd rather be than with you lot.'

I said that knowing deep down that I wasn't going to be with them the next year. Even then I knew I was going to have to let go.

Football is unique. And weird. In any other profession, when you get to the age of thirty-seven/thirty-eight, you're coming into your prime. As a footballer, you're on the way out. It felt so wrong. It hurts to the core when you finally have to hang up your boots, especially if playing football is all you ever wanted to do, for as long as you can remember.

It's even worse if you've spent your best years in a dressing room full of some of the best players to have ever pulled on a red and white shirt, and more importantly, players who are great characters and good people.

Then suddenly it's snatched away. 'What if I never see any of those guys ever again?' That was one of the hardest parts to accept.

Having to let go is tough. Knowing that the joy, spirit and camaraderie of achieving great things, and the chance to achieve more is being eradicated because you're too old. That's hard to process.

You win, you lose, you cry, you shout, you scream, you hug, you hurt, you laugh, and you sing together. Then they clap you to the exit door. I knew it was time to accept defeat. But I am a bad loser.

In civilian life, for want of a better phrase, it may take a decade or more to experience all those emotions with friends and loved ones. In football it can all happen in a single season. Sometimes in a single match. Simply put, nothing in life replaces what you can experience in football.

And so back to that bath in the dressing room at Highbury the day of my testimonial.

I dragged myself out of the water, got into a new suit instead of my usual club tracksuit, and headed up to the Highbury players' lounge. There were all kinds of people in there: family, friends, directors, one of my school PE teachers, teammates. And, of course, the boss.

And then Callum read the poem again, the entire room hanging on every word of a twelve-year-old.

We stayed, we chatted, people had a drink and I didn't, and then that was it: I went home. And nothing happened. Silence, the phone stops ringing. The diary is suddenly a desert of football-free weekends. What are you going to do? Play on at a lower level? Can you even bear the thought of running out in the second or third division, on a cold winter's night, in front of a half empty stadium. So do you pack it in? And if you do, what's the point of you?

So I threw myself into half a dozen different projects to prove that once I came away from Arsenal, I could survive without football. Of course, I was lying to myself. Football was there the whole time. I loved it too much. I knew I was going to have to play football somewhere, anywhere.

I still have a recurring football dream, even now. I am transported back to the Wenger years and he brings me out of retirement to play one more game. I start on the bench but at half-time he subs me on, saying, 'I believe in you, Martin, you can do it. I trust in you.'

As I walk down the tunnel towards the pitch, I notice my laces are undone. I bend down to tie them up and the lace breaks. Wenger is shouting at me to get on to the pitch, but I can't do my lace up.

In a panic I walk on to the pitch, but then suddenly I wake up. Initially I'm relieved I don't have to play because my lace is undone. But then the disappointment hits me. It was only a dream and my football career has really gone for good.

Sometimes it can feel like it all happened to someone else,

another person. My life has been split in two, a life with football and a life without.

Fans still stop me in the street, which makes me feel proud. They congratulate me on everything I did for their club, but what they need to know is that the pleasure, and the privilege, was all mine.

Capping it All

Like a lot of my Arsenal teammates, I had a parallel career in international football. I won forty-three England caps, captained my country, played in two European Championships and went to two World Cups. That feels like a pretty surreal and amazing sentence to write, the dream of a hyperactive kid who spent hours kicking a ball against the wall in his back garden.

I was almost thirty-six years old when I won my last cap, just ahead of the 2002 World Cup against Cameroon. Only seven older outfield players have ever played for England, including the great Stanley Matthews, Tom Finney and Arsenal's Leslie Compton. But it's fair to say that things could have worked out very differently; I was qualified via my parents to play for either the Republic of Ireland or Northern Ireland, and it was only FIFA bureaucracy that stopped me from playing for the Republic.

Before that came the Northern Ireland approach. It came through legendary Arsenal goalie Pat Jennings, when I was still just an apprentice. I told him I wasn't really sure what I was going to do, and he told me they'd been watching me and that they really wanted me, which was amazing to me.

Pat was – and still is – one of the most well-respected people in the game. My dad was a massive fan of his because of what he'd done in the World Cup in 1982, when he only let in one goal in the first group stage and Northern Ireland somehow beat Spain.

Arsenal manager Terry Neill had also been Northern Ireland manager, and he worked on me too.

I explained to Terry that I had the option to play for the South too. Arsenal always seemed to have a lot of terrific players from The Republic – Liam Brady, Frank Stapleton and John Devine, to name a few – which was one of the reasons my mum and dad were such big Arsenal fans.

Then, with me still working out what I wanted, Don Howe, who was involved with the England youth set-up, picked me for England Under 17s. A letter came to the house, and it was totally unexpected. In hindsight, it was probably too soon to make such a big decision.

There was no family discussion about it, but it was a big deal because, in those days, if you played for the youth team of a country, that was it. It's not like today, when the nation you choose to represent only becomes permanent once you have played a senior competitive game. Declan Rice, for example, was able to play three friendlies for the Republic of Ireland before switching to England, but my decision aged seventeen was going to determine the rest of my international career.

I didn't really make a decision – I just went along with it. I remember as it gathered pace until, when I went to play for England, there were a lot of relatives who said to my dad: 'Raymond, how did you allow him to play for England?' And my father always used to say, 'Look, son, I've come here, I've taken the benefits of this country. You're English, so you should embrace that and play for England.'

Lots of youngsters play international youth football and still don't make it in the game. But that first Under 17s group included Tony Adams and Teddy Sheringham, as well as me. And Teddy and I were still in the England squad at the 2002 World Cup, nearly 20 years later, which is pretty incredible.

Tony and I roomed together on our first international away trip, but never again. The sound of him listening to his CD Walkman all night drove me mad! It may have helped him sleep, but I didn't get a wink.

Despite my England youth appearances ruling me out of playing for any other country, Jack Charlton, the Republic's England born manager, thought he'd try his luck anyway ahead of the 1990 World Cup.

Jack, a 1966 World Cup winner with England, asked FIFA to allow me to switch – not that I knew anything about it!

I had no idea he'd written to FIFA about it until a journalist called my house to ask me about it. I was pretty shocked and, obviously, a little excited about maybe going to the World Cup, but FIFA said no, so I didn't have a choice to make in the end. And I never once heard from Jack about it.

I can't deny it would have been an interesting offer. Ireland had some fantastic defenders: Paul McGrath, who I later just missed out on playing with at Aston Villa; Manchester United's Kevin Moran; David O'Leary, who was of course at Arsenal; Mick McCarthy; and then Steve Staunton coming through. It would have been fun to play with so many great defenders. At that time they had more defensive strength than England.

If FIFA had allowed it, I would have said yes to the Irish, one hundred per cent. I still felt just as much Irish as I was English, and at that point it was a more realistic opportunity to go to a World Cup. If I had gone, I could have ended up playing against England as they and the Republic drew 1–1 in the group stage at Italia '90.

However, I'm completely comfortable with how things

panned out, despite it looking like a bad call for many years. I got to play over forty times for England, go to major tournaments and captain my country.

But there was definitely a period when I believed I was being ignored by my country, and several centre-halves got picked over me, when I thought that I was the better player.

It certainly felt strange when the 1990 World Cup came round and England and Ireland faced each other. I was at Everton at that point, and I spent the whole summer training, trying to build up my strength. I thought my international career was passing me by and I needed to go back to the drawing board, so I spent the whole summer doing weights, squats, sit-ups – you name it.

I'd had the chance to work my way into the England 1990 squad, in early 1988. Des Walker and I were playing for the Under 21s and we both had a really good game for England away in Scotland, but – stop me if you've heard this before – I was injured for the return leg, the victim of a horrific challenge from striker Billy Whitehurst that almost broke my leg.

I think it's worth a quick diversion from the England story to tell this one. It all goes back to the fact that my mum worked at the physiotherapy centre where Whitehurst happened to be getting treatment. She used to bring me up in conversation, and he'd say how lovely it was that her son was a player too. But on the pitch, a couple of years later when our paths crossed, he used that against me, saying she was driving him crazy, and promised to smash me all over the pitch. He was elbowing me so much that I was ducking out of the way while trying to get the linesman's attention.

I was at Villa at this point and late in the first half the ball bounced between us. He was probably favourite to reach it, but he hesitated, took a poor touch, and I won the ball. But then he followed through, late.

One shin pad broke in two; the other one ended in the stand. On a sunny day in the light, you can still see the scars now from the tramlines from where he scraped down from my knee to my ankle. He was one of the toughest and dirtiest players I ever faced.

Anyway, I was out injured, Des Walker played the return game, did very well and made his full debut in September that year. Bobby Robson said to me what a shame it was that I didn't play, as he would have loved to have watched me that night.

So while Des ended up at the World Cup, I didn't make my England debut for another four years, by which point Des had worn the Three Lions shirt thirty-eight times.

When Graham Taylor came in as England manager, I wasn't sure if it would help my case, having worked with him at Aston Villa, because there was some bad blood about the way I had left the club.

In the end it was the Everton fans who got me the call-up. They were really fantastic and kept singing my name for England. Once I struck up the partnership with Dave Watson, we were one of the best pairings in the league, I like to think.

I didn't know if Graham was keeping an eye on me or not at that stage. Sometimes you'd see his Jag in the car park, but I just told myself that I had a job to do. I'd almost given up on international football. I thought there was something in my game that made people think I didn't belong at that level.

I was suffering badly with my chronic back injury at that point, so instead of running around, trying to cover everybody,

I had become much more measured and controlled. I'd pick and choose when to run, because my back would break down if I did too much, and suddenly my performances were at a much higher level and I looked much more like a Rolls-Royce than a Land Rover.

I was hardly able to train but was playing my best football and had a manager in Howard Kendall who was purring over my performances.

Then, one evening, Nicola and I were at home and there was a knock at the door. It was Howard.

'Boss,' I said. 'What are you doing here?'

He said, 'I've got some really good news. You've been chosen, you're in the England squad. So I wanted to share it with you.'

I invited him in of course and he said to Nicola and me, 'We need to celebrate. Go and get one of those Man of the Match champagnes you've got gathering dust.'

So we did. I don't know whether he simply liked having an excuse to open a bottle, but I do think he mainly wanted to share the good news with me.

I poured Howard a glass – in fact, I poured him more than one glass. He wasn't in a hurry to leave and was genuinely pleased that I was called up to the squad.

And then he threw in a curve ball: 'By the way, you're not going to be joining up with the England squad. You came off with a slight hamstring in the last game, so you won't be joining up.' He wanted to protect my body so Everton could get the most out of me.

I was so disappointed! I tried to change his mind, but he said not to worry, it was just the first step and that I'd be involved next time. And he was right.

Twenty five is quite old to join up with England for the

first time, considering I had made my Arsenal debut at nineteen. If I'd been savvier and made the right decisions about where to play my club football, I could've been in the squad much earlier.

But I was here now, with a chance to launch my international career and, although I'd faced many of these top players many times before, the likes of Barnes and Lineker, it still felt a bit daunting trying to become their new colleague.

Most of the players seemed to keep their distance, but Liverpool winger John Barnes was really easy-going, and I got on well with Sheffield Wednesday midfielder Carlton Palmer, who was the glue in the group.

Graham Taylor did his utmost to entertain the players at get-togethers. One time we visited Pinewood Studios where the Bond movies and Carry On films were made.

A group of stunt men spent the day showing us some of their work. We thought the demonstration was finished and sat down to eat. Then two guys suddenly dived through the patio windows (which were actually made of sugar, we later found out) and jumped on Carlton, pushing him to the floor and pretended to try and kidnap him. They were dragging him out but Carlton thought it was a real kidnap because he started fighting back. He must have been wondering why the rest of us didn't come to his aid. Things got a bit messy, but we all thought it was hysterical.

Bizarrely, we also were taken to the London Palladium to watch the play *An Evening with Gary Lineker* – with Gary Lineker there with us. The play's star, Nick Hancock, was saying how nervous he was that Gary was in the audience, and Gary seemed embarrassed that the show was about him.

You name it, Graham took us there. We even went to

Clivedon House, the location of the 1963 Profumo scandal which helped bring down the government. It was now a luxury hotel, where we were treated to an extremely posh meal.

Graham made everything really enjoyable, until we got to the actual tournament itself, when we just had to stay in our rooms, bored stiff. More of that in a second.

Playing for England was always an honour, but for me it was almost always tinged with injury and disappointment.

When I got into the international set-up, Graham was under extreme pressure. His mind always seemed to be racing, worried about all manner of things, especially Paul Gascoigne's form and mood. Graham had lost the certainty of control he had as a club manager. He was so different from the incredible, super-confident Graham of Aston Villa.

But he did give me my debut – at Wembley against France, on Wednesday, 19 February 1992. I wore the No. 4 shirt, and it was a night of debuts. Alan Shearer and Rob Jones both made their bows that night, and I was reunited with Des Walker in central defence, in a three with Liverpool's Mark Wright.

Was I nervous? Well, before, whenever I was playing in a big match, I'd always tell myself, 'It's not like you're playing for England at Wembley – it's just another game.' Now, suddenly, I was playing for England at Wembley. It was a level of anxiety that I'd never experienced. I'd had to wait such a long time for this moment.

These days, whenever I see young players getting their debut out of the way early, I'm pleased for them. The sooner it happens, the better, because you've less time to build up the nerves and put pressure on yourself.

My first game for England was a huge occasion for me, and I was expecting Mark Wright, an experienced international centre-half from my neck of the woods, might help me through my first outing. But he didn't.

I knew Mark's family and really got on with his brother, Carl, who played local rugby with my brother John. You couldn't find a more sociable chap. But whether Mark was aloof or just shy, he didn't seem interested in helping me through my first international.

That was a pity: lots of players have a terrific on-field understanding without being overly pally in real life. Dwight Yorke and Teddy Sheringham were a pair of deadly strikers for Manchester United, but off the pitch they hardly spoke to each other.

That night, Mark, Des Walker and I were set up as a back three, and I could tell we had the makings of a really effective defensive trio. We never got the chance to develop together, because after Mark pulled out of the Euros, we never played in the same international side again.

Still, that day, against France, we three struck up an instinctive understanding and beat the French for once, and I was proud of my performance.

In the tunnel before, the legendary Jean-Pierre Papin was staring at me, thinking I was going to mark him. But I was picking up Eric Cantona. He was obviously hugely talented and went on to be the catalyst for success at Manchester United. But whenever I played against him, I found it manageable, because I didn't think he was quicker or stronger than me. I wasn't going to lose any sleep playing against him. Pace was the thing I feared most at international level.

My whole family was there that night. It was an ordeal. I remember saying, 'Look, guys, I can't wave to everybody in the crowd, I've got a job to do.' But they saw me play well and keep a clean sheet in a 2–0 win, with Shearer scoring on his debut.

Though, as it turned out, I was soon level on England goals with Shearer (albeit he nudged past me by the end of our careers).

The next month, in my second game against Czechoslovakia, I scored a goal that you have to see to believe, smashed into the top of the net from the left-hand side of the box. It was an absolute thunderbolt, though, when I tell the story to people now – and in the future, the distance might get further and further . . .

It felt important, too, as I had lost my man for their opening goal and so I thought, by scoring, it put me back in credit. It was our second equalizer in a 2–2 draw.

What you learn at international level is that things can be very quiet for long periods. You have to concentrate every minute of the game and then, all of a sudden, top players come alive and can embarrass you with one moment of brilliance.

At last I was first choice. But then, because nothing is ever simple, things took a turn. I played nine times for England, but before the ninth game – the final Euro '92 group game against Sweden – I was injured. But Graham asked me to play, and I felt I owed it to him. So I went into that last game and tried to play through the pain. It turns out I had a partial tear of the tendon in my left knee. It was becoming chronic, and I went straight to hospital after that match. England went out in the group stage, winless and bottom of the four-team group.

When I went back to Everton, they were, understandably, not happy. And neither was I – I felt like I'd gone above and beyond, and paid the price – I was out for months.

But, looking back on Euro '92, I feel there were extenuating circumstances to England's early exit, whatever the Press said.

Mark Wright got injured very late on, after the deadline for naming the squad. He had to pull out and Graham couldn't name another player to replace him. We went to Sweden with just nineteen players. Gareth Southgate went to the last Euros with twenty-six.

Even more significantly we lost John Barnes, simply our best player, to a horrific injury, snapping his Achilles tendon in the last warm-up game against Finland. He would've made a very big difference to our team and general confidence of the group. Another key absentee was Paul Gascoigne, who was out with a torn cruciate ligament.

We drew our opening game 0–0 against Denmark, who were the eventual winners; we drew 0–0 with France; and then lost a tight game to Sweden 2–1, having been ahead.

England's learned national journalists wrote that we were a disgrace for drawing with Denmark. But there was very little between those four teams.

However, I'm certain that the ridiculous 'preparation' we had before the tournament didn't help.

Graham took us off to Lahti in Finland to try to get the team to bond.

We all took a psychological profile test and, based on those results, everyone was put into five different teams and we then had to do various challenges across a number of days. Everyone who ticked the same boxes were in the same team, as they wanted to put the same personality types in the same groups. But this created frequent clashes.

I remember the challenges ended on the last day with us

doing orienteering and having to find various locations with a map and a compass. Most of our team split into pairs.

Carlton was determined that he could use a map and compass better than anyone. He kept running through the forest, but the problem was that two or three hours after the finishing time, nobody could find him. It was starting to get dark – and in Finland the summer days are virtually endless – so we had to send out a search party for him. Carlton was eventually found miles away, looking very dishevelled and disappointed. He'd been gone for about five hours.

All I cared about was making sure I wouldn't be voted the worst player of the day in training. Because each player was encouraged to vote for their worst performer of the day, and the next day you had to wear the bright yellow T-shirt saying 'I am the worst player in the team' or maybe a slightly ruder version. And if you came last in Graham's nightly quiz, he made you wear a dunce's cap.

At Villa I had never seen Graham attempt anything like this, but having spoken to John Barnes for this book, it turns out he did the same at Watford. Had I known that, I would have had a word. I think all it did was create fear and friction. Groups of players began voting for certain teammates to piss someone else off. It wasn't ideal preparation for a major tournament.

On top of that, in the rooms there were no TVs, no phones, barely any communication with anyone back home. We were rooming on our own, and everyone was so bored. And being the summer in Scandinavia, it was so light it was almost impossible to sleep. The sponsors gave us this hand held gaming device – I think it was a Sega Game Gear – but it didn't make any difference as far as I was concerned. We also got a phone card with a one-hour credit for the hotel telephone, an hour to last for the whole week! The queue to ring home was about ten deep every night so a private conversation was pretty well near impossible.

It felt like a prison camp.

I think it pushed everybody apart. The only person who was allowed a proper connection with the outside world was Gary Lineker, because his son was very ill and he needed to keep in touch with his loved ones.

As you may have noticed, I didn't enjoy that trip. It soured the experience of being part of the England set up. But I don't think Graham was enjoying it either.

He was getting slaughtered in the press. After we lost to the Swedes, the *Sun* had a photo on their front page making him look like a turnip. Some of the younger journalists were vicious. I suspect they thought they should have been on the pitch instead of us. Some of the things they wrote were a disgrace.

Their poisoned typewriters were ruining the joy of playing for England. There were a posse of about ten of them, all aiming quick-fire questions at you. One set of quotes would be written in three different ways in each of their papers the next day. I never had any trust for them whatsoever back then.

When Terry Venables came in to replace Graham after England failed to reach the USA '94 World Cup finals, things got even worse for me. I thought it was a little bit like the London mafia again, me being this outsider from Oxford, despite being back at a London club.

I never understood why Terry Venables didn't pick me for England in '96 when I was Arsenal's player of the year. My manager, George Graham, was a pal of Terry's; you'd think he'd have put in a word for me.

So I never heard from Terry. Instead he picked a young Sol Campbell for Euro '96, which was taking place in England. Those Euros were horrible for me. I had been in top form; it was in many ways my breakthrough season and I was at my peak. I could play in a back three, which was Terry's preferred system, and I was a good man-marker. It was one of the biggest disappointments of my career, not to be involved.

I think Terry was wrong. I could have helped that team, even though they did a pretty good job, getting to the semi-finals. That Germany game (The one we lost on penalties after Gareth Southgate tamely passed his effort to their goalkeeper. Sorry to bring it up, Gareth.) was made for me. I went on to prove that four years later when we beat them at Euro 2000 and I had a pretty decent game. But it was so hard, watching a tournament being played on your doorstep and you're not allowed to be there. I couldn't bear it, to be honest, and in the end I took Nicola and the boys off on holiday to France.

I think maybe if I'd have had some sort of previous working relationship with Terry Venables it would have been fine. But I only met him years later. I said, 'Terry, we've never met.' And he said, 'No, I don't think so.' And I said, 'Well, that's because you never picked me!' And he laughed and I really enjoyed his company. I think he would have been quite an easy person to work for. But maybe it was my fault for always standing up to George.

When Terry left and Glenn Hoddle came in as England manager, I never assumed the door would open for me. I just figured I had to keep performing well at club level. But then Arsène Wenger revolutionised everything. Soon there was an influx of foreign players into the league, so there were a lot fewer English centre-halves. But this French guy was picking me every week, picking Steve Bould, picking Tony Adams in a back three. And we were playing fantastic football, so no one could say to me again that I couldn't play football and I'm just a man-marker. I remember our goalkeeping coach, Bob Wilson, pulling me aside after a game, and he said, 'I've just sat with Glenn Hoddle, and he said to me, "How long has Martin been playing like this? Tell him he's in the next squad."'

As you may have heard over the years, training with Glenn had its moments, and he liked you to know how good a player he was.

He used to unwittingly do something really intimidating when we were in camp. There were these miniature footballs that Glenn preferred for training, because it was harder, and he thought it made the game easier when you then used a full-sized match ball. He'd organize a little keepy-uppy kickabout in the car park before we got on the bus at the Burnham Beeches Hotel, and his touch was amazing. You could see one or two players would skulk on to the coach to avoid the session. But I used it as a chance to prove myself. He'd smash the ball at you, and you'd have to take a touch and then smash it back. You can imagine who won most of the time. (Clue: it wasn't me.)

Glenn was trying to make everyone better, but it made some people think, 'I don't know if I could do this.'

The two summers we spent away under Glenn were eventful, to say the least, but I always enjoyed his professionalism and attention to detail.

In 1997, we had Le Tournoi, a four-nation warm-up tournament before the 1988 World Cup finals. England won, beating France and Italy – though not Brazil. It was England's last international tournament triumph. That gave the team and the country a good deal of optimism ahead of the 1998 World Cup.

We stayed at an incredible hotel. There was an amusement arcade in the basement with games, pool, darts – you name it, it was all there. Not to mention the adjacent nine-hole golf course, offering us plenty of walks and fresh air.

The massage room became the place to socialize. It was run by Steve Slattery and Terry Byrne, both great guys. There was lots of banter flying around, and Gareth Southgate and Beckham were regular visitors to that room.

In the evenings at Le Tournoi everybody would go to Paul Ince's room. It was like a pub. Players aren't supposed to get tanked up during a tournament, but the drinkers in the squad all wanted booze, so they'd order a pot of tea and say to the waiter, 'We don't really want tea, we want wine. We want you to put it in the teapot.' They were throwing him money. So he comes up with wine. The 'tea' was polished off, and then the same happened again. This went on until the next time we ordered 'tea', there was a knock on the door, it was Glenn's assistant, John Gorman, with a teapot.

He handed it over and said, 'Make sure this is the last one.'

A year later at La Manga for our now infamous pre-World Cup camp, Gazza was given a warning not to drink because Glenn wanted him to prove he could stay on the straight and narrow.

Gazza, bless him, was good as gold. Then, at the end of the camp, Glenn said, 'Right, we're going to have a drink tonight, a controlled drink.' But by the time Glenn joined us, Gazza was singing away at the piano, merrily centre stage. Glenn saw the state of Gazza, and I think that was when he decided he wasn't taking him. But by permitting 'controlled drinking' that evening, Glenn had sent a mixed message to someone who had huge problems with alcohol. It wasn't smart, and it wasn't fair.

I never got to play that much with Gazza. We were in the same Under 21 squad, and he was always getting into scrapes. I put it down to youthful over-enthusiasm. But at senior level, well, he was out injured during the 1992 Euros in Sweden, when he might have made a big difference. Then, in 1996, when he became a national hero again, I wasn't picked.

I did play with him against Holland in a qualification game in 1993 when he went off with a cracked cheekbone, after they targeted him because he was running the show.

By 1998, when he played his last game for England, against Belgium, he wasn't the same player. He seemed short of confidence, a nervous wreck.

I remember arriving at some of the England get-togethers, determined to help Gazza as much as I could. But within two or three days it was obvious that I needed to pull away, not just for my own sanity, but because it was so hard. Trying to help Gazza was like trying to push water uphill with your nose.

In the summer of '98, when we were all about to be told whether or not we would be in the World Cup squad, he left poolside to go up to his room, saying we should send his flip-flops on to him if he didn't make it. You could tell he wasn't really that confident.

None of the rest of us thought for a minute that Paul Gascoigne wasn't going to be on the plane. I still think he should have been. When we heard how he had trashed Glenn's hotel room when he was told he wasn't in the final twenty-two, it very nearly derailed the rest of the squad. It would have been a lot easier just to take him with us to France.

Now I regularly work with Glenn as a TV pundit and find him to be fantastic company, with a great sense of humour. Back then, though, once we were at the tournament, Glenn became more and more uptight, and he would take it out on the subs. It culminated in a bizarre set-piece session where he shouted at Rio Ferdinand for not knowing the set-piece codes.

I was very much one of the subs.

I don't draw a distinction between World Cups and Euros. They're both major tournaments. What was weird was that both times I went to a World Cup, Arsenal had just won a domestic Double and I was at the top of my game. All right, In 2002, I was a veteran at thirty-five, but in 1998 I should have been playing. Gareth Southgate – and this gives you an idea of what a lovely man he is – confided in me that he was embarrassed that he was playing, after the season I'd had. And when Glenn started playing Gary Neville in a back three, instead of selecting me, I thought that was just odd. But then it was odd being in the same squad as the Manchester United players; it was so hard to feel like teammates after spending the whole season trying to knock each other off their perches.

Gareth Southgate managed to inspire his England players with a team ethos, but in my day, it was difficult. I don't think there was enough open sharing of minds taking place for it to be successful. You have to be completely comfortable around your teammates, and that wasn't the case.

The United players in Glenn's squad didn't seem very sociable. Maybe they all sat together because they were more comfortable as a group, and it wasn't a deliberate snub to everyone else, but it didn't help. Andrew Cole and Teddy

Sheringham were different, they had played for other clubs and would integrate more. But the Nevilles, Scholes and Butt had been at Old Trafford all their playing lives and seemed very introverted to me.

David Beckham was another story, his own man, and I still think he doesn't get enough credit. I wonder if people don't bother to say nice things about him because of his stardom, one of the best to have ever played for England. On a personal note, when I asked him if he could play at my testimonial, there was no hesitation. Despite his club's objections – he was at Real Madrid by then – he made his own way to Highbury, and I thought that was a massive gesture.

A part of me admired how the United players stuck together. We Arsenal players felt we ought to mix in with players from all the other clubs. Maybe we didn't have the arrogance of the United boys. Not that we saw much of them. Dinner was at 7 p.m., but Gary Neville and his followers would always be down fifteen minutes early. By the time the rest of us arrived, the United players were two thirds of the way through their food. You were lucky to see them for more than ten minutes before they were back up to their rooms. They were a manager's dream, though, those United players. One evening, after lending something to Phil Neville, I knocked on his door at 9.30 p.m. When he answered, you would have thought it was the middle of the night. He explained that he and roommate Paul Scholes always went to bed at 9 p.m.

I did admire the way that Scholes went about his career – no fuss, no limelight, just a suitcase full of medals. In fact, I swore he tackled the United players in England training with much more venom than he tackled anyone else.

To further emphasize the professionalism of these United

players, when we warmed up, the Neville brothers went straight to the front of the group, and when the coach said, 'Knees to chest,' they were nearly knocking themselves out, such was their keenness to do everything to the nth degree. Fergie had indoctrinated them well.

Gary and Phil were fiercely competitive siblings. I remember them once playing table tennis and there was so much rivalry I set up a cheerleading group in the corner of the room as Phil, trailing 20–17, dragged himself back level in the game. I shouted to Phil, 'You know you're better than Gary. You've always been better than Gary. Now prove it.' Phil was buzzing, and Gary was getting more and more angry. Phil won the game and we all ran around the room to tease Gary. It didn't really go down well, as the table tennis bat was launched through the air as Gary left the room.

Gary did rub me up the wrong way with some small things. When we travelled abroad, there was no assigned seating on the plane and Gary was always first on so that he could take the seat right at the front with the extra legroom, even though he was far from being the tallest in the squad. When it came to the dispute about whether we were going to land in London or Manchester after international duty, you can bet Gary was having his say on Fergie's behalf. He was like a union shop steward.

Whenever we played United, I would seek out the referee and point out that Gary was taking an illegal throw-in, with one hand behind the ball and the other to the side rather than one on each side. It drove me mad and, rightly or wrongly, I recently asked two top former referees on their interpretation of the throw-in law to see if he had been cheating all those years. One said yes and the other no, so maybe I should just get over it!

CAPPING IT ALL

At one England get-together, Gary approached me and said that somebody at our club had been complaining about his throw-ins and did I know who it was. I said I had absolutely no idea.

Anyway, back to my meeting with Glenn, which was somewhat delayed after Gazza decided to smash the place up. Glenn told me that when we got to the latter stages of the World Cup I'd be playing.

I wanted to know why I wasn't going to be picked in the early stages. Glenn just repeated that when the competition gets more difficult, I was going to play. And I said, 'Call me old-fashioned, but it's a World Cup and I thought it would be hard from the off. I've just played in a Double-winning team and I want to play.' But he said there were marking jobs for me and I was earmarked to play in the knock-out stages. So I trained really hard, thinking that chance would come, but then the Beckham red card and penalty defeat against Argentina in the last sixteen put paid to that.

It was crazy, the abuse that David got for that red card. The person who deserved the blame was Diego Simeone for play-acting and getting him sent off, and he's admitted that since.

On a personal note, it was frustrating. Back in England, as the bags came round the luggage carousel, Glenn's assistant, John Gorman, meaning well, told me I would have definitely played in the quarter-final against the Netherlands because of my deep knowledge of Dennis Bergkamp and Marc Overmars. It wasn't much of a consolation then, and it isn't now.

For Glenn, of course, it was the beginning of the end. He was relieved of his duties soon afterwards, which I thought was a shame. But his exit ushered in a new England manager, my childhood hero, Kevin Keegan.

People look back at Kevin Keegan's time as England manager as a failure, but it was my most enjoyable spell playing for my country, under the man who I had idolized when I was growing up. Kevin came in on a temporary basis and did well enough to stabilize the group and guide us towards Euro 2000 via a dramatic play-off win over Scotland.

He was able to benefit from the professionalism that Hoddle had put in place, but he also made it fun. The epitome of that were the race nights. Kevin would get a videotape of a horse or greyhound race that nobody had seen before, we'd all gather and he'd put it on the TV.

Kevin played the bookie and he would lay out tempting odds for us to bet on. He'd run through the form, we'd all lump our money on, and then the race was played on the screen.

Then Kevin would sit on the kit skip, which had wheels on it, like he was a jockey, and Arthur Cox would push him along in front of the screen as if Kevin was taking part in the race.

It was hilarious and really good fun. Gareth Southgate and I would confer about how much money to put on, usually a cautious £10 or £20. But some of the lads were putting on a grand. The money was all placed on the skip with Keegan's legs either side of it while Arthur shoved Kevin towards the winning post. Sometimes one of us would win, but often Kevin was the big winner, leaving the heavy gamblers feeling devastated. You can imagine his look the time his horse nicked the race at the line to win him more than £10,000 of our money.

When it came to the serious stuff, I actually thought Kevin was a very good coach.

He was hands on and his finishing sessions were first-class. There was detail in the sessions, there was a tempo to the work, it was always very enjoyable and competitive.

I think his problem was that his staff were quite inexperienced in terms of international football.

Kevin's difficulties became evident during matches. There are always issues in games, things that need tweaking, and he seemed slow to react to them. For example, we'd be getting overrun in midfield, which sometimes happens when you play three at the back, and we'd need an extra body in the middle of the park. I'd often try to indicate things like that to him, but he wasn't proactive enough at in-game management.

But we had enough quality to win that play-off against Scotland and qualify for the 2000 Euros.

The build-up to that game was classic Kevin and very unconventional. We met at the Burnham Beeches hotel, in Buckinghamshire, where every time you looked at the TV, Sky were doing a countdown clock: 'Seven days to Hampden play-off.' It was going to be a long week. On Monday, Kevin said, 'Right, guys, we don't play until Saturday, so I've organized a game of golf.' So off we went and had a really good day, lots of banter, as you always could with Kevin.

We came to day two, we had our tracksuits on, our boots in hand, ready to go, and Kevin would say, 'It was really good fun yesterday, wasn't it?' And then, quick as a flash, he'd say, 'You know what, let's do it all again. Arthur, ring the golf club; we're not training. We're playing golf.'

On Wednesday, we just did a warm-down, we didn't really train properly. It wasn't until Thursday that we had any kind of notion who was going to play.

It was masterful, really, the way he dealt with the pressure. It was all lifted off us.

We went to Hampden Park for the first leg, and you could see the hatred in the whites of the home fans' eyes. And when they sang 'Flower of Scotland', it was a 'hairs on the back of the neck' moment, the sort of thing you don't get with 'God Save the King'.

It was a truly hostile environment, but we were the better side and Scholes scored a couple of goals to get us the win. I was described as having one of my best games for England and there was no doubt that in this period I was among the best centre-halves in the country, if not the best.

And then, almost inevitably, I got injured in between the two games, thanks to the poor quality of the playing surface at the National Sports Training Centre at Bisham Abbey. It was one of the last sessions we ever did there because Kevin went berserk at how bad the pitches were.

So I didn't play in that second leg. We lost 1–0 at Wembley but went through on aggregate.

I was fit in time for Euro 2000, but Kevin didn't start me in the first game, against Portugal. I'm not sure why not, because after we qualified he told me I was his number one centre-back. Instead he brought Tony back into the team. We were 2–0 up and somehow lost 3–2.

One of his most confusing selections against Portugal was in midfield. Steve McManaman had just won the Champions League for Real Madrid playing in a central position. He ran the show for them, but for us he was stuck out on the left wing in the opener. He then got injured, which was an even bigger blow. Steve was a top player, and a midfield with him, Beckham and Scholes would have been quite something.

Anyway, the Portugal collapse meant I got my chance against Germany, and that was a big deal for me. After the anguish of missing out on Euro '96, I was going to make sure we won. I was throwing everything on the line, up against Carsten Jancker, a 6 foot 4 striker with a huge build. When I was behind him, I couldn't even see the ball most of the time; I had to pop out to the side to get some light to see the ball. I felt like a human missile trying to head the ball.

We won 1–0 that day thanks to Alan Shearer's goal, and I think it was my most significant performance in an England shirt. It was also the first time I'd heard English fans singing my name. It was a great feeling, being abroad, winning a big match.

Afterwards, Kevin came up to me and said he'd made a mistake leaving me out against Portugal and that I was starting every game from then on. It felt very satisfying.

And then it all blew up in our faces against Romania, when it really didn't need to. Things started badly when David Seaman got injured in the warm-up. Nigel Martyn, was an excellent goalkeeper, but he had played so rarely for England and now he was being thrown into this huge game with no preparation.

I think if Nigel had been given longer to prepare, if he'd known the night before, things probably would have been different as well.

As it was, he had a tough game as we threw away a 2–1 lead to lose 3–2 and go out of the tournament, with Phil Neville infamously giving away a penalty late on.

As that happened, I was thinking that a year before, in 1999, Neville had given away a penalty against the team I was playing for (the FA Cup semi-final at Villa Park) and got away with it. But now I was playing alongside him, there was no such luck.

We went back to the team hotel and packed our things.

When you go out of a tournament, it cuts to the bone. It's brutal, and it's all over so quickly. You leave your room and, in a blink of an eye, you're heading home.

I sat up into the wee small hours with Gareth Southgate, combing through where we went wrong and why it was that we didn't perform.

Then things really kicked off on a personal level.

At the time, I was writing a column for the *Telegraph* newspaper for the duration of the tournament, something that would be discouraged now. Because it was a broadsheet newspaper, not a tabloid, I thought I was safe.

I was working with Gareth Davies, a journalist I trusted implicitly. After England were knocked out of the tournament I had what I thought was an off-the-record conversation to help him mould the column. I thought I'd then rework it with him and get final sign-off.

Instead Gareth told me that things had been taken out of his hands and despite his protests, the paper was going to run what I'd said as a big story. I protested as well, but they ran the story without my blessing.

What had I said that was so controversial and newsworthy? Thinking my words were for background, not public consumption, I'd said the reason England were eliminated was that we were tactically inept, which was down to Kevin. It became a huge news story, and instead of coming out of the tournament with some credit, I was wondering if I actually had an international future.

I was devastated because I'd formed a strong bond with Kevin. When I first got into the squad under him, I told him, 'I only came into the game because of you. You were my childhood hero.'

And he went, 'Ah, you're not the first person to say that.'

And then I was on my way downstairs to play snooker in the hotel, and he said, 'Rack 'em up, I'll be down in ten minutes.' So every squad I was in, I'd be playing snooker with Kevin and thinking how surreal it was.

So Kevin Keegan was the last person I wanted to piss off. I felt I was taken advantage of by the Telegraph. David Davies from the FA rang me and asked me to call Kevin to apologize. So I rang him to explain. I told him the whole story.

Kevin said, 'I believe you.' And he picked me for the next squad.

In those days, the football press considered England managers to be fair game from minute one, and by doing that column I'd been silly enough to get involved. I realized that you couldn't get too close to most journalists.

But nobody could have foreseen how quickly things would unravel for Kevin after that.

Wembley, 7 October 2000. The last game at the famous old stadium before it was knocked down and rebuilt.

It was Germany again, this time a 2002 World Cup qualifier, and we'd lost 1–0.

Tensions were high before the match because Kevin was incensed that our line-up had been leaked to the media. It certainly wasn't me; when I first got into the squad, under Graham Taylor, a journalist asked me if I wanted to leak him the team in return for £500 each time. No chance!

The Germany game itself was so frustrating. We conceded a poor goal from a free kick and just didn't get going.

As we were coming off the pitch, there was discontent

from the fans and a bit of booing. And that was hard for Kevin, for he is one of those guys who just has to be loved.

So that game really cost him his job in his own mind. I think he could have carried on quite comfortably and we would have still qualified for the World Cup, which we did instead under Sven-Göran Eriksson.

But that day, we trudged into the dressing room, Kevin said to Arthur Cox, 'That's it. I've always said if I hear any grumblings, I'm out of here.'

Arthur told Kevin to think about it, but he was insistent that he already had. It was incredible, Kevin having this sort of conversation openly, in front of the team.

The next minute, Arthur, the boss, the club doctor and David Davies from the FA went into the shower areas at the back of the dressing room to discuss it. I think the others were trying to change Kevin's mind because the last thing anybody wanted was for him to go. He didn't need to. This was all about learning and growing and getting better. But Kevin was all about feeling.

And so Kevin was gone, and it was really strange timing because we were between two internationals. We were due to play Finland in a few days – without the manager.

In among all this chaos, bizarrely, came my one game as England captain. Howard Wilkinson, once a Division One-winning manager at Leeds United, had been brought in as England caretaker manager and, on the plane out to Helsinki, he came up to me and said he was thinking of giving the captaincy to somebody else (it's not fair to name them) and what did I think?

I said, 'Well, I wouldn't have minded being captain.' He

said he didn't think I'd be interested so I made it clear that I'd be more than happy to captain my country.

'You're captain, in that case,' he said.

It was an unusual exchange, and I don't know if he was testing me, but I guess, if he was, I passed.

We got out there, and Howard and I had to do a press conference that was obviously going to be a bit intense after Kevin quitting. I was OK with that because I was thirty-four and experienced enough to handle myself. A lot of players had pulled out of that squad after Keegan went, which was probably why I was captain, but it was an honour nonetheless.

As for the game, it was 0–0, but it shouldn't have been. Ray Parlour hit a shot that clearly crossed the line, but it wasn't given. It wasn't quite the level of controversy of Geoff Hurst in 1966, but we weren't happy as we'd played well in difficult circumstances. The result left us bottom of the group, seemingly with a mountain to climb to qualify for the 2002 World Cup. But we'd got an admirable point in tricky circumstances – really, Kevin should have stuck around till after that game.

Peter Taylor was the caretaker for the next game – against Italy – and ahead of that squad being announced, Arsene Wenger told me that Taylor wasn't going to pick me for the squad. Apparently he wanted a younger group, but it felt like a poke in the eye to me. You're pushed into the limelight, you captain your country at a difficult moment and then you're on the scrapheap.

Except I wasn't. Taylor was only there for one game, and in came Sven-Göran Eriksson, whom I was so sad to see pass as I was finishing writing this book. I liked Sven, a lovely man, and he wasn't dissimilar to Arsène Wenger. He was structured, calm, almost to the extent of being dispassionate.

He had a little tactics board the size of an A4 pad, and spoke really quietly, so I had to start sitting at the front of team meetings because otherwise I couldn't really see or hear. I thought about offering to have a whip round to buy Sven a proper whiteboard, but I wasn't sure whether he had a sense of humour.

Steve McClaren came on board as his sidekick and was a decent coach, even though he later struggled as a manager. I had to have a go at him a few times because I felt he was taking the piss — some sessions weren't realistic, like throwing the ball back into play quicker than could ever happen in a real game, then shouting at me to close it down.

I also watched open-mouthed as he walked into a meeting with the back four and said it was very obvious what the problem was with them. Of course it was — he'd just asked my advice and then repeated it almost word for word.

Steve created a good tempo and team spirit, but I wasn't convinced he had a strong tactical brain. After a while, I got so fed up with it that I started going to Sven directly with any ideas I had. For example, at the 2002 World Cup, I flagged things about Brazil's shape that I saw on an overhead camera shot on late-night TV and Sven was grateful as he said he hadn't spotted them.

In fact, Sven told me to do my coaching courses and then come and work for him, but I thought he was just being nice so I didn't really push that through.

When Sven was all over the papers for having affairs with TV presenter Ulrika Jonsson, and Faria Alam, who worked at the FA, things became strange, to say the least. Normally a player would be apologizing to the manager, but in this case, it was the manager apologizing and trying to justify his relationships to us. There was quite a lot of laughter in that meeting.

We played a qualification game away to Greece deep into June, and before the game we were based at La Manga, in Spain, which had a lovely golf course. Sven told the media we were only allowed to play golf on one day, but we actually played every day of the week and Sven just told us to keep it to ourselves and that we needed to be able to breathe. It worked perfectly, as we won the qualification game 2–0 away in Greece.

The Under 21s weren't happy, though, staying at the same hotel, looking out the window watching us play golf.

Although Sven gave us lots of freedom, he had a line you didn't cross. After Steve McManaman and his former Liverpool teammate Robbie Fowler were late back from the golf course, Steve hardly played again for England and Robbie's international career took a definite downturn.

I had a few injuries during the rest of that 2002 qualifying campaign, but Sven always picked me when I was available. And he thought about bringing me back in 2003, too, until I picked up another knock.

The World Cup squad was a great group to be a part of. West Ham and Chelsea midfielder Joe Cole was chosen as my running partner. He thought that was a result because of my age, but he soon realized it wasn't, because I was as fit as anybody at the time.

There was enormous talent in that group, even though injury denied us of the services of the immensely talented Steven Gerrard, whose style of play I really loved. Rio Ferdinand was starting to excel, he and Sol were forming that partnership at the back, Ashley Cole was coming into his own, there was Beckham, Scholes, and now Bayern Munich midfielder Owen Hargreaves as well. He was pacy and intelligent.

That squad had a couple of players who weren't first choice because of injuries. Leeds United right-back Danny Mills played right-back instead of Gary Neville, and West Ham winger Trevor Sinclair came in on the left of midfield. Trevor had a lot of talent, but I wasn't sure how much he believed in himself, and I tried to guide him.

There were tensions, especially when we went to Dubai with our families, ahead of the tournament. There were some partners of the players annoyed that they couldn't bring all their kids on the trip as the FA were only paying for two children each.

Nicola and I were happy to have our kids at the foot of the bed, all four of us in one room.

Apart from the football, my main memory from that tournament, though, is Beckham Mania. It was insane. We had one security team for David and one for the rest of us. Whenever we went anywhere, the clamour for David was unreal, I'd never seen anything like it. We went out for the evening once and they had to close a department store for us so we could go shopping in peace.

There were England fans outside the hotel twenty-four hours a day, but these were local Japanese fans, a new level of hysteria, and every time any of us stepped outside, the flashguns almost blinded you. Security used to go running after David each time we went out and we were wondering, 'What about the rest of us?' It was quite funny, really. It was certainly the first time I realized just how much of a superstar he was.

One of the big concerns in the build-up was around David's world famous broken metatarsal. Would he be fit to play?

Everyone was on tenterhooks when, very tentatively, he joined his first training session.

So when I clattered into him firmly (and I would like to add, fairly) everyone suddenly stopped in horror as he lay on the floor. Then, very happily, he rose to his feet with a big smile, and we all knew he was going to be absolutely fine to play in the World Cup.

As for the tournament itself, we did well in the early stages, beating Argentina in the group, conceding only one goal in our first four matches. We looked solid.

However, Michael Owen was playing in those games, and he didn't look completely fit to me. He needed hour after hour of treatment on his hamstring. It just wasn't the Owen of old.

Yes, he did score a goal in the quarter-final against Brazil, but he probably should have come off in that game. I think he was being a typical striker, wanting to score that all-important goal, but he wasn't fully fit.

We lost 2–1, and it didn't help that it was brutally hot in the Shizuoka Stadium, in the unfortunately named city of Fukuroi. The Brazilians adapted to the conditions better than our players, though I'm still not sure if Ronaldinho's winning goal was meant to be a cross or a shot – we'll never know.

After the match I said to Sven, 'Were you even aware that Michael was struggling?' and he replied, 'No. Why didn't you come and tell me?'

I didn't think it was my place to tell the England manager his job, but Sven said next time, if we were in that situation he'd like me to speak to him.

I was an unused sub in that tournament, my last cap coming in the warm-up game against Cameroon. I'd been hoping to get some minutes, hoping to play at a World Cup finally, but it wasn't to be, with others ahead of me in the pecking order.

Some unkind people are quick to point out that I didn't play in a World Cup, and add that the two European Championships I went to ended in exits at the group stage. But I didn't think of it like that. I just wanted to get into each squad, and the World Cup thing is just an anomaly.

I have all my caps still in a safe place. They mean so much to me. But one I took more pride in than the others – my first. I put that one in a lovely display box and gave it to my parents.

And that was the end of my England career. Except that in 2023 every player who either captained England or made fifty international appearances was awarded a silver salver on the pitch before an England game. It was wonderful sharing that experience with my former teammates.

The Final Frontier

I thought I was going to Portsmouth. I'd spoken to Harry Redknapp and he gave me the impression that it was all going to happen. But then it dragged and dragged, and out of nowhere they said to me that they didn't realize how old I was, coming up to thirty-eight years of age, and they didn't want to take the risk. I reckoned he was spinning a bit of a yarn — to put it politely.

There was also a call from an intermediary suggesting Spurs might be interested in signing me, but that was never an option — how could it be, after all the Arsenal meant to me?!

With no other top-flight destinations, I had to look at the Championship.

Ideally, I wanted to find a club near my Oxford home, for the sake of Nicola and the boys. I was talking to my friend and former teammate Matthew Upson the other night about how when you stop playing, it's probably the biggest game of your life trying to keep on the straight and narrow, be a good husband and father, a good member of your local community. That becomes the victory, because so many footballers end up getting divorced and/or going bankrupt, in the five years after they retire — it's such a big change to your life. I didn't want to start moving us all around for some selfish reason.

So when Leicester City came in for me, it made a lot of sense in terms of location. Wolves were interested too, but it was a bit further, so I decided to go with Leicester. My first contact was with Dave 'Harry' Bassett, who was head of football, and he was very positive and said he'd talk to the manager, Micky Adams, and get back to me.

Adams was persuaded, but when I arrived he seemed very insecure and suspicious of my motives for going there. I was signed as a player/coach, but it felt like Adams never had any intention of letting me coach the players. Maybe he thought I was after his job. He kept blocking me, even when I wanted to do some work with the youth team.

Equally paranoid was his assistant coach, Alan Cork, who I felt was trying to intimidate me, acting like a schoolboy, in my face.

From a playing perspective, I joined quite late, so I hadn't done a proper pre-season, so I was eased in, coming on as a sub in the first game.

I still played in eighteen matches, showing I was fit enough to deal with the gruelling schedule in the Championship.

Micky wanted to know everything that Wenger did – all the training sessions, the mindset. He was hungry for information. He was very different from Wenger in his management style, which I guess should not have been a surprise, but initially I thought I could learn something from him as I was convinced I was going into coaching.

Our second away game of the season, away at Millwall, set the alarm bells ringing.

We got caught in two hours of traffic because of a detour to pick up two players near Birmingham. Six hours into our journey, all we had was a box of KitKats to eat, and things started getting quite agitated.

I shouted out, 'For fuck's sake, have we got any food for the players?' but we didn't, and we didn't get to London until 9 p.m. with a game to play the next day.

On the day of the game the manager cancelled the hotel team talk, with players speculating that he was too hungover to take it, though I don't know if that was true.

At the stadium it was over 32°C and our third-choice all-black kit was all laid out. I asked the kit man if we could change to our lighter second strip for heat reasons, but he said the commercial department said we had to wear it.

Adams could hear me complaining so said in the team talk that if anyone wanted to use the journey or shirts as an excuse, they could fuck off.

I thought he was going to talk about key points for us to focus on and the weaknesses of our opponent, but not a bit. He just slagged off Dennis Wise, the Millwall manager, for the next ten minutes. We lost 2–0.

Leicester had lost a lot of players that summer, and there were big holes in the squad. But there were some notable arrivals (beside me). One was Dion Dublin, who I knew and liked. Another was David Connolly, a perfectionist, a good finisher, but desperately frustrated with the club he had signed for.

Jason Wilcox, who is now Technical Director at Manchester United, was in the squad too, but you'd have never guessed he would end up in such a high-profile role. He was very unassuming, almost to the point of invisibility.

Leicester was almost too easy to travel to, with players coming from London, Manchester and Birmingham every day. It was nobody's home.

Of course, dropping down a level was always going to be different. It was dreamlike at Arsenal under Wenger. Everything was so stable. The routine, the fantastic people, and then suddenly you come out of that environment and see what the football world is really all about. Arsenal was light years ahead with its professionalism and attention to detail.

At Arsenal, I used to pass the ball into midfield to Vieira and I never got it back. At Leicester, I got it back at chest height and I had to try to volley the ball away.

It was worlds apart.

Leicester brought in a dietician to run through what food we should be eating, picking out Everton as the benchmark. Then he recommended every kind of sugar and bad food you could imagine. Wenger would have had a heart attack – if he wasn't so fit.

I think if you are used to winning things and you demand high standards, it creates change which other like-minded people embrace. But for those in the comfort zone or who were worried about their own positions, what I said next must have made me sound like a troublemaker. I listened, I thought about whether to intervene, and then I picked my words, asking the dietician:

'What was Arsenal's diet last season, the team that won the league without losing a game?'

And he said, 'I don't know.'

I said, 'I can tell you what it was, and it was none of the stuff you just described. We were the complete opposite.'

I could see Adams looking at me, wondering why I was causing trouble. But I wasn't, I was trying to create change.

I had to say it. He was telling us we could have bacon sandwiches, even a lager, the night before a game! It was typical of the attitude of so much of the place.

That was 2004, and if you'd have told me then that Leicester would be Premier League champions before Arsenal won the title again, I'd have questioned your sanity – and that's putting it politely.

First thing in the morning when I went to use the loo next to the changing room, there was a lighter in there and you could smell smoke in the toilet where someone had been smoking a crafty cigarette. Every day I took the lighter and threw it in an outside bin. Every day it was replaced. They weren't lucky enough to have had the same education about how to treat their bodies.

In the dressing room, everybody was on their mobile phones, which made it difficult to build a team spirit. Under Wenger, you didn't touch your phone once you were in the building.

I said to Adams, 'You need to ban phones. We need to communicate.'

Instead, he banned them on the bus before matches, the one time you need to connect with your family, a time you often feel calmer by speaking to a loved one. He was getting it all wrong.

Some of the rollickings he gave players, I'd never seen anything like it. It was just too much and showed no patience. He was like an assassin, with total contempt for his players. When on the bench, I tried to encourage him to be calm, and one time he snapped, saying, 'I can't take any more of this Wenger bollocks. I'm going to let them have it.'

When I signed, Adams told me that after each game I didn't have to come in until Tuesday, so I could rest my body. But when the season actually started, he was bringing everyone in the Sunday after the game, including me, saying we needed to sort things out.

Despite that, he didn't come in himself. I'd ask the physio, 'Where's the manager?' and then he'd tell Adams I was asking.

Things soon blew up with me. He took me out of the first team, claiming that I'd been talking about him behind his back. I had been talking to some friends outside the club about how hard it had been, but I wasn't expecting things to make their way back to Adams. I'd said to someone that it was like a Christmas club, not a football club. I was telling the truth. I think he thought I wanted his job, but I really didn't, though I felt I couldn't have done any worse.

Adams didn't last long, as he was sacked shortly after.

Dave Bassett, who had bags of experience, then took over for a while and brought Howard Wilkinson alongside him. It was a relief to see some coaches around me who I could feel respect for. However we should have been renamed Set Piece City, as they both spent hours on the training pitch working on free kicks and corners.

I thought things had improved, but the board made the decision to make a change. Craig Levein was the next man through the door. He'd done well managing Hearts, in Scotland, and I was determined to give him a chance. But it was torture.

After each match, the next day, before training, he would take the whole team into the video room and sit for an hour watching the weekend match back.

That was fine in theory, but he would just batter everybody for their poor performance.

He was very good at telling us what we couldn't do — a black belt in finding fault — but absolutely useless at putting on a training session to develop the style he was looking for.

We needed to improve with constructive coaching, but it never arrived.

We just ran our bollocks off. There were no intense sessions with the ball, just repetitive runs backwards and forwards called doggies. There was never a concession for anybody who was thirty-eight or thirty-nine. Everyone was running the same distance and, if you couldn't keep up, then off you go, we don't want you here.

I didn't give him any trouble.

I just bit my lip through all of the criticism, put my head down and worked.

But then an incident around a game at Blackpool was my point of no return.

I'd played in a league match at Preston, was making lots of headers, and started to get double vision and was feeling dizzy. It wasn't the first time in my career when the ball had caught me at an awkward angle on my head.

I had an MRI scan which found nothing serious. But afterwards, I still didn't feel right.

A few days later we were playing at Blackpool in the FA Cup and I told the physio I wasn't fit to play. I assume he relayed that to Levein, but I was told the boss wanted me to travel. I was told he needed me on the bench – for my influence with the players – but I wouldn't be coming on. It seemed ridiculous, but I got on the team bus like I was told.

Then, guess what? Half-time came, and Levein said, 'Martin, you're coming on.' I reminded him about the dizzy spells. And he just looked at me with total disdain. Maybe the physio hadn't told him I was suffering from double vision.

'Right,' he said. And then the next morning when I came in for training, Levein sat me down in his office and told me he wanted me out of the club. Head injuries weren't taken all that seriously back then, and maybe he thought I wasn't committed to the club.

When you look back now, and at the problems the game is having with concussion and dementia, it's incredible really.

I'm so pleased that I stood my ground and didn't go on. Because when I was younger I might have done what I was told and put myself at risk.

To get rid of me they were going to have to buy out my contract, which seemed mad to me. I could have helped them, and wanted to. But Levein wanted to show the board that he needed young players to make a promotion push, not old pros. He wanted a new direction.

I tried to tell him that I was just the player that they needed at the club. He was saying, 'If I could get rid of you and get someone else in, we can make the play-offs.' I said that if I went, they might struggle to avoid relegation.

He won, I left at Christmas, and Leicester went on a run of one win in fourteen league games, only staying up by grabbing a handful of wins in the last few games.

You might wonder why I didn't retire then, but at that point I'd been playing almost every week and I didn't want my career to end on a sour note.

Reading had shown interest in me in the summer but hadn't a coaching role for me, which is why I, foolishly in hindsight, picked Leicester. It made a lot of sense now to join Reading to work with Steve Coppell, who had a reputation as a good man and manager.

Unfortunately, I joined Reading with an injury, picked up while trying to keep fit after leaving Leicester. I had injured my knee, and I needed sugar injections in the tendon in the back of my right knee, like they give to horses. Reading's physio, John Fearn, was brilliant. He trusted me, knew it was serious, but it took a long time to get right.

Reading had a good group of players but their back four wanted to play together and didn't want to let me in. Another downside was the assistant coach, Wally Downes, who was

THE FINAL FRONTIER

convinced I was disrespecting him. On one away trip on the bus he crept up on us – I'm telling you, the guy was on his hands and knees, on some sort of spying mission – to see if I was having a go at him.

There were lots of really good people at the club with an Arsenal connection. Brian McDermott (a former teammate) was head of recruitment, and Nicky Hammond (a youth team colleague) was director of football.

Eamonn Dolan was head of the youth team and later signed my son Niall, one of the proudest moments in my entire life.

I finally made my Reading debut in early February, but then my age caught up with me and my body called time. I wasn't to play again until April. I went to see Steve to tell him I was embarrassed to be taking wages from the club. I told him not to pay me for that period because it didn't seem fair. He said, 'You're the first player that's ever come into my office in all the years I've been managing who has said, "I don't want to take my wages."' He said to leave it a couple more weeks and, within a fortnight, I was fit – and ready for the final four games of my career.

My last ever match against Wolves was a 2–1 defeat, and it doesn't particularly stay in my mind. What does was sitting on the bench a week later, watching Wigan beat us 3–1 to seal their first ever promotion to the Premier League. It was somebody else's time to celebrate.

My last chat with Steve started with the truth. He told me that he didn't have a role for me for next season and I thanked him for the honesty.

Then I asked him if he wanted the truth from me.

He said yes. I gave him my view on how he could secure promotion for his team next season, but he needed to change.

Steve, who I really rated, didn't interact with the players that often, he let the coaches coach. The players all had massive respect for him, but I felt that he needed to offer more of himself to them to get that extra bit back.

The next season I was delighted to see them reach the Premier League with two Arsenal academy graduates, James Harper and Steve Sidwell, playing major roles in Reading's success.

Coppell thought I could play another year somewhere else, and maybe I could have. There was an offer to go to Oxford United, but I didn't want to be in a team that was on a downward trajectory. People in the city sometimes criticized me for never playing for my local club, but I couldn't have saved them at my age. As a young man, I would have jumped at the chance. I saw that relegation was coming and, sadly, it did.

I didn't really want to finish, but I couldn't walk into another dressing room and start all over again. So I decided to retire. It's such a weird word, isn't it, when you're not even forty years old and everyone outside of professional sport is still climbing the career ladder?

My only regret regarding Reading was that I should have gone there in the summer. Then they could have seen the best of me, and I could have had more of an impact.

Was that final year of any value? I don't know. I try not to look back with regret, but perhaps I could have stopped after leaving Arsenal and gone into coaching with Wenger straight away.

I didn't particularly feel sad when I finished at Reading. I had been through my grieving at Arsenal, that last season, coming back from training every day in the car with plenty of time to think.

And so I hung up the boots and went back to the club and

man I knew and loved most – my football father, Arsène Wenger. He'd always said there would be a place for me at the club to coach when I wanted it, and here I was.

The boss brought me into his inner circle. I loved working with the players and learning from Arsène, one of the all-time greats, but I could see that it was difficult for his staff to know where I fitted into the pecking order.

I wasn't really truly welcomed into the fold by Pat Rice and Boro Primorac. As good people as they were, I think they'd have preferred it if I hadn't been there, Pat especially seemed nervous about having me around. They were worried that my presence was changing the connection they had with the players, maybe because I had known so many of them as teammates only a year earlier.

Was I talking too much to the players? Were my thoughts really welcome? It didn't feel like that. I worked with the defence, I tried to make a difference, and I helped that side get to the Champions League final with a superb defensive record. The boss asked me to train Monday to Friday to improve the intensity of the sessions. I even played in the XI against the first team ahead of that final against Barcelona.

At one point I was taking pain-killing injections to keep going. Another time I broke my nose trying to help Johan Djourou attack the ball. There can't have been many coaches who have broken bones!

I helped persuade Mathieu Flamini to convert to left-back when the boss had hit a bit of a brick wall. Some of the players really seemed to appreciate my input. But when a couple praised me in public, there were media requests for interviews with me, and the boss told me to be careful as certain members of the staff were anxious about where the credit was going.

Maybe I'd have stayed longer if my coaching role had been clearly spelt out to Pat and Boro at the outset, but it was becoming an uncomfortable experience, and when it came to the end of the season, I didn't continue.

How that year unfolded has bothered me a lot in recent years. It's weighed on my mind. I'm not sure the boss truly understood how I felt.

So there was only one way to finish this book, really: to go and see him. To reminisce, to say thank you and to unpack the way things ended.

To Play Without Fear

Arsène Wenger. No person has had a bigger influence on my footballing life. And so many of the highs and lows (though mainly highs) are down to him. So what better way to finish this book than by going to visit him in Zurich, where he now works for FIFA, to discuss our time together.

Some of this chat was a fantastic trip down memory lane. In fact, I haven't felt as creative as I did during these hours together since the last time I was in his company. He makes you feel like that.

But other parts were deeper than that, more meaningful. It was a chance to ask him questions and get things off my chest that have been there for a long time.

When I arrived at FIFA's offices to see him, I was told to wait in the plush reception area. But I had spotted the full-sized pitch next to the office straight away, so headed out into the penalty box, knowing it would tease him out there as he just loves being on the grass. And, true to form, he appeared after two minutes, just as I was going through imaginary set-piece routines. Then it was straight into football chat, as if we hadn't been apart all these years.

Martin: Boss, hello, how great to see you.

Arsène: You, too, Martin.

Martin: You're looking great, boss. In fact, you might even look better now than when I first saw you all those years ago in your ill-fitting suit and big glasses!

Arsène: I was forty-seven! Anyway, welcome to Zurich, my home now. So what is this book about?

Martin: My life and career, up until I retired. I've spent the past few months putting it together, revisiting all the great moments, the tough moments, the painful moments, and it became pretty clear that the journey wouldn't be complete without coming to see you. How could it be? You changed my life. So, thank you for agreeing to this chat.

Arsène: You're welcome, Martin, of course.

Martin: I thought I was in trouble with you right near the start when you took us away to Henlow Grange and I came to tell you that we were going out for a drink for Nigel Winterburn's birthday. You took some persuading as you said alcohol was poison and then told me I was responsible if anything went wrong. Do you remember that, boss?

Arsène: Yes, of course.

Martin: And then the lads got very drunk, some missed the curfew, and you and Pat Rice were not very impressed.

Arsène: Yes, but that time at Henlow Grange was good. We had team meetings, analysed things. I always tried to stay in the UK for trips like these. So many teams went away to Dubai or wherever and they'd get in trouble and end up with scandal in the newspapers. Then their season would so often unravel. I thought it was better to keep the players near home, where their wives controlled them.

Martin: During that early period, you were working us so hard that the back five thought you were trying to get one of us injured so you could play a four. Nobody wanted to be that player who got left out.

Arsène: Ha, that was not true, but I was surprised by you all when I arrived. I knew the Arsenal team, of course, and when I was in Japan waiting to come across, I watched videos of all the games. David Dein sent me the tapes. During the day I was the manager of Nagoya Grampus Eight and during the night I was preparing for Arsenal. So by the time I arrived in London, I knew the team. I called Patrick Vieira to ask him if the players were any good, and he said he didn't know because he was training with the reserves. I knew I was getting good defenders, but I discovered when I arrived just how good you all were.

Martin: So is that why you played a back five in those opening months, because you couldn't pick between us?

Arsène: I always played with a back four in my career, but you had started the season in a five so I thought it was better for the squad to keep that rhythm and balance until the end of the season.

Martin: That makes sense. Your first real game in charge was against Borussia Mönchengladbach, despite it not being listed.

Arsène: Yes, I made the decisions that day, and I took Tony off at half-time. And when I made that decision, I thought it was like dropping a bomb. Nobody could understand.

Martin: I thought you were right and brave – he wasn't having a very good game.

Arsène: What struck me was that there was always tension between you and Tony. When you play together at youth level, it should create harmony.

Martin: The club pushed us against each other as kids.

Arsène: It was always there.

Martin: Was it a good tension?

Arsène: Yes, but sometimes I felt it went a bit overboard. Sometimes he wanted to push you down. I always believed you complemented Tony and Bouldy well. They were dominant, tactically good, but not quick like you. You always need one guy who is quick. In 2004 we had four, in Kolo, Sol, Lauren and Ashley. When I look at teams now, it's the same. If you take Saliba out of Arsenal, it's terrible. If you take Walker out of City, it's terrible, because they rescue situations when you get caught once or twice in a game.

Martin: When I was younger I was much quicker than when you worked with me! Can I ask what you made of me generally as a player?

Arsène: First of all, you had the stature of a defender. You were quick, strong, determined and had a desire to learn and improve. You always wanted to understand why we did things. Curiosity is the first sign of intelligence. Also, you were never happy with yourself and carried that dissatisfaction that the top players carry.

There are two types of players: those with intrinsic motivation and those with extrinsic. People motivated by extrinsic factors care most about money or winning something big or status. Those who are intrinsic are motivated most by a deep need inside to improve their quality and show their quality. They're not happy people, but they're very often successful.

Martin: Yes, that is me, I agree. Though I'd never been happier than playing under you. Maybe you hid it well, but you gave me the feeling that there was nothing wrong with my game.

Arsène: I encouraged you to play with the ball. That part was a gamble, but you were all much better technically than I expected. And by encouraging you, we found even more potential.

Martin: Yes, the emphasis changed and then we felt fulfilled.

Arsène: That defence had character and quality before I arrived. And you were reliable too. Maybe during the week I'd look at one of you and think you weren't in the shape to deliver at the weekend. But then you'd dig deep and find the resource to perform on a Saturday and win the game. And once you were 1–0 up, the game was done. You hated to concede goals.

Martin: I felt lots of the English managers were ganging up against you, especially in those early years. They would send messages through the media.

Arsène: Yes, of course.

Martin: It was xenophobia. Did you feel that too?

Arsène: I was not very welcome because I was different.

Martin: I don't think people knew you either. I always felt one of the best things about you was that you were able to laugh at yourself. I remember you getting tangled up in the net in training and laughing with us at it, and also the time ahead of the 1999 FA Cup semi when you went up to get your dessert, turned round and didn't realize it had slipped off of your plate. We were all laughing so hard, you looked up, pleased at the general happy atmosphere, and finally you sat down, picked up your spoon and suddenly looked down at your plate to see there was nothing on there. We were all pointing at the floor, where your dessert was. It was comedy gold, and you took us laughing at you so well. You used to say you liked to see your players happy. Was it important to you to laugh at yourself?

Arsène: I think so, yes. People often said to me that they didn't know I had a sense of humour because I was so often serious because I wanted to win football games.

Martin: I feel the same about myself.

Arsène: I needed you all to be happy because 'game' is happiness. When you go to school and you finish the day or it's break time, you play with your friends. You're happy because it's the opposite of boring. Game is to express yourself and, once it becomes only a job, you lose the ability to express yourself.

In professional football the main job is to fight against fear, more than it is to encourage players to work. Because it's not work, it's a game. And what you're feeling goes straight to the crowd. You can't cheat the crowd. They know if you're happy to play or if you're scared or whatever. Fear is the root of all evil. Fear of humiliation, fear of missing something, fear of failing – it's the biggest problem for players.

Martin: You're right. And you created an environment for me to express myself, to be myself. I remember us all singing 'Simply the Best' on the bus on the way to games. We'd come off the bus bouncing.

Arsène: And what was special about that bus, and about playing in London, is you really feel like you are in the city. You're driving past the houses and you don't even realize there's a stadium close by. The second thing is that back then you got off the bus and had to walk through the supporters. They'd been waiting for an hour or two just to see you. Now, the bus goes under the stadium and you don't see them.

Martin: And we've lost our front door too. There's no obvious place that is the entrance to Arsenal Football Club like at Highbury, and I'm asking the club to change that. I wish we'd been consulted.

Arsène: You are right.

Martin: I'm trying to learn from you. You decided we needed a new training ground, you decided we needed a new stadium, and you told the people in charge and then let them get on with it and think that they'd come up with the idea themselves.

Arsène: Exactly. I designed those places, every piece myself. And with the stadium we had to – we had huge waiting lists and couldn't turn down customers for ever if we wanted to compete. And now the club makes more money from gates than Manchester United.

Martin: And now they're closing the gap at Spurs in that department. Back to the football for a minute. Why did you protect me in the moments when I made mistakes? Red cards or things like the van Nistelrooy incident? You never told me off. You always waited for me to come to you to apologize.

Arsène: Yes, on that one you came to me and said you were sorry. I said, no, no, you did well! The only thing I regret is that you didn't headbutt him completely! Of course, I'm joking. But actually, I felt that the incident brought the team even more together, so I really didn't mind. I felt proud to see you fighting for each other – that's what you want. You just don't want sendings-off and bans. Let's not forget that it was never a penalty.

Martin: That game was the beginning of the end for me. I then got sent off in a League Cup game against Middlesbrough and let you all down. It killed the team. And so every day I was coming into training thinking it was about to be over.

Arsène: It killed you because you felt guilty about it.

Martin: I didn't want to be the one who let the group down. I was one of the experienced players, probably the most by that point, and didn't want to be a reason for us losing games.

Arsène: Your enemy was yourself. When you played with freedom you were fantastic, but you didn't allow yourself to express yourself on the ball enough. You were always scared not to do well enough. Do you agree?

Martin: Yes, but you helped me find that in my game. You taught me to play five-yard passes when I wanted to hit the long ball. You taught me to play simpler.

Arsène: We worked a lot technically. I feel that today players don't work enough on their technique. I watch a lot of training sessions across the world, but they are so pragmatic and focused on passing and systems. Very little is done on individual technique, how to control the ball, move the ball.

Martin: Boss, I want to ask you something which is maybe a bit uncomfortable. When Ray Parlour and I left, physical, nasty but nice players, you didn't replace that type of player. So if you had arrived and we weren't there, would you have brought us to the club?

Arsène: Yes, of course. But after you left, you have to understand that we moved into the new stadium in 2006 and we faced a cap on the wages we could pay. We could only spend 50 per cent of our turnover on wages due to financial restrictions and then Roman Abramovich came into Chelsea and changed the market. Then City came in a few years later. We had Song, Diaby, Coquelin, who were physical, but they were young and had bad luck with injuries.

Martin: But did you go away from the blueprint of your success?

Arsène: When Vieira and Henry left, everyone wanted me to replace them. But we've been waiting almost twenty years for someone to find the next Patrick Vieira and Thierry Henry and there still isn't one. And I understood that they had to go. When a player has given you seven or eight years and they want to go to clubs like Barcelona or Juventus, it's difficult to block them. And anyway, to keep them, you need to offer them three or four years on wages you cannot afford. It was the same with van Persie.

Martin: I understand the human element of that, letting him go to a rival so he could win the league. I'm not sure I could have done it.

Arsène: But what else could I have done? He had one more year on his contract, he was thirty-one and we got £23 million for him. United would have beaten us that season whether van Persie had stayed or not.

Martin: Is there one game that stands out from my time under you?

Arsène: There were many, but I think the 2003 FA Cup final against Southampton was when I most relied on you. You played alongside Luzhnyi, who never played centre-back, so I needed you as a coach and player at the same time to get him through the game. I thought, 'Only Martin can save us today!'

Martin: I had one game at Newcastle which I think was the perfect game in 2000.

Arsène: Yes, you were outstanding. Perfect on that day, just before the UEFA Cup final. That day I made a mistake. I rested too many players against Newcastle for the Galatasaray game and the players weren't sharp enough. It's always the balance between what you gain physically and what you lose mentally. When you rest players, you create stress in their mind and you give them too long to think about the game ahead.

When you have a big team, you know the best eleven or twelve players you have, which is why you don't see managers resting players that much even now when they complain about the schedule.

Think back to the 1999 Champions League final and how Bayern took Lothar Matthäus off with ten minutes to go. Even though he was dead on his feet, the whole mood changed when he came off. Sometimes coaches forget that after seventy or eighty minutes, players have a feel for a game. And changing them can cause more damage than good.

Martin: Which of the three league-winning teams do you think was the most important?

Arsène: The title that meant the most to me was '98 because I arrived as Mr Nobody and in my first full season in charge I won.

Martin: Yes, I feel that team were the pioneers.

Arsène: 2002, nobody speaks about, but we also won the Double. I always felt the best way to win the Double was to win the cup first. It takes a weight off the team and brings them the euphoria of winning.

Martin: That was when I thought we were on top of the mountain, when the momentum in English football had changed.

A couple of years later, you sat me down at the end of my last season, on the bus on the way to the last game, to tell me you didn't need me any more. How did you find that, and why then?

Arsène: For every single player, when you have to tell them that, it's always difficult. When I arrived in England, I had so many players who were twenty-nine or above. I was thinking, 'Oh God, I have to tell all these guys that they're finished.' And they were big characters. So I took them as far as I could so as not to cause problems for the squad and the club.

I always left it late to tell people if they were being let go, because often I had to make up my mind, or I didn't know if we were getting a new signing. And you couldn't do it after the end of the season because everyone goes off on their holidays. Some managers don't actually tell players they're being released, but I always did it face to face.

Martin: I appreciated that, but doing it on the bus on the last day didn't leave any time for a constructive chat about what I might want to do next in my career.

Arsène: I spoke to you many times about you being a coach, because I think you had all the qualities for it.

Martin: Yes, and that's how I ended up coming back as a coach for a year in 2005/06.

Arsène: Yes, but I should have made you one of my assistants. I realize that today, Martin. You would have kept the team alert. But I didn't think you were sure you wanted to stay in the game.

Martin: I'm glad we can speak about this. It was difficult for me, because somewhere along the way I turned from an Arsenal man to a Wenger man. I was willing to give up other ambitions to work for you. But then I didn't want to break up the ambience that you had going with Pat Rice because I sensed insecurity. So that was one of the reasons that I stepped away after a year.

The other was that my mum was very ill. And my dad said, 'If Wenger doesn't need you, I do. I've supported you my whole career and I need you around me now.' My mum would get into bed at night and, after five minutes, she'd think she'd had eight hours, so my phone would be ringing all the time to come and help. Someone needed to be with her and in the meantime I was travelling every day from Oxford to London, I wasn't being paid and I didn't think you were sure about me being there.

I needed that reassurance of a job title as the players were looking at me, thinking I was doing it for a bit of fun. And because Pat was giving me a hard time too. So I decided it was best to step away. Don't ever think that I didn't want to do it. There's nothing in my life I would rather have done, but I couldn't say that to you. I tried to, but the timing was terrible as we'd just lost the Champions League final. I wonder how different things would have been if we'd have won that match. But you should never have let me step out of that building. I came back again in 2012 to say, 'Hey, I'm here and I'm ready,' but I don't think you thought I wanted it enough by that point.

Arsène: It was a missed opportunity for me and for you.

Martin: I don't want to say anything to you that will upset you, boss.

Arsène: You can upset me, Martin, it's OK. I just want you to be honest.

Martin: I think you had so much on your mind that we never spoke about my career. I remember bringing my notes to you, and I'm not sure you wanted that analysis at that point. I thought you thought it was just all too intense. I needed you to manage me, but you had all the players to manage. I remember telling you you needed to speak to Kolo Touré and you told me, 'No, you should.' But you were the one with the magic. He needed you. Does this surprise you?

Arsène: No, no.

Martin: This book was supposed to finish when my playing career did, but I had to talk to you about this. It is too important to me. Some of us players wanted you to share the club more with us. You could have had Vieira, Henry, Bergkamp and myself around you. Then you'd still be there now – because I don't like it that you're not there.

Arsène: It's difficult to know how to use all these players when they finish playing. I'm sad not having done that, but look at Liverpool. How many former players are there on the coaching staff? Look at Man City – how many are there? Look at Man United – how many? After players finish, they move on. Now when you hire a manager, you hire their whole team.

Martin: You didn't even have too much say with the youth team. Maybe I should have taken on that role and helped to unify the club.

Arsène: My job definitely changed, and I had to do much more work regarding the media and transfers. The whole club became more distant from me.

Martin: I think they're missing out on you now.

Arsène: But that's what they wanted.

Martin: It's not what I want. I remember you telling me that if you were in charge of the youth team, you'd put the two central defenders into central midfield and the two midfielders into centre-half to learn. Brilliant. But the club wasn't and isn't getting that link, that magic.

If we played for the village team, we'd retire and then come back to watch them when we want. We'd be part of it. With Arsenal we have to be invited back. It's not our club any more. We're on the outside, but no one's going to tell me it's not my club.

Arsène: It is your club in your heart and your mind, but once your body stops you from playing, there is nothing you can do.

Martin: It's like there's a wall and you can't get through. I always thought, boss, that you would move to the Arsenal boardroom eventually and you'd have been just as good there as you were in the dugout. But you're here at FIFA instead, and it feels wrong to me.

Arsène: No, I don't feel part of Arsenal at all.

Martin: I remember telling you, boss, that one day you would be on the outside too. And you looked surprised.

Arsène: I gave ten years of my career, Martin, to keep them at the top while we paid back the money for the stadium. After I left, they raised the wage ceiling again because they realized they wouldn't survive otherwise. The Kroenkes invested again, but did it once they had full ownership. If they'd have done it before, the price of the 30 per cent they didn't own would have been much higher. It wasn't in their interest to have the share value go up.

Martin: Yeah, it could look like they artificially kept the club below its potential to keep the price down of the chunk they wanted to buy. That is a depressing thought, and we'd have to ask the Kroenkes whether that is true, as I'd imagine they would say it isn't.

Arsène: I never had shares, because I didn't want to be accused of doing anything because I had them.

Martin: Ah, boss, it's emotional, sitting here talking to you like this. No one has done for me what you did for my footballing life. You unravelled the coil. I couldn't do it on my own, for some reason.

You're our father figure, a symbol of what we achieved, and it's not right that you're not still there now. I know you enjoy FIFA, but in my ideal world you're still there and I'm there, too, working with the youth, helping the next generation.

Anyway, that is just a dream, sadly.

Boss, I'm so grateful for you giving me the time and for us having such an honest chat. It really has been eye-opening for me and helped to clarify quite a lot of things that have sat with me for a long time. Thank you.

Arsène: You are welcome, Martin. Now, shall we go and have some lunch?

Postscript

I've always been competitive. Matthew Upson recently reminded me that when we were in the dining room at Arsenal's training ground, if some players on another table were laughing at a joke, I'd urge the people on my table to laugh even louder, as if we'd just heard the best joke in the whole world. Why am I like that? I don't really know, even after writing this book.

But what I can tell you is that my new role, as a co-commentator and pundit, gives me huge pleasure, and I approach it as if I was taking part in the match myself, because it's the nearest thing to being out on the pitch. Instead of a football at my feet, there's a microphone in my hand. With the ball, I had to be effective in possession and make things happen, then pass the ball on to a teammate. With the microphone, I can make my point with impact and colour and then hand it over to my colleague, the way I used to find Patrick or Dennis with the ball. It's thrilling, commentating in real time, more so than analysing the game afterwards in the studio.

I must be fairly good at it, because in 2007, I was asked to join a new team, BBC Sport. I've since had the honour and pleasure to commentate and/or pontificate on four World Cups, four Euros, and countless other matches. In 2018, our coverage of the World Cup quarter final between England and Sweden, with Guy Mowbray and myself as commentator and co-commentator, was watched by an audience of almost 20 million. England won that game and so did we – awarded the 2018 BAFTA for best sports programme. How could I top that? Well, by commentating on the World Cup Final itself, Croatia v France, Moscow, July 2018 – the pinnacle of my television career, so far.

Not bad for Brain of Britain.

Acknowledgements

To Josh Landy, my agent, without whose perseverance, attention to detail and love of the Arsenal, this book wouldn't have happened.

To Alex Kay-Jelski for faithfully telling my story, and to Daniel Bunyard at Penguin Books for his support and patience.

To Laurence Marks and Maurice Gran, legendary comedy writers, for inspiring me at the beginning and helping me bring my sense of humour to the page.

To Lee Clayton, my good friend and boss at the *Daily Mail*, for his honest feedback and encouragement.

To Arsenal historian Andy Kelly, photographers David Price, Stuart McFarlane and Andy Exley at Arsenal and Andy Cowie at ColorSport – thank you all for opening your archives to help me enhance this book.

To Bill Edgar, a diligent football statistician whose attention to detail was second to none.

To Tony Adams, my long-term centre-back comrade, who put his hand up, not to appeal for offside, but to volunteer to reminisce about our twenty-year football partnership.

To Arsène Wenger, my footballing father, who gave me another opportunity to sit down and relive how he brought my football career to life in 1996.

And to all the teachers, managers, coaches, physios, teammates and fans who enabled me to fulfil my dreams.

Thank you.

Picture Credits

Alan Walter: 14a top centre

Bill Smith/Popperfoto via Getty: 4a top centre

Bob Thomas via Getty: 6b top right

Clive Rose via Getty: 22b top right

Colorsport Images: 5b bottom right; 7b top right; 9b bottom centre; 10a top left; 10b top right; 10c bottom centre; 13a top left; 13b bottom right; 16a top left

Frank Tewkesbury/Evening Standard Ltd: 9a top centre

Gary M. Prior via Getty: 16b top right

Glyn Kirk via Getty: 22d bottom right

Images courtesy of Arsenal Football Club: 16c bottom centre; 17a top left; 17b bottom right; 18a top right; 19b bottom centre; 20b top right; 21b bottom centre; 22a top left; 24a centre

IMAGO/Team 2: 11a top left

Mark Leech/ Offside via Getty: 11c bottom centre

Michael Regan/The FA via Getty: 22c bottom left

Michael Steele via Getty: 15b bottom centre

Mike Capps via Kappa Sport Pictures: 7a top left

PA Images/Alamy Stock Photo: 6a top left; 14b bottom centre; 15a top centre; 23a top left; 23c bottom left

Paul Barker via Getty: 18b bottom left

Paul Popper/Popperfoto via Getty: 7c bottom centre

Popperfoto via Getty: 11b top right

Professional Sport via Getty: 23b top right

Shaun Botterill via Getty: 20c bottom centre

Stuart MacFarlane via Getty: 20a top left

Tom Purslow via Getty: 19a top centre

All other photographs courtesy of Martin Keown's personal archive.

Every effort has been made to ensure images are correctly attributed, however if any omission or error has been made, please notify the publisher for correction in future editions.